CRITICAL LIVES

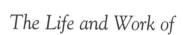

The Life and Work of

Malcolm X

Kofi Natambu

ALPHA

A Pearson Education Company

International Standard Book Number: 0-02-864218-X

Library of Congress Catalog Card Number: 2001094709

04   03   02   8   7   6   5   4   3   2   1

Interpretation of the printing code: The rightmost number of the first series of numbers is the year of the book's printing; the rightmost number of the second series of numbers is the number of the book's printing. For example, a printing code of 02-1 shows that the first printing occurred in 2002.

Printed in the United States of America

Publisher:
Marie Butler-Knight
Product Manager:
Phil Kitchel
Managing Editor:
Jennifer Chisholm
Acquisitions Editor:
Randy Ladenheim-Gil
Development Editor:
Tom Stevens
Production Editor:
Billy Fields
Copy Editor:
Heather Stith

Cover Designer:
Ann Jones
Book Designer:
Sandra Schroeder
Production:
Mary Hunt
Michelle Mitchell

Dedication

For Chuleenan

Malcolm X

Chapter 1

A Troubled Childhood
in a Racist Society

Malcolm was born on May 19, 1925, in Omaha, Nebraska. He was the fourth child of his mother, Louise, and the seventh of his father, the Reverend Earl Little (whose three other children from a previous marriage lived in Boston, Massachusetts). From as early as Malcolm could remember, his parents had been deeply embroiled in racial and social conflict. In December 1924, shotgun-brandishing members of the Ku Klux Klan terrorized Louise, who was pregnant with Malcolm at the time, and the children while Earl was miles away preaching in Milwaukee, Wisconsin. The Klan demanded that the Little family immediately leave Omaha because Earl, an itinerant Baptist minister, was a dedicated organizer for Marcus Garvey's black nationalist organization, the Universal Negro Improvement Association (UNIA), and was "spreading trouble" among the "good Negroes" of Omaha from his pulpit.

Marcus Garvey (1887–1940) was a native of Jamaica who had emigrated to the United States in 1916 to meet with Booker T. Washington, the African American educator, politician, and founder of the famous Alabama Negro college, Tuskegee Institute. Garvey greatly admired Washington's emphasis on self-reliance and economic independence despite Washington's political conservatism and accommodation to racial segregation and the absence of voting rights that his program called for (and for which

1

Washington was openly criticized and attacked by such prominent black intellectuals and activists as W.E.B. DuBois and his interracial colleagues in the newly formed NAACP). Garvey wrote an impassioned letter to Washington saying that he was coming to America and very much wished to meet with him. However, unbeknownst to Garvey, Washington had died in 1915, so Garvey decided to travel to New York's large, thriving black community in Harlem to establish a new political base.

For years Garvey had been searching for an international forum for his eclectic ideas about black racial pride, economic and cultural nationalism, and global political independence from all forms of white racist oppression and exploitation. He already had a reputation as a radical trade unionist in Jamaica and throughout the Caribbean. Garvey had so angered the authorities in what was then known as the British and French West Indies that he was under constant surveillance and was finally asked to leave Jamaica because of his attempts to organize black workers there.

By the time Garvey reached the United States, his utopian political ambitions had greatly expanded to include not only the liberation of the Caribbean, but the entire black world in North and South America as well as Africa. Within five years, Garvey had amassed the largest black nationalist organization the world had ever seen, with over two million members in the United States alone. The Pan-African and international scope of Garvey's many organizations and programs galvanized black people everywhere, from Jamaica, Trinidad, and Cuba to major American urban centers such as Harlem, Chicago, and Detroit, as well as west, central, and southern Africa.

An integral part of what soon became popularly known as "Garveyism" was his repatriation-to-Africa idea, which proposed that all those of African descent who wished to return to Africa be able to leave the lands of their former slaveholders and find independence, peace, and prosperity in all-African societies. This aspect of Garvey's program was especially appealing to Earl and Louise Little and many other poor African Americans who were deeply alienated by the extremely cruel and oppressive racism they found in the United States during this time. The proselytizing that Earl Little did on behalf of UNIA was perceived as a threat by white governmental authorities as well as local white supremacist groups such as the Black Legion (whose members wore black robes instead of white ones) and the Klan (which by the mid 1920s had become a major national political force and whose members held political offices in Indiana, Michigan, and Illinois, as well as many cities and towns in the deep South). Malcolm and his three siblings, brothers Philbert and Wilfred and sister Hilda, were raised in this tension-filled atmosphere.

Soon after the Klan incident and Malcolm's birth, his father decided that the family should move, first briefly to Milwaukee, and then to Lansing, Michigan. There his father bought a house and resumed his freelance work as a Christian minister while continuing to spread the secular doctrine of Marcus Garvey. As Earl Little began to put away savings for a store he had always wanted to own, local authorities caught wind of his political work on behalf of Garveyism, and the Black Legion began to stalk and harass him wherever he went, attacking him for being an "uppity nigger" who had the nerve to assert himself as an independent black man and whose family lived outside the designated, segregated ghetto district. As in Omaha, the Littles were reviled for stirring up trouble and "dissension" among the "good Negroes" of Lansing, Michigan.

The constant pressure, fear, and tension that Malcolm's family was under from the larger society was mirrored within their own household as Malcolm's parents constantly fought, both verbally and physically. A deeply frustrated and anger-filled Earl Little frequently beat his wife and their children.

A fourth son, Reginald, was born in 1927. In the summer of 1929, the Little family purchased a two-story farmhouse in a semi-rural, all white neighborhood. This led to even more grave and dangerous problems for Malcolm's family. Local whites were appalled that a black family had been allowed to move into "their" community and soon demanded that something be done to get rid of the Littles. The brutal response came just three months after Earl Little had purchased the property. In September 1929, the

Littles were notified that the deed to the property contained a clause stipulating, "This land shall never be rented, leased, sold to, or occupied by ... persons other than those of the Caucasian race."

The owner of the adjacent lots, a land development company, insisted that the Littles' presence was damaging its efforts to sell to white customers and persuaded James Nicoll, the white farmer who had sold the farmhouse to Earl, to collaborate in an effort to evict the Littles. The ensuing lawsuit was successful. Judge Leland Carr did not even give the Littles time to seek new lodgings, ordering them to vacate immediately and denying them reimbursement. The judge compounded this flagrantly racist act by levying all the attorneys' fees and court costs against them, despite the absence of any culpability on their part.

An enraged Earl Little refused to relinquish his property and had his lawyer buy time by posting an appeal bond and serving notice that he intended to appeal to the Michigan Supreme Court. However, like thousands of previous legal cases brought against racially restrictive land and housing covenants (and in the case of Jewish Americans, religiously restrictive contracts), the Little appeal was denied. It would be another thirty years before the U.S. Supreme Court would declare these covenants to be unconstitutional and a violation of civil rights.

On November 7, 1929, soon after Malcolm's baby sister, Yvonne, was born, two white men burned down the Littles' house. The Littles lost everything in the blaze, yet the police accused Earl himself of setting the fire. Speculation was rife that because Earl felt he was being evicted from property that was rightfully his, he also felt that neither Nicoll nor his white neighbors should be allowed to have it. Thus, the police reasoned, Earl Little had a strong motive to set the fire and then pretend that whites had.

Malcolm's father was charged with arson and illegal possession of a firearm (the revolver Earl allegedly had used to shoot at the white men who he testified set the fire). The inconsistencies in the testimony of Earl, Louise, and their son Wilfred made the police even more suspicious, and Earl was later arrested and jailed. However, the county prosecutor later dropped the charge of arson due to lack of evidence.

The family had escaped the fire unhurt, and Earl was able to move his family into temporary lodgings with clothing provided by friends and neighbors. Soon the Littles moved again, this time into another house on the outskirts of East Lansing. After their white neighbors repeatedly threw rocks at them and harassed them in other ways, they finally moved out into the country, some two miles away from the city. There Earl Little, who was also an accomplished carpenter, built a four-room house and bought a six-acre plot of farmland that enabled them to raise chickens and rabbits and grow most of their own food, in direct accordance with Earl's Garveyite convictions that blacks should always be economically self-sufficient and capable of surviving independently without any outside assistance (especially welfare). But racism again stymied the hopes of the Little family when it was discovered that the white widow who had sold them the land had concealed a tax lien on the northern three acres of the property. Mired in litigation once again, the Littles discovered for the second time in eight months that they had to forfeit land they had purchased in good faith.

In 1931, Louise had one more child (her seventh, and Earl's tenth), Malcolm's youngest brother Wesley. That same year Malcolm began attending kindergarten at Pleasant Grove Elementary School. Now six years old, Malcolm had already directly experienced more grief and terror, both socially and at home, than many adults. Yet he and his family were about to endure even more. On September 28, 1931, Earl Little was found near death after being run over and cut nearly in half by a streetcar. After two agonizing hours in the hospital, he died. Louise Little insisted that the Black Legion had murdered him. Others disputed this charge and said that his death was an accident. Whatever the truth, Earl Little's death left the conflict-ridden yet close-knit family in shock.

Color, Caste, and the Effects of Racism

From the beginning of Malcolm's life he had been assaulted because of the color of his skin. His parents were a distinct contrast in skin tone, and this incidental physical difference took on very significant implications in Malcolm's life. Malcolm's father Earl, a native of Reynolds, Georgia, was very dark, and his mother, who was born Louise Norton in the small Caribbean nation of Grenada, was so light-skinned that to many observers she looked white. Racism was such an insidious force in the personal and psychological lives of many African Americans that this banal fact became a source of much emotional rancor and endless social conflict within both Malcolm's family and the larger society. As a result, Malcolm's light brown skin, kinky reddish hair, and green (later gray) eyes were a source of pain and isolation to him.

Teased, bullied, and baited relentlessly by white schoolmates and even by his older and darker-skinned brother Philbert, Malcolm found himself alternately resenting and then absurdly admiring his skin tone as the mixed signals that society gave him confused and hurt him in a myriad of ways. At school, the white children called him "Chinaman" (or "chink"), "Eskimo," and "snowflake" in addition to "nigger." He was also sometimes called "Milky," and his brother Philbert was nicknamed "Blackie."

His own parents often demonstrated conflicting and ambivalent feelings about color and social status as well. Malcolm's mother Louise despised her white father, who had abandoned her and her unmarried black mother before she was born. As a confirmed Garveyite in her own right, she had proudly endorsed the same fiercely black nationalist positions as her husband, yet she favored her light-skinned relatives over the darker ones. She always proudly insisted that she was West Indian and not African American.

Louise displayed the opposite attitude with Malcolm because she wanted to make sure that he would not think his fair skin made him superior. She insisted that Malcolm spend more time outside so that the sun would darken his skin. He felt that she favored the darker children partly because his light skin was a painful reminder of her own "illegitimate" status. This feeling was reinforced by the severe beatings he received at the hands of his mother, who was known as a strict disciplinarian and who, in the view of some, lacked normal affection. (Her mother had raised her in much the same way.) Despite this treatment, or perhaps because of it, Malcolm was by far the most rebellious of all of Louise's children.

Malcolm's father was a hardworking, ambitious, assertive, highly intelligent, yet uneducated man (like so many black children of his era, he had to drop out of school in the fourth grade to help support his family by working on the family farm) who chafed at being subjected to the punitive and overwhelming power of white racism and was never able to fulfill himself as either father, minister, political organizer, or construction worker. Perpetually angry and embittered, he routinely took out his frustrations on his family and in some cases on other black people who resented his sometimes overweening ego and personal sense of entitlement. These strengths and weaknesses led Earl Little to be alternately respected and despised by family and friends alike.

Malcolm was clearly his father's favorite child. As Malcolm pointed out in his autobiography, his father would sometimes beat his older brothers "almost savagely" if they broke any of his endless rules (Malcolm ruefully notes that his father had so many that it was hard to know or remember them all). But he also noted that his father rarely ever touched him in this manner and even doted on him.

Unlike his mother, his father seemed to be proud of Malcolm's color and made no secret of his preference for Malcolm's highly precocious presence. For example, Earl would take Malcolm with him to the Garvey UNIA meetings, an experience that Malcolm cherished and remembered fondly. Malcolm's theory about his father's preference was that as anti-white as his father was, he subconsciously favored the light-skinned children because, like so many other blacks afflicted with the white man's vicious brainwashing concerning color, he felt the "mulatto" (or mixed-race) child was somehow "better" because he or she was visibly nearer to white. Indeed, consciously or unconsciously, many black parents of that time treated lighter children better than they treated the darker ones (even if the parents were themselves dark). Of course, the converse was true in many cases as well.

This racist attachment of social status to skin color haunted Malcolm and distorted his perceptions about himself and the world. At home, he and his brother Philbert were highly competitive and sometimes hostile rivals for their parents' approval and affection—Philbert for his father's and Malcolm for his mother's. Neither was successful, which only increased their wariness, envy, and suspicion of each other.

Despite their mutual misgivings, Philbert, who was two years older than Malcolm, was fiercely protective of his younger brother. Malcolm was often bullied by the other kids and was perceived as being not very tough. Even though Malcolm was smart, charming, articulate, and adept at talking himself out of fights at school, he longed to be seen and treated as tough and strong like his brothers. This longing led Malcolm to try desperately to emulate his older brothers' behavior, especially Philbert. (The always intellectually rebellious Malcolm felt that his other older brother Wilfred conformed too much to the dutiful image and behavior that his parents demanded of their children.) Philbert was similar to Malcolm in that he was independent, self-confident, and intelligent. Yet Philbert was also an accomplished athlete, a graceful dancer, and even at an early age, a disciplined devotee of religion and spiritual matters.

When Philbert, inspired by the legendary Joe Louis, the heavyweight boxing champion in 1937, became a successful amateur boxer in Lansing, Malcolm, then thirteen, tried and failed to become one, too. Tall, skinny, and never particularly athletic, Malcolm was twice beaten soundly in local bouts by a young white boxer named Bill Peterson. Humiliated, Malcolm felt doubly embarrassed because the other black kids felt that losing to a white boy was absolutely the worst thing any black boy could possibly do (after all, black athletes generally were considered superior to white athletes) and because his younger brother Reginald, who had previously looked up to Malcolm the way Malcolm looked up to Philbert, began to view Malcolm differently.

The boxing defeat bothered Malcolm not only because his ego was so tied up in competition with his brother but also because, in his view, his lack of athletic prowess reflected badly on his ability to impress his male peers (and of course, girls) that he was as "tough" and "hip" as the people he admired in the black community. This intense identification with other accomplished African Americans in any area (legitimate or illegitimate) remained a fundamental part of Malcolm's personality throughout his life and was often a great motivating factor in Malcolm's quest to excel among his contemporaries.

The Great Depression Breaks Up the Little Family

The devastation of Earl Little's death in the fall of 1931 coupled with the national disaster of the Depression took a tremendous toll on Malcolm's mother, Louise. Widowed with seven children, she found herself completely adrift and without a sufficient means of economic support. Holding tenaciously to the tenets of racial pride and independence (no reliance on whites for anything, especially government) taught by Garvey, Louise sought desperately to maintain the facade that she was going to be able to survive without help in the midst of the greatest collapse of capitalism in history. But the illusion that self-reliance was possible in such difficult economic times was soon shattered.

The immediate breakdown of the once booming automotive parts industry in Lansing, which was only thirty miles from the massive automobile production center of Detroit, resulted in widespread poverty among local residents. By 1933, the industrial unemployment rate in Michigan was 50 percent. A family of four on relief had to exist on sixty cents a week, plus whatever free food was available at the soup kitchens that were located at the city's fire stations. Near Lansing, white men who were lucky enough to find factory jobs were paid twenty-five cents per hour. White women were paid fifteen cents. African Americans, many of whom had migrated to Lansing because of the employment opportunities created by the first World War and its prosperous aftermath, received only half as much as their white counterparts. Like everyone else caught in this horrific trap, Malcolm's mother scrambled for whatever employment she could find.

The bitterness that Louise Little had always felt toward whites increased greatly in the wake of her husband's sudden death. The grim reality that she was thirty-four years old with eight mouths to feed took not only a great physical toll on her but a severe psychological and emotional one as well. Adding to her stress were her often highly contentious and frustrating battles with various state governmental agencies and creditors. Louise's exhausting attempts to collect on the two life and accident insurance policies that her husband had left the family were sources of endless conflict (one of the policies had not been fully paid up when Reverend Little died). One insurance company even falsely insisted that Earl Little's death was a suicide so that it would not be legally compelled to pay Louise the proper premiums.

Her oldest daughter looked after the other children as Louise Little looked for work. Eventually, she found part-time employment as a seamstress. She also worked as a domestic servant, but as soon as her white employers, who had assumed that she was white, discovered she was half-black, they fired her. Malcolm never forgot how his mother often came home crying while trying to hide her tears.

This merciless environment of racial discrimination and limited economic opportunity made providing adequate food and clothing for the family almost impossible for Louise. All of the Littles wore ragged hand-me-downs that were often too small. Malcolm, as fiercely proud as his mother and determined not to accept what he considered charity from anyone, often spent time outdoors shivering in the very cold winters in Michigan. But when offered a scarf or gloves by parents of friends, he declined them. "I'll be all right," he would say. During the summer, Malcolm and his siblings went barefoot because shoes were scarce and too expensive. During the rest of the year, he wore beat-up sneakers, so his feet nearly froze from having to endure the long, harsh Michigan winters. On top of everything else, many white children (who were almost as destitute as Malcolm and his family) ridiculed and chided the Little children for wearing ragged, cast-off clothing. However, no one could make fun of them for wearing dirty clothes; Louise Little made sure their clothes were impeccably clean.

The small, four-room cottage that Earl had built for his wife and children was in no better shape than their clothing. There was no running water or indoor toilet. The furniture was very sparse with no rugs on the floor. A single, bare lightbulb hung from the ceiling in each room, and an uninsulated, tar-paper shingle exterior presented virtually no barrier at all to the cold.

As the Depression raged on, hunger became a severely worsening problem for the Littles. Malcolm and his younger brother Reginald would periodically walk two miles to the local bakery and buy bread. It was stale surplus bread, but it helped to keep his family alive. In Malcolm's autobiography he recounts how his overworked mother found endless ways to make whole meals out of bread by making bread pudding, stewed tomatoes with bread, French toast (if they could afford any eggs), and even bread burgers on those very rare occasions when they had some hamburger. However, Louise was often penniless, and the children were so hungry that, in Malcolm's words, "they were dizzy." Sometimes, if they were lucky, they would subsist on oatmeal or cornmeal mush three times a day. His mother would boil a big pot of dandelion greens, and the family would survive on that. Some white children, emulating the hurtful comments of their parents, teased Malcolm and his family about eating "fried grass."

In the semi-rural area just outside Lansing that Malcolm lived in, nearly all his schoolmates were poor whites. Even some of the blacks in the city proper who were a little better off than the Littles (and for whom Earl Little had once preached in their churches) began to refer to them contemptuously as "farmers" or by the dreaded epithet "country." During this time, Malcolm's oldest brother Wilfred dropped out of high school to help their mother with the rapidly mounting bills and expenses. The quiet, steady, and responsible Wilfred took a series of any odd jobs he could find and often came home at night exhausted by the grueling labor, the wages from which he would give to his mother.

Soon the state welfare bureau social workers began coming to the family home, questioning Louise about her economic condition and seeking to determine what they could do to contribute assistance to her family. Soon after, Louise began to receive two small checks: one a welfare stipend and the other a widow's pension. However, the debt that the family incurred from having to take credit from the local grocery store and other bill collectors ensured that the small stipend was gone as soon as the money appeared at the first of the month. There was never enough money available to make ends meet.

The reliance on credit and state agencies, which Louise and her late husband had always despised, absolutely infuriated this stubbornly proud and dignified woman. As Earl had always preached, and Louise firmly believed, "Credit is the first step into debt and back into slavery." Of course, she had no choice in the matter, but it stuck deeply in her craw.

Especially well educated for a woman of her time and very articulate, Louise's high-toned manners, aristocratic bearing, and acerbic tongue rubbed whites and many blacks the wrong way. She was thought "uppity" and far too intellectually aggressive "for a [black] woman" and was resented by racist whites, who saw her as flagrantly violating the written and unwritten laws of "racial etiquette" under Jim Crow segregation. When local merchants and the grocery store owner tried to cheat her by padding the bill, Louise sharply remarked that she was far from ignorant and knew exactly what they were trying to do.

She also told the state welfare workers that she was a grown woman, fully able to raise her children without them coming to the house so often to question her and meddle in her family's affairs. However, as Malcolm points out, the monthly welfare check was the social workers' free pass into his family's home. He states that the all white social workers acted as though they "owned" his family. His mother hated their presence, but she could not keep them out. She would get particularly angry and upset when the workers insisted on drawing the older children aside one at a time away from their mother to ask insinuating questions or, even worse, tell the children certain negative things about their mother and then inquire about her conduct as a single parent. In response, Louise expressed her great reluctance to accept the free food that the state of Michigan provided. Not surprisingly, Malcolm and his siblings could not understand why. Later Malcolm understood that it was a matter of pride and dignity.

Shame about the family's poverty and anger about having to publicly acknowledge it by accepting the state's largesse left Louise even more resentful of her plight. When friends or social workers asked her if they could get her anything, her response was usually negative. When she did accept their offers (as when they offered to repair and improve the house), she insisted that she give them what little she had in return—even if it was only a freshly baked pie. She always maintained that the slight public assistance she received was a loan, not a gift.

As the national crisis intensified, Louise Little became increasingly religious and spiritually ascetic. She began to stress self-denial as a way of coping with her many problems as a parent and to consciously embrace fasting and other forms of personal religious discipline. She also became much more puritanical in her response to the daily pressures of life by categorically rejecting all "worldly vices." She joined a new church called the Seventh-Day Church of God, an offshoot of the Seventh-Day Adventist Church, which demanded a very strict adherence to doctrine. Members of this church were not allowed to eat pork and were also required to abstain from tobacco, liquor, drugs, gambling, and extramarital sex, as well as movies and dancing. These dogmatic edicts struck the Little children as excessive, but for a time every child in the family tried, with varying success, to practice these beliefs—that is, everyone tried except Malcolm, who had always questioned Christianity and its tenets, which struck him even as a child as overbearing, emotionally overwrought, and oppressive.

Though his brother Philbert, who was somewhat devout and loved church and his other siblings dutifully, if not enthusiastically, went along with their mother and the church, Malcolm openly rebelled against the strictures of organized religion. He found black Baptist ritual and ceremony "confusing" though he remained "amazed" by the amount of emotional and physical energy expended during church services. He admitted that he could not believe in the Christian concept of Jesus as a divine figure. He much preferred the "more rational" behavior of those blacks, like his father, who advocated the political and ideological activity of Garveyism. As he grew older he became totally disaffected and alienated from religion, which he viewed as hypocritical, ineffectual, and irrational. Despite his parents' religious activities, he expressed the view that he had "very little respect for most people who represented religion."

At nine years old Malcolm had a stoic maturity that was both poignant and disturbing. He was also beginning to deeply resent and openly curse the endless racism and economic brutality that marked his childhood and that of his family and friends in the black community of Lansing. Already he had begun to rebel at school and at home in ways that soon lead to confrontations with the white authorities he despised. By 1934, the worst that the Depression had to offer was about to hit Malcolm and his family so hard that their very survival was at stake.

As the Depression years wore on, Louise became much more withdrawn and isolated from the world and even her own children. Never fully recovering from the shock and pain of her husband's death, she soon retreated behind a psychological and emotional wall. Her once regal physical appearance began to deteriorate as her beautiful mane of black hair began to gray rapidly and her expressive face became dull and listless. As she devoted less and less time to her family, her friends and neighbors also found her unapproachable and strangely aloof. As a result, the county welfare authorities began to actively intervene in what was clearly becoming a major crisis in Louise Little's life as her mental state began to worsen.

Malcolm's response to his mother's withdrawal was to further withdraw himself. He began to steal, not only from his mother's purse but also from local grocery stores. Each time he was severely punished by his mother, he would admit stealing from others but never from her and his family. Clearly his stealing was a perverse and desperate way to get attention, even if it was a negative response. No punishment deterred him from his self-destructive course. At a mere eleven years of age, he was becoming incorrigible just as his mother was quickly heading for a complete mental collapse. Every time his mother whipped him, Malcolm yelled so loudly that even his neighbors heard his cries. This internal family chaos coupled with Malcolm's constant stealing provided authorities with evidence for their accusations that Louise Little was unfit to raise her children.

As Malcolm refused to perform his household chores and ignored the demands of both his mother and the local school for punctuality, good behavior, and attendance, he demonstrated that he was not willing or able to assume the heavy responsibilities that had been forced on him and his siblings by his father's premature death. The older children tried in vain to get Malcolm to mend his ways, but nothing worked. By the time Malcolm turned twelve in 1937, the once proud and independent Little family was in shambles, and all eight members of the family were once again about to undergo another major traumatic change.

Chapter 2

Family Separation and Estrangement

Poverty, the endless snooping of state welfare workers, and strained relations with his mother caused Malcolm to drift away from the family, especially at mealtimes. As he recounts in his autobiography, instead of going home from school he sometimes walked the two miles up the country road into Lansing where he either hung around outside different stores to steal fruit from their displays or dropped in about dinnertime at the home of some family he knew in the hopes of being invited to stay for supper.

Some of Malcolm's favorite people to visit were the Gohannas, an older couple who were raising a nephew whom everyone called "Big Boy" and whom Malcolm especially liked. An elderly woman named Mrs. Adcock also lived with them. The Gohannas and Mrs. Adcock had all been very active members of Earl Little's church and were known to be extremely caring and charitable; Mrs. Adcock in particular was known for visiting people who were ill and bringing them food and medicine. At the height of Malcolm's outlaw period, years later, she told him, "Malcolm, there's one thing I like about you. You're no good, but you don't try to hide it. You are not a hypocrite." Malcolm said this remark was "something I remembered for a long time."

As Malcolm began to stay away from home more often, he became more aggressive and impatient. He sensed that the attitude of whites toward him had something to do with his late father's activities as a Garveyite and that the rumors that a white supremacist group had murdered his father had some truth to them. Malcolm also believed that the insurance company that had refused to pay his mother her policy money had pulled a fast one and that its actions were also tied to "racist revenge" for his father's political work.

During this time, which was about 1935 or 1936, the Seventh-Day Adventists religious group began visiting Malcolm's mother, having long talks that lasted hours at a time about their faith, and leaving various booklets, pamphlets, leaflets, and magazines for her to read, which she did. Malcolm's oldest brother Wilfred, who had finally started back to school after the family began to receive the relief food supplies, also read a lot. As Malcolm recalls, Wilfred's head was "always buried in some book."

The entire family soon began to go with their mother to the Adventist meetings that were held farther out in the country. For the children, the main attraction was the good food that was served, but they also went because they were the dutiful offspring of their devout mother. Though a handful of African Americans from small towns in the area attended the church, 99 percent of the congregation was white people. The Adventists felt that the world was soon coming to an end, but as Malcolm recalls they were "the friendliest white people I had ever seen."

During this period, the state welfare people increased their monitoring of Malcolm's family by constantly questioning Louise. By this time her annoyance with them had turned into hatred, and the sessions became increasingly tense. Malcolm believed that the social workers planted the seeds of division in the children's minds by asking such insidious questions as who was smarter than who in the family. They also asked Malcolm why he was "so different."

From this point forward their professional objective became getting the family members into foster homes by any means available. The state also felt that this "solution" would be far less troublesome for them than dealing with the anger and suspicion of Louise Little. Initially the authorities made their case for Mrs. Little's alleged incompetence as a mother through Malcolm. The fact that

Malcolm stole and was becoming a disciplinary problem at home implied that his mother was not properly taking care of him. The word *crazy* began first being applied to Mrs. Little during this time. Malcolm distinctly recalled that when the state learned that the black farmer who lived in the next house down the road from his family had offered to give them some butchered pork (two whole pigs) and his mother had refused, the state had reacted in this way. All of the Little children heard the social workers call their mother "crazy" to her face for refusing "good meat." Of course, her explanation that the family had never eaten pork and that eating pork was against her religion as a Seventh-Day Adventist meant nothing to them.

Malcolm's memories of this period are especially excruciating. He stated that the social workers "had no feelings, understanding, compassion, or respect for my mother." Despite all the problems Malcolm caused and the now constant trouble and worry that he inflicted on his mother, he truly loved her. By this time, however, the state had already interviewed the Gohannas, and they said that they would take Malcolm into their home. Mrs. Little became furious when she heard that, so they held off for a while.

Around this same time a black suitor began visiting his mother. Malcolm remembers the man as large and dark, and that he looked somewhat like his late father. The man was single, independent, and strong, and at only thirty-six years of age, Mrs. Little was not ready to lead a lonely widow's life. She was more lighthearted and happier generally when she was with him, and the children, Malcolm included, were very happy for their mother. The relationship went on for a year, and then suddenly the man from Lansing just stopped coming to see her. He had backed away because he was not prepared to take on the immense responsibility of helping to provide for seven children. As Malcolm put it, "He was afraid of so many of us. To this day I can see the trap that Mother was in, saddled with all of us. And I can also understand why he would shun such a tremendous responsibility." However, the suitor's departure was a great shock for Louise. Malcolm recalled that she began to sit at home and to walk around talking to herself as though she were completely unaware that he and the other children were there. This behavior terrified them.

At this point, the state began to take definite steps to remove Malcolm from the home. Social workers began to tell Malcolm how nice it would be if he could live with the Gohannas permanently; they and Mrs. Adcock had all said how much they liked him and would love to have him live with them. Malcolm liked them, too, but he did not want to leave his brothers and sisters, not even Philbert with whom he had had so many arguments and conflicts.

Mrs. Little's behavior worsened; she increasingly talked to herself and gradually lost all contact with her children. She was less responsive than ever and no longer responsible for their welfare. As a result, all domestic chores now fell on the children. Malcolm's oldest sister Hilda cooked and did much of the housework. At the same time, the younger members of the family, Reginald, Yvonne, Malcolm, Philbert, and Wesley (ages six through twelve), all leaned heavily on the two eldest members, Wilfred and Hilda (both in their late teens) for support, nurturing, and guidance. The general feeling in the Little family was one of great uncertainty mixed with a terrible sense of impending doom.

Thus, when Malcolm was finally sent to the Gohannas' home it was a great relief. Malcolm remembers that when he finally left home with the state's representative, his mother's one statement was "Don't let them feed him any pig." From this point on Malcolm settled into a regular domestic routine with the Gohannas family, their nephew Big Boy, and Mrs. Adcock. As he did so, his brothers and sisters were also being systematically displaced or separated from each other. Wilfred and Hilda were considered old enough by the state to be allowed to stay in the four-room house that Malcolm's father had built. Philbert was placed with a Mrs. Hackett in Lansing while Reginald and Wesley went to live with the Williams family, who were friends of their mother's. The youngest children, Yvonne and Robert (whom Louise Little gave birth to out of wedlock following the end of an affair in 1938), went to live with a West Indian family named McGuire. The pride, independence, and indomitability of the once closely knit family unit had finally succumbed to the ravages of the Depression and a relentlessly cruel, indifferent, insensitive, and racist state bureaucracy.

Malcolm was permanently scarred by the experience and always maintained that his mother, brothers, and sisters did not have to become the social statistics that they became in the wake of this tragedy. He firmly believed that the state social workers had destroyed his family, as well as thousands of other black families of the period, because they lacked mercy, simple human decency, and compassion. The bitterness of this realization hit the highly sensitive, rebellious, and intelligent child like a thunderbolt and made him even more resentful and suspicious of whites in general. The breakup of his family was to have a profound effect on Malcolm's adolescence.

Louise Little suffered a complete nervous breakdown and was declared legally insane. She was then officially committed to the Michigan State Mental Hospital at Kalamazoo on January 9, 1939, where she remained for the next twenty-four years.

Malcolm Is Sent Away to a New Community

In the fall of 1938 Malcolm was still living in Lansing with the Gohannas family when a prank incident in his local middle school led to another major change in his life. Occasionally still acting out in school, he came to class late one day with his hat still on. As punishment for being late and violating the rules by wearing one's hat in class, the white teacher ordered him to keep his hat on and to walk around the room repeatedly until he was told to stop. "That way," the teacher announced, "everyone can see you. Meanwhile, we'll go on with class for those who are here to learn something." Malcolm was still walking around the room as instructed when the teacher got up from his desk and, with his back turned to the class, went to write something on the blackboard. As everyone in the classroom watched, Malcolm passed behind his desk, snatched a thumbtack, and deposited it on the teacher's chair. When the teacher sat back down he sat on the tack, yelled out in pain, and shot up as Malcolm dashed out of the door and his classmates howled in laughter. Given his school record of misbehavior, Malcolm was not surprised when the school board expelled him.

Instead of being angry or sad about it, Malcolm felt relieved and happy to be out of school. He thought that he would be allowed to stay with the Gohannas family, where he was quite content, and wander around town or maybe get a job for pocket money if he wanted. Thus, he was very surprised and disappointed when a state bureaucrat he had never seen before came to the Gohannas home and took him to court where the thirteen-year-old Malcolm was told that he was going to reform school. He was informed that he was first going to the detention home, which was located in Mason, Michigan, about twelve miles from Lansing. Malcolm was told that the detention home was where all "bad" boys and girls from his county were held on their way to reform school while waiting for their hearings.

The state bureaucrat to whom Malcolm was assigned, Maynard Allen, was nicer to him than most of the state welfare people had been. As Malcolm points out in his autobiography, he even had words of consolation for the Gohannas, Big Boy, and Mrs. Adcock, all of whom were crying when Allen came to get Malcolm. But Malcolm himself did not cry. He took the few clothes he owned and stuffed them into a box and rode in Allen's car to Mason. As they drove along, Allen told Malcolm that he was very intelligent and that his school grades indicated that if he would straighten up, he could "make something of himself." He also told him that reform school had the wrong reputation, that it did not have to be a negative experience. He talked about the word *reform*, which means to change and become better. He went on to say that the school was a place where boys like him could have time to repair their mistakes, start a new life, and become somebody everyone could be proud of. Finally, he said that the people in charge of the detention home, Mr. and Mrs. Swerlin, were very good people. This statement turned out to be true.

Malcolm remembered Mrs. Swerlin fondly as a large, robust, and joyous white woman and Mr. Swerlin as a thin white man with a black mustache and red face who was always quiet and polite, even with him. They liked Malcolm from the start. Malcolm's stay in the detention home was also the first time Malcolm had ever had a room of his own. Malcolm also discovered with surprise that everyone except the most "difficult" boys and girls at the detention home ate their meals with the Swerlins sitting at the head of the long tables. Malcolm also recalled how Mrs. Lucille Lathrop, who was the Swerlins' white cook and helper, also treated him well and lived at the home with her husband, Duane.

Soon Malcolm was doing daily chores such as sweeping, dusting, washing dishes, and mopping at the Swerlins' home in much the same way as he had worked at the Gohannas' family house. For the first time in a number of years, Malcolm felt accepted by others the way he had sometimes felt in school by a few of his early white friends. However, this feeling of acceptance soon began to erode as Malcolm discovered that the whites were treating him in a condescending and patronizing way. He later described it as being treated as a mascot.

Many white adults would talk in front of Malcolm as though he were a pet. They would often talk about him or "niggers" in front of him as though he could not understand what they were saying. They used the word *nigger* many times during the course of the day, creating a constant barrage of racism. Malcolm felt that in their minds they meant no real harm and that using this word was a cultural "habit" of speaking. Even the Lathrops did it. Malcolm even recalled one day when Mr. Swerlin came in from Lansing where he had been through the "black section" of town and right in front of Malcolm said to his wife, "I just can't see how those niggers can be so happy and be so poor." He went on to talk about how they lived in shacks but had those big, shining cars out front. In response, Mrs. Swerlin remarked, "Niggers are just that way ..."

This casual racist ignorance had a profound affect on Malcolm even as he passively went along with the commonplace expression of these attitudes. One of the judges who was in charge of Malcolm's specific stewardship for the state would periodically visit the Swerlins and ask about him, and they would call Malcolm in to be "inspected" by the judge, who would proceed to look at him as if he was examining a "fine colt or pedigreed pup" as Malcolm later put it. But at the time Malcolm was only vaguely conscious of the implications of this behavior.

Malcolm continued to do his chores and proceeded to behave as a model ward. As each weekend approached, the Swerlins did not mind Malcolm catching a ride over to Lansing for the afternoon or evening. Even though Malcolm was still in his early teens, he was a quickly growing boy, so no one ever questioned him for hanging out in the "Negro section" at night. Malcolm was growing to be even bigger than his older brothers Wilfred and Philbert, both of whom had begun to meet girls at the school dances and other places and even introduced Malcolm to a few.

Malcolm, however, remained very shy around girls. One problem was that he "couldn't dance a lick," as he put it. Besides, he defensively thought, why squander the little money he had on girls? Instead Malcolm spent those Saturday nights hanging out and around the black bars and restaurants. There Malcolm first indulged his lifelong love for jazz and blues music. The jukeboxes were sources of great pleasure for Malcolm, who would spend hours listening to musical giants of the era such as Erskine Hawkins, Count Basie, Billie Holiday, and Duke Ellington. Sometimes the legendary big bands from New York came to play one-night stands in the "sticks" and played big dances in Lansing. There Malcolm first heard and saw his favorite musicians play live. Later, Malcolm would get to know many of the artists personally when he moved to the east coast in the early 1940s.

As the other kid's dates came up and they were sent off to reform school, Malcolm remained at the detention home. When his dates came up on two or three different occasions, the event was always ignored. Malcolm was glad and grateful that Mrs. Swerlin always intervened on his behalf with the state authorities. Therefore Malcolm saw many new young people come and go at the home. For all of the conscious and unconscious negative racial attitudes of the Swerlins and other adults, Malcolm was settled in and enjoyed living with the other kids at the home.

One day Mrs. Swerlin informed Malcolm that he was going to be entered in Mason Junior High School, which was the only school in town. More importantly, Malcolm's enrollment marked the first time that any ward in the detention home had ever gone to school there. Apparently the Swerlins and the state were impressed so much by Malcolm's precociousness, hard work, and improved attitude that they were willing to "gamble" on him again as a regular student. After all, he was still only thirteen years old.

So Malcolm entered the seventh grade. He and some younger students from a family named Lyons were the only blacks in town. Malcolm found some of the white kids at school were even friendlier than those few who had befriended him back in Lansing. However, some people, including the teachers, still called him "nigger," though curiously not in an overtly hostile manner. Malcolm also began to feel like a mascot in class, albeit an extremely popular one. Malcolm attributed this popularity to being a kind of exotic novelty as the only black person in his class. He was in demand and given priority among his classmates. But Malcolm also perceived that a major part of his notoriety stemmed from having the "public seal of approval" from Mrs. Swerlin, who was both well known and respected throughout the town of Mason. Because many whites were determined not to get on her wrong side, Malcolm was even more fawned over by them. As a result, hardly a day went by when Malcolm was not asked to join this or that club or school team. The debating society, the basketball team, and many other extracurricular groups all asked Malcolm for his participation. Flattered, Malcolm never turned down an offer.

Soon after Malcolm began attending school at Mason Junior High, Mrs. Swerlin, knowing that Malcolm needed spending money of his own, got Malcolm a job after school washing dishes in a local restaurant. Malcolm's boss was the father of a white classmate whom Malcolm spent a lot of time with. Malcolm enjoyed working there and noted that it was the first time in his life he had ever had any money all his own. Soon Malcolm was able to afford a green suit and some new shoes.

Malcolm excelled in school. His favorite subjects were English and History. Although his English teacher, Mr. Ostrowski, was encouraging and full of advice about doing well in life, his history teacher, Mr. Williams, was an outright racist who reveled in telling "nigger jokes" to his students. One day during Malcolm's first week in school, he walked into the classroom, and Mr. Williams began singing a racist ditty "Way down yonder in the cotton field, some folks say that a nigger won't steal." Malcolm recounts how when the class came to the paltry one-paragraph section on "Negro history," Mr. Williams laughed aloud while reading to the class about how the "Negroes had been slaves and then were freed, and how they were usually lazy and dumb and shiftless." He went on to add in between laughs that "Negroes' feet were so big that when they walk, they don't leave tracks, they leave a hole in the ground."

This relentless racism continued while Malcolm played basketball for the school team. As the team traveled to neighboring towns, whenever Malcolm showed his face on the court the opposing team's fans would openly hoot and holler "nigger" and "coon" from the stands. Or they called him the derogatory name of "Rastus." Malcolm found very little support from his teammates or his coach when this behavior occurred, which was all the time. By this time, however, Malcolm was nearly numb to the treatment, which continued after the games at school dances.

As Malcolm walked with his teammates into another school's gym to attend a dance, he could feel what he called "the freeze." The racial tension lessened a bit when Malcolm would indicate through body language that he did not intend to mix with the others or break the ancient racial taboo of dancing with or being friendly toward white girls. The result was that Malcolm often kept to himself even amongst his teammates. At his own school he could sense that beneath all the superficial "beaming and smiling" he, their mascot, was not supposed to show any interest in or dance with the white girls, especially when they displayed overt interest in him, which happened from time to time. At these events Malcolm would just stand around with a forced smile, talk, drink punch, and eat sandwiches before making some excuse to make an early exit. Thus loneliness, fear, and alienation in a nearly all-white environment remained a major feature of Malcolm's life as a student.

At the same time many of his white male schoolmates, especially those he knew well or hung out with, began to ask Malcolm peculiar questions about sex, or they would push him to sexually proposition certain white girls, sometimes their own sisters. The reason behind this behavior, as Malcolm discovered, was that the white boys could get the girls in the position of having broken the taboo of interracial sex and then use that knowledge against the girls to make the white girls give in to them as a form of sexual blackmail.

As Malcolm was quickly learning, an integral part of the pervasive psychosis of white racism in America was deeply rooted stereotypes and lies about black sexuality as well as ironically profound feelings of sexual insecurity and even inferiority among the whites. Malcolm also found that the white boys felt that he, a Negro, "just naturally knew more about romance or sex than they did," and that he instinctively knew more about what to do and say with white girls. Malcolm, who was just under fourteen years old at the time, recalled that although some mutual attraction existed between himself and some of the girls, an impenetrable wall went up between them anytime they found themselves in any close conversation or potentially intimate situations. Thus any sexual activity was impossible. Anyway Malcolm really liked a couple of black girls that his brothers Wilfred and Philbert had introduced him to back in Lansing. But whenever he got around these girls he would be tongue-tied.

Despite Malcolm's personal sexual reticence, he did observe that a great deal of clandestine interracial sexual activity took place in Lansing where white men and women would often try to pick up black men and women. It was then that he learned about the racist mythology on the part of many whites about the allegedly prodigious and superior sexual prowess of Negroes.

As Malcolm entered the second semester of the seventh grade he was elected class president. Although he was surprised at the time, it was not difficult for Malcolm to figure why this happened. His grades were the third highest in the entire class, and as the only black student, he was, in Malcolm's own words, "unique ... like a pink poodle." But Malcolm was very proud and honored to be elected by his classmates and later described his intense efforts to be liked by everyone as "trying to be white." Mrs. Swerlin exclaimed that she was very proud of Malcolm when she heard the news of his election and soon word spread throughout the restaurant where he worked. Even the state bureaucrat who had initially taken Malcolm to the detention home, Maynard Allen, had words of praise for Malcolm. Allen also said that he never saw anyone prove better exactly what the word *reform* meant. However, although Malcolm liked and respected Mr. Allen, he bristled whenever the man hinted that Malcolm's mother had let him and his siblings down somehow.

During the same period, Malcolm would visit the Lyons family, and the black family acted as though Malcolm were one of their own children. Malcolm also found warmth and affection whenever he went into Lansing and visited his brothers and sisters and the Gohannas family. The only negative memory that Malcolm had of this generally happy period in his life was seeing the wildly popular epic film *Gone With the Wind* at the local movie theater in Mason. He was the only black person in the theater, and he recalled that when the heavily stereotyped black characters such as Butterfly McQueen went into their minstrel act, he felt deeply ashamed and "felt like crawling under the rug."

Malcolm visited Lansing and his brothers and sisters just about every Saturday. His older siblings Wilfred and Hilda, now nineteen and seventeen respectively, were taking very good care of their parents' house and lived there harmoniously. Wilfred, always the steady and reliable one, was still working odd jobs and was a voracious reader. Hilda was also working very hard and kept the house in immaculate condition. Philbert, then sixteen, was getting quite a reputation as one of the better amateur boxers in Michigan. He was so good that many people expected him to become a professional. The studious and disciplined Philbert, although he loved boxing and sports in general, had other plans. Malcolm also had frequent opportunities to visit his younger siblings Reginald, Wesley, Yvonne, and Robert, who were staying with other families in the Lansing area.

Although Malcolm was always happy to see members of his family, he and the others rarely talked about the plight of their mother. His father was mentioned even less. No one knew what to say, given the depth of the tragedies that had befallen them, and none of the children wanted anyone else to say anything about their mother. From time to time, all of them would get together and visit her in the State Mental Hospital in Kalamazoo. More often the older kids went to visit their mother individually. Malcolm recalled that the experience of visiting her was so painful that he and the others did not want to have to experience it with anyone else present, even a brother or sister.

The visit that Malcolm remembered most occurred during his seventh grade year when his older half sister Ella, his father's child from his first marriage, came from Boston to visit the family. Wilfred and Hilda had been exchanging letters with Ella, and Malcolm, at his sister Hilda's urging, had written to her from the Swerlins' home in Mason. Malcolm and his family were very happy when her letter to them said she was coming to visit. For Malcolm, the meeting with his then twenty-seven-year-old half sister Ella Little-Collins turned out to be a major turning point in his life and a harbinger of his life to come.

Ella Little Enters Malcolm's Life

The major impact that Ella Little-Collins had on Malcolm was immediate and profound. Malcolm thought she was the first truly proud dark-skinned black woman he had ever met. In Malcolm's view, Ms. Little-Collins was a "commanding woman" whose pride, grace, dignity, intelligence, strength, and independence "bespoke somebody who did and got exactly what she wanted."

Malcolm recalled how his father had often boasted about his daughter Ella to his family. He said that she had single-handedly brought many of their family out of Georgia to Boston and helped them to get settled financially. She owned some property, had worked very hard to save money, and had investments that she had built up in value. Soon she started sending money to Georgia for her sister, brother, cousin, niece, and nephew to escape the Jim Crow South and come north to Boston. For Malcolm, all that he had heard about Ella was conveyed in her striking appearance and bearing. Malcolm had never been so impressed with anybody.

From letters sent to her by Wilfred and Hilda, Ella had taken an immediate liking to Malcolm and asked Wilfred and Hilda many questions about how Malcolm was doing. She had already heard about his election as class president and asked about his grades in school. Ella praised him for his academic excellence. Malcolm, in turn, inquired about his half brother and other half sister, Earl, Jr. and Mary. He was informed that Earl, Jr. was a professional singer with a band in Boston and that Mary was also doing well. Ella told Malcolm, "We Littles have to stick together," which greatly pleased him. She also told him that various members of the family, such as cousins and other relatives, were working in good jobs in the North, and some even had small businesses of their own. Most of them were homeowners.

Ella suggested that the entire family in Lansing accompany her on a visit to Malcolm's mother at the state hospital. For the first time, all eight of the children went to Kalamazoo with Ella. It was a joyous occasion for the family because Malcolm and his siblings left feeling for the first time very positive about the possibility of their mother recovering from her illness and joining them once again. A few days after visiting all the various homes where each child lived, Ella left Lansing and returned to Boston, but before she left she told Malcolm to write to her regularly. She also suggested that, if he wanted, Malcolm could spend his summer vacation visiting her. As Malcolm exclaimed, "I jumped at the chance."

In the summer of 1940, fifteen-year-old Malcolm caught the Greyhound bus for Boston carrying a cardboard suitcase and wearing his green suit. Conspicuously green in more ways than one, Malcolm felt as if he were wearing a huge sign with the word *hick* emblazoned on it. Still, he was ecstatic about leaving Mason for a time to find out what the rest of the world had to offer. Ella met him at the terminal and took him home to Waumbeck Street in the black middle-class section of Roxbury, the Harlem of Boston. There Malcolm met Ella's second husband, who was a soldier (her first husband had been a doctor), and his two half siblings, Earl, Jr. and Mary.

Ella was heavily involved in dozens of activities in the community. She belonged to countless civic and social clubs and was a leading light in black society circles. Malcolm was absolutely fascinated and mesmerized with the many black people whose sophisticated talk and behavior left his mouth hanging open in awe. For the first time in his life Malcolm saw an entirely different side of black America. Malcolm had been unaware that the world contained as many African Americans as he saw daily thronging downtown Roxbury at night, especially on Saturdays. He was amazed at the many neon lights, nightclubs, pool halls, bars, cultural centers, and restaurants in the black community. The beautiful cars that many of the black people drove also impressed him, and he loved the great down-home cooking he found in the black restaurants. And the music! The jukeboxes blared all of Malcolm's jazz and blues favorites: Hawkins, Ellington, Holiday, Basie, and others. Malcolm saw all the biggest and best black bands up close at the Roseland Ballroom, on Boston's main thoroughfare, Massachusetts Avenue.

On Sundays when Ella and Mary took Malcolm to church, he saw extraordinarily beautiful and large black churches with incredible choirs that rocked with black Baptist fervor and soul-baring energy. Despite Malcolm's aversion to religion at the time, he was transfixed by the majesty, pomp, and grandeur of the services and remarked that he had never seen any churches in the white communities of Mason or Lansing that were anywhere near as fine and stately.

Malcolm was hooked on experiencing a new, different, and much more exciting way of life in a nearly all-black cultural and social milieu. When he returned to Mason at the end of the summer, he could barely contain his excitement. He found himself unable to fully convey to his brothers and sisters all the wonderful things he had seen, heard, and experienced. He was now determined to go back and live in Boston as soon as he could. Malcolm's quickly growing dissatisfaction with life in Michigan made this move happen sooner rather than later. Like so many events in Malcolm's life, his decision to leave Michigan was heavily influenced by the racial dynamics of the era.

Chapter 3

From Country Boy to Urban Hipster

The experience in Boston induced a radical change in Malcolm's perspective and behavior. Everyone in Mason noticed it. Malcolm was now extremely restless living in such a small town, and he was especially impatient with and restless around whites. As soon as he returned to school in the fall of 1939 to enter the eighth grade, he felt the urge to leave. His mind drifted, thinking often about Boston and all he had seen there. He also thought a lot about how differently he felt in an environment that was predominately black. For the first time he had a real sense of what it meant to be a part of a mass culture in which he felt comfortable and relaxed, as opposed to the constant tension he had become accustomed to in the virtually all-white environment of Mason.

During this time Malcolm remembered that many of his white classmates, the patrons in the restaurant, and the Swerlins remarked that he was acting strangely. They pointed out that he did not seem like himself. Malcolm usually ignored or dismissed such questions and concentrated on his studies. He was still near the very top of his class in grades. Then an incident occurred that was to become another major turning point in his life.

One day Malcolm happened to be alone in the classroom with Mr. Ostrowski, his English teacher. Malcolm had received some of his best marks in the class, and he had always liked and respected Mr. Ostrowski. Malcolm was convinced that Mr. Ostrowski felt the same way about him, too. Malcolm saw him as a natural-born advisor who would often suggest to others what they ought to read, do, or think. He was so full of opinions about nearly everything that Malcolm and the other students often made jokes about him, asking if he knew so much about success in life why was he teaching in a small town like Mason instead of working somewhere he could acquire some of the same success he spoke about to his students. But Malcolm felt that Ostrowski meant no harm in freely offering his advice. So it was a shock when he offered his latest advice to Malcolm. The conversation began innocently enough when Ostrowski told Malcolm that he should be thinking about a career. He asked Malcolm whether he had given the question any thought. Malcolm replied, "Well, yes sir, I've been thinking I'd like to be a lawyer." Ostrowski looked surprised at Malcolm's answer. He leaned back in his chair and clasped his hands behind his head. He kind of half-smiled and said, "Malcolm, one of life's first requirements is for us to be realistic. Don't misunderstand me, now. We all like you here, you know that. But you've got to be realistic about being a nigger. A lawyer—that's no realistic goal for a nigger. You need to think about something you *can* be. You're good with your hands, making things. Everybody admires your carpentry shop work. Why don't you plan on carpentry? People like you as a person—you'd get all kinds of work."

Stunned, Malcolm was very hurt and confused. He could not imagine why Mr. Ostrowski, of all people, would be so casually insensitive and dismissive of his ambitions. Though Malcolm was too shocked to say anything in response to Mr. Ostrowski, his disturbing comments stayed on Malcolm's mind. He felt uneasy in the teacher's presence, and where once he had trusted Ostrowski and was open to him, Malcolm now began to draw away. What also especially rankled Malcolm was that Ostrowski's advice to the white students, most of whom had told the teacher that they wanted to become farmers, was markedly different in tone and content from what he had said to Malcolm. Ostrowski made a point of openly encouraging those white students who had other ambitions for their lives and who wanted to pursue professional careers and college training to do just that. A number of these students told Malcolm that Ostrowski had helped and encouraged them despite the fact that none of them had earned grades and academic accolades equal to his.

Malcolm began to realize that even though he was a much brighter student than nearly all the white students in his school he was still not considered intelligent enough in their eyes to become what he wanted to be. This racist treatment led Malcolm to change inside. He became withdrawn from his classmates. Although he continued to come to class and to answer when he was called upon, sitting in Ostrowski's class became a physical and psychological strain for Malcolm. Where before the term *nigger* and other racial epithets had slipped off his back as he tried desperately to fit in and accommodate his classmates, he now quickly noticed and looked hard at whomever made such remarks. And they look surprised that he did. Because of his open resentment, he did not hear these remarks as often as he had before; many classmates and teachers simply wondered aloud what had come over him. As Malcolm put it, "I knew I was being discussed."

As weeks passed, Malcolm's attitude at the restaurant where he worked as a dishwasher and at the Swerlin home became much like that at school. One day Mrs. Swerlin called Malcolm into the living room where he met with the state official Maynard Allen. Malcolm could tell from their faces that something was about to happen. Mrs. Swerlin then told him that none of them could understand why, after he had done so well in school, on his job, and living with them, that he had lately made them all feel that he was not happy in Mason, especially because almost everyone in the town had come to like him. At that point Mrs. Swerlin said there was no need for Malcolm to stay at the detention home any longer and that arrangements had been made for him to go and live with the black family in town, the Lyons, who also liked Malcolm. Mrs. Swerlin then stood up and put out her hand, saying, "I guess I've asked you a hundred times, Malcolm, do you want to tell me what's wrong?" But Malcolm shook her hand and said, "Nothing, Mrs. Swerlin." Then he calmly went upstairs, packed his clothes, and came back down. At the living room door, Malcolm saw Mrs. Swerlin wiping her eye. She had been crying, and now Malcolm felt very bad. He then thanked her warmly and went out front to Mr. Allen who took him to the Lyons family home.

During the two months that Malcolm lived with the Lyons family, they all tried to get him to tell them what was wrong. But Malcolm could not tell them, either. He was now nearing the end of the school year and was more anxious than ever to leave Mason. He wrote almost every other day to his half-sister Ella in Boston. Without saying why, Malcolm told Ella that he wanted to come to Boston and live. Ella soon arranged to gain official custody of Malcolm, and he was transferred from Michigan to Massachusetts as her legal guardian. The very week he finished the eighth grade, Malcolm boarded the Greyhound bus to Boston. The big city beckoned, and he was more than ready to begin a new life. As he later acknowledged, no physical move in his life had been more pivotal or profound in its repercussions.

Life on the Hill, 1940–41

When Malcolm arrived in Boston, small town Mason, Michigan was, as he later put it, "written all over me." He described his appearance as that of Li'l Abner, the backward country boy character made famous by the satirical cartoonist Al Capp. His kinky reddish hair was cut in a bowl-like hick style, his green suit's coat sleeves stopped above his wrists, and his high-water pant legs showed three inches of white socks. His Lansing department store topcoat was a narrow-collared, three-quarter length monstrosity that was just a shade lighter green than his suit. His hayseed appearance was too much even for his loving sister Ella. However, she told Malcolm that she had seen "countrified" members of the Little family come up from their native Georgia in worse condition than he was. Ella had fixed up an upstairs room for him, and Malcolm deeply appreciated her generous support and excellent cooking!

Malcolm remained transfixed and deeply impressed by Ella's intelligence, sophistication, and outspoken manner. He was also taken with her tough, independent spirit and leadership qualities.

She seemed to have inherited all of their father's very best traits without the residual frustration and bitterness. Malcolm quickly found that she was a force to reckon with. He admired her greatly for this quality and paid close attention to her wise counsel until the streets began to sway him in a far different direction.

Ella advised Malcolm to learn all about the city before he started to look for a job. "Walk around, ride the buses and the subway, and get the feel of Boston," Ella insisted. She pointed out that before he tied himself down to a job somewhere he should take this opportunity to see and get to know the city they were living in. After all, he would never again have such leisure time to get his bearings and find out what the city had to offer. Ella assured Malcolm that she would help him find a job when it was time to go to work.

Malcolm and Ella lived in the "Sugar Hill" section of Roxbury, which was Boston's major segregated black community, where African Americans who called themselves the "Four Hundred" acted as if they were an elite class and looked down their noses at the blacks in the poorer ghetto area called the "town" section. This neighborhood introduced Malcolm to the emerging class system among African Americans during the 1940s. Those who could claim professional status, such as teachers, nurses, doctors, and ministers, often considered themselves superior to poorer black people and sometimes acted pretentiously. Even some postmen, porters, and dining car waiters acted in a haughty and aloof manner. They prided themselves on being more cultured, dignified, and better off economically than their counterparts in the nearby ghetto. Malcolm viewed the African Americans who acted in this way as self-deluding and sadly imitative of bourgeois whites. After meeting some of these people with their affectations and smug attitudes, he was determined to go in an entirely different direction. He was no snob and despised those who engaged in snobbery. He much preferred people who were open, honest, and sincere, whatever their class position.

Soon Malcolm's wide-ranging interests took him out of Roxbury, and he began to explore Boston proper. Malcolm went everywhere in the city. He walked long distances and took his first subway ride. Following the passengers at various stops, Malcolm soon arrived in Cambridge where he saw the campus of Harvard University. He also explored the downtown district. He even wandered along the city's many piers and docks soaking up the many historical landmarks that Boston was especially known for. Malcolm poured out his feelings and impressions in letters to Wilfred, Philbert, Hilda, and Reginald back in Lansing about the many large department stores, restaurants, and hotels he saw in downtown Boston. Being a movie fanatic, he was also impressed by the large, air-conditioned movie theaters.

The most exciting place in the city for Malcolm was the huge Roseland State Ballroom, a famous music hall where all of the nation's best jazz bands and singers played. Malcolm was always looking at the big posters out front advertising the many great orchestras that performed there. Malcolm soon became a regular at its concerts and dances.

Meanwhile Ella became concerned that Malcolm did not stick around very much on the Hill, where they lived. She kept dropping hints and then insisting that he spend time and mingle with "nice young people" his age in the district. However, Malcolm, who was then only sixteen, often felt and acted older than other kids his age. When he used to visit Lansing on weekends to get away from Mason, he had already started hanging out with his brothers Wilfred and Philbert and their friends in the black part of town. All of them were several years older than Malcolm, but he was bigger than many of them and looked older. So Malcolm rejected Ella's advice and began hanging out in Boston's ghetto section. Malcolm felt much more relaxed there and viewed it as more exciting than the much more staid and conservative Hill section. Malcolm thought the blacks in the ghetto were being their natural selves and not putting on airs. Before long Malcolm found out about the more unsavory aspects of life there, but in the meantime, he was having too much fun to notice.

Malcolm did take note of the sharply dressed young men who hung out on the corners and the poolrooms, bars, and restaurants. They were usually unemployed, yet they always seemed to have money to buy liquor and cigarettes and to gamble. Malcolm recalled being "entranced" by these young men called *cats* in the parlance of the era. He also could not get over how their hair was straight and shiny like white men's hair. Ella told him it was called a *conk*.

At the time, Malcolm had never tasted alcohol, smoked cigarettes, or gambled. Yet he saw black children who were ten and twelve years old shooting craps, playing cards, fighting, playing the numbers, and cursing up a storm. Malcolm was also fascinated by the highly inventive slang words and vernacular phrases that were completely new to him, such as *stud, cat, chick, cool,* and *hip.* He also witnessed interracial couples drinking and partying together in bars. Malcolm had never seen white women and black men hanging out together in such an overt way before. Where he was from even the mere hint of such activity was extremely dangerous. He wrote to his brothers about that, too.

Malcolm decided to try to find a job himself to surprise Ella. One afternoon while looking through the front window of a poolroom that he often hung outside of watching others play pool, he decided to go inside. There he met and talked with a stubby young man, whom Malcolm called "Shorty," who racked the balls for the players. (Shorty is a fictional composite Malcolm used in his autobiography to describe a number of real-life people that he knew.) Shorty remembered Malcolm as the boy he had seen many times before loitering outside the poolroom. When Malcolm inquired about a job racking balls, he was told that nothing was available. Then Shorty asked Malcolm what kind of work he had previously done (in the black street vernacular all work was referred to as "a slave"). When Malcolm told him he had washed dishes in a restaurant in Mason, Michigan, Shorty excitedly exclaimed, "My homeboy! Man, gimme some skin! I'm from Lansing!" From that point on, Malcolm and Shorty were fast friends and nearly inseparable.

Shorty's genuine joy at meeting someone from his hometown made him feel protective of Malcolm. Because Shorty was ten years older, he was like a surrogate big brother to Malcolm and, unlike many of the young men and women on the Hill, Shorty treated Malcolm like an equal. Malcolm felt happy and lucky to have found a friend as hip and "down" as Shorty was. "Man, this is

a swinging town if you dig it," Shorty said. "You're my homeboy—
I'm going to school you to the happenings."

New Teachers, a Different Education

From the beginning Malcolm's friendship with Shorty was like
that of mentor and protégè. Shorty was everything that Malcolm
most admired and wanted to emulate: He was hip, fun-loving, honest, sincere, tough, and a real go-getter. Shorty told Malcolm that
he should be grateful that his sister Ella was willing to let him live
at her "pad" without having to pay rent or rushing him to "find a
slave." He also explained that he was working in the poolroom just
to make ends meet while he practiced and developed his skill on
the saxophone. Shorty's aspiration was to be a professional jazz
musician. He was already taking lessons "with some other studs"
and intended to organize and lead his own small band one day. He
stressed how important it was to be independent and find one's
own way in the world. As Shorty put it, "I don't dig joining some
big band, one-nighting all over just to say I played with Count or
Duke or somebody." Malcolm listened closely to him and thought
that he also needed to develop a particular skill of his own.

Shorty also began to "school" Malcolm about street life in the
city. He told him which hustlers standing around or playing in the
poolroom sold "reefers" (marijuana), which had just come out of
prison, and which were "second-story men" (professional burglars).
Shorty pointed out that he played at least a dollar a day on the
numbers. He said as soon as he hit a number he would use the win-
nings to organize a band. Malcolm was ashamed to have to admit
that he had never played the numbers or done any gambling in his
whole life. Shorty replied that there was nothing to be ashamed of
because he had never had any money to play with. But he also said
that once you got a "slave" and you hit the number, then you had
a stake in something of your own. Shorty also pointed out who the
big gamblers and pimps were. He began to introduce Malcolm to
the players and other hipsters and told them that his "homeboy
was looking for a slave" and to contact him if they heard anything.
They responded that if anything turned up they would let him

know. He told Malcolm to come back the following day and that he was sure "some of the cats will turn you up a slave."

Shorty's friends found Malcolm a job as a shoeshine boy at the Roseland Ballroom. Ella was not happy about this development. She felt strongly that the job was beneath him and told Malcolm that he was smart and could do a lot better. Ella gave Malcolm daily pep talks telling him that if he stayed in school and studied hard he could eventually become a lawyer. Like her father Earl, Ella was very ambitious and was also a critical perfectionist like Malcolm's mother. Despite her good intentions, this combination of traits often left Malcolm feeling heavily pressured to please her. When he found that he could not please her unless he did exactly what she wished at all times, Malcolm, as he had in the past, rebelled and went his own way.

By now Malcolm's own way included becoming a regular denizen at the Roseland where the jazz giants playing there mesmerized Malcolm so that he did not mind shining shoes and providing fresh towels to customers in the restrooms for tips. Just being near the musicians and the dynamic ambiance of the ballroom scene satisfied his thirst for excitement and "kicks." Before long Malcolm was smoking marijuana, gambling a dollar a day on the numbers, and engaging in the fast living that Shorty introduced him to. Shorty was becoming the most influential teacher Malcolm had ever had.

Impressed by the highly stylish dress of many of the hustlers, dancers, musicians, pimps, and gamblers who frequented the Roseland and the rapidly growing vogue for what was called the *zoot suit*, Malcolm decided to purchase one himself. It was quickly becoming a cultural requirement for the truly hip, young, black urban male, and Malcolm was determined to fit into the club. The zoot suit was a sartorial emblem of social defiance and joyous rebellion among young black males. The brightly colored jackets to these ensembles had huge padded shoulders and a narrow, constricted waist that made one's torso look triangular. Wide, baggy Punjab pants were tapered to the ankles with a matching wide-brimmed hat, gold-plated watch chain, and monogrammed belt.

When Shorty took Malcolm to a clothing salesman near the ball-room, Malcolm selected a sky-blue zoot suit with a hat that contained a feather protruding from its large, saucer-like brim. Malcolm was ecstatic as he left the department store. He later recalled, "I took three of those twenty-five-cent, sepia-toned, while-you-wait pictures of myself, posed the way hipsters [did] wearing their zoot suits … hat dangled, knees drawn close together, feet wide apart, both index fingers jabbed toward the floor."

As black cultural historian Robin Kelley points out

The combination of his suit and body language encoded a culture that celebrated a specific racial, class, spatial, gender, and generational identity. East Coast zoot-suiters during WWII were primarily young, black (and Latino), working-class males whose living spaces were confined to Northeastern ghettos, and the suit reflected a struggle to negotiate these multiple identities in opposition to the dominant culture … zoot-suiters appropriated, even mocked, existing dominant styles and reinscribed them with new meanings drawn from shared memory and experiences.

This perspective was certainly borne out in Malcolm's emotional attachment to the style. While his haughty Hill neighbors looked on horrified, Malcolm openly flouted the conservative traditions of the striving black middle-class by "profiling" on street corners in his impeccable new outfit, twirling his long, gold-plated keychain that hung low from his trouser belt. From time to time his hand eased into his wide pockets and jangled some loose change. In the hip black parlance of the era, he was now "reet, petite, and gone" and "as sharp as a tack."

Malcolm had several photographs made of himself during this time that showed a man transformed by his new image. The first of these he gave to Ella, who had by now resigned herself to his new attire even though she thought it made him look "unsophisticated." Wisely, she did not say anything. She and Malcolm often quarreled about how Ella thought Malcolm should behave on the Hill. Malcolm also sent pictures of his new identity to his brothers and sisters in Lansing.

By this time Malcolm's hair had grown long enough to be conked like Shorty's so that it would be straight like that of a white man. Following Shorty's instructions, Malcolm purchased some lye, two potatoes, and a couple of eggs. Shorty cut up the potatoes into thin slices and put them in a jar. Then he added the lye and eggs. Malcolm touched the jar and could feel how hot it was. "Damn right, it's hot, that's the lye", Shorty said. "So you know it's going to burn when I comb it in—it burns *bad*. But the longer you can stand it, the straighter the hair." When Shorty combed the yellow starchy paste into his hair, Malcolm confessed, "My hair caught fire. I gritted my teeth and tried to pull the sides of the kitchen table together. The comb felt as if it was raking my skin off." But after enduring watering eyes, soap-lathering, and a pain so intense it made his knees tremble, Malcolm had finally survived his first conk.

Despite the pain and the fact that his scalp still flamed and hurt a little, Malcolm was impressed with the twisted results of combing out all of the normal kinks in his hair and vowed he would never be without a conk in his life (a practice that Malcolm continued for another decade). The conk had also turned Malcolm's hair a bright red. For the first time Malcolm felt he could be truly proud of his overall appearance. Years later, Malcolm reflected that enduring all of that pain and literally burning his flesh to have his hair look like a white man's hair was his first big step toward self-degradation. Violating and mutilating his body to try to look "pretty" by distorted white standards demonstrated that he, like many other blacks of the time, had bought into the racist notion of inferiority.

Malcolm reveled in his new job at the Roseland. There he met Freddie who had shined shoes before Malcolm but now had hit the numbers and was quitting. Freddie taught Malcolm how to work for tips by not only shining shoes but also providing other things that the club regulars might want. For example, he instructed Malcolm to purchase a couple dozen prophylactics to sell to men who wanted to purchase them after picking up women at the club and to charge a dollar each for them. As Malcolm later discovered, Freddie also sold reefers and liquor and acted as a procurer of black prostitutes for various white johns. These illegal activities brought in even more tips and income. Freddie even taught Malcolm how to make his shoeshine rag pop while shining shoes and informed him that people often tipped better because they figured that the loud sound meant he was working harder. Before leaving, he told Malcolm to never forget that "the main thing you got to remember is that everything in the world is a hustle." At the time, the sixteen-year-old hipster thought it was sage advice from a very wise young man who had "chumped all the squares." Yet this kind of negative philosophy eventually led Malcolm into the depths of criminality.

Malcolm reserved most of his energy for "black dance night." Like nearly all ballrooms across the nation, the Roseland had a segregated policy that allowed black people to dance only on a special night each week. Individual whites could attend these black dances if they chose, but blacks were strictly forbidden from attending the white dances during the rest of the week. Roseland only had white bands for six days during the week, but on black dance night the greatest black jazz bands were allowed to play. Malcolm saw, heard, and shined the shoes of such musical legends as Duke Ellington, Count Basie, Lionel Hampton, Cootie Williams, and Jimmy Lunceford. Malcolm even met many of the great musicians from these bands as he shined their shoes before shows.

An enraptured Malcolm wrote letters to his brothers and sisters back in Lansing about the sheer majesty and beauty of it all. The incredibly agile and creative dancing of the black lindyhoppers rocked the Roseland so much that in Malcolm's words "it felt like a big rocking ship." The bands blasted, and the electric energy of the dancers consumed the building. Malcolm often became so caught up in the intensity of the action that he would jump up and down in his gray work jacket listening to the music and watching the dancers. The manager had to come and shout at Malcolm that he had customers waiting upstairs.

It was around this time that Malcolm took his first drink, smoked his first cigarettes (and reefers), and shot craps for the first time. He began playing cards for money and betting a dollar a day on the numbers, hoping in vain to "hit." Malcolm also began staying out late at night with Shorty and his friends, much to the chagrin of his sister Ella who warned him in no uncertain terms that he was "hanging out with the wrong crowd" and that his lifestyle was unacceptable, especially for a member of the proud Little family. In the fall of 1941, Malcolm dropped out of school. Why continue schooling, Malcolm reasoned, if he was precluded from any future success as a lawyer because he was a "nigger," as his old English teacher Mr. Ostrowski put it? Malcolm's disillusionment and cynicism, however, masked a deep and lingering hurt over the fact that his intellectual ability was never fully appreciated or supported by his teachers (all of whom had been white). From now on, Malcolm vowed, he would rely only on a much different kind of teaching and learning that came from the streets and mentors like Shorty. At least they were encouraging.

Shortly thereafter Malcolm quit his job shining shoes at the Roseland and decided that he wanted to learn to dance so that he could participate in the Roseland dance competitions. Ella was so overjoyed when Malcolm informed her that he had quit the shoeshine job that she went out and found him work that she approved of. The new job was at the Townsend Drugstore, where teenyboppers from the Hill hung out after school. Malcolm worked behind the soda fountain. It was his first full-time job. His white employers were highly pleased with him. He had a lot of initiative and worked very hard; when their delivery boy was sick, Malcolm would volunteer to deliver medicine in addition to his other duties. Although he impressed everyone as a model employee, inside he seethed. It was one thing to have to endure the snobbish attitudes of his neighbors on the Hill; it was unbearable to have to cater to them.

However, it was a relief and a source of great joy for Malcolm to finally learn how to dance. He approached learning this new skill with the same thoroughness, discipline, and tenacity that he brought to anything he truly loved or coveted in his life. First, he learned how to lindyhop at a friend's house. Then he attended every party he could in order to practice his footwork. Very soon Malcolm developed such extraordinary skill that girls were asking *him* to lindyhop. He bought a new zoot suit for his debut at the Roseland, a gray ensemble with cuffs so narrow he had to take off his knob-toed, orange shoes to put on the tapered Punjab pants. During this time Malcolm met the first girl he was ever truly serious about: Laura.

Chapter 4

New Choices, Different Consequences

Laura was a sweet, soft-spoken girl who would come into the drugstore where Malcolm worked after school and order banana splits while intently reading a book. She was always reading some material from school such as algebra, Latin, or history texts. Watching her read and study so intensely during her daily sessions at the store made Malcolm feel guilty and uncomfortable about no longer taking any interest in reading books himself, something he had always loved to do when he was living in Mason.

After nearly six weeks of watching Laura every afternoon and serving her banana splits, Malcolm began to notice that she was a different kind of person than he had grown accustomed to on the Hill. She was not pretentious and snooty, but warm and polite. She was obviously intelligent, and she kept to herself. She never participated in the petty and snobbish gossip of so many of her peers. Although Laura never said much, Malcolm could see that she was not aloof or disdainful of others. He liked the fact that she never put on airs like so many of the others who came to the drugstore.

Malcolm finally let down his reserve and struck up a conversation with Laura. She responded in a very open and friendly manner. He found out that she was a high school junior and an honor student. Her parents had split up when she was a baby, and she had been raised by her very strict and religious grandmother. Laura had one close friend who she would talk on the phone with every day. Other than that, her grandmother rarely allowed her to go to the movies, let alone date.

But Laura loved school and had definite plans to attend college. She was very good in math and planned to major in science. She was a year older than Malcolm, but she looked up to him as having had a world of experience in life beyond what she had known. But whenever she left, Malcolm felt depressed about having turned away from the books and the learning that he loved back in Michigan. Laura was so stimulating for Malcolm in every way that he looked forward to her coming to the drugstore every day after school. He paid for her banana splits and gave her extra ice cream, and she let him know that she really liked him.

Soon Laura stopped reading her books when she came to the drugstore; instead she and Malcolm would just sit and talk about everything under the sun. Malcolm confided to her that he had once thought about becoming a lawyer. Laura was very encouraging and supportive. She told him that there was no reason why he could not pick up right where he left off in school and become a lawyer. She even suggested that Ella would help Malcolm financially as much as she could. Malcolm was certain Laura was right about that. Ella was forever telling Malcolm that he should go back to school and become a professional man.

Malcolm never mentioned Laura to Shorty or his other friends in the hipster world. He was sure they would not understand his admiration for her. After all, Laura had never been kissed or had a drink, and she definitely knew nothing about marijuana. So Malcolm was surprised when one afternoon Laura mentioned that she "just loved" lindyhopping. Malcolm asked her how had she been able to go out dancing when her grandmother was so strict about allowing Laura to go anywhere. Laura explained she had been introduced to lindyhopping at a party given by the parents of some friend just accepted to Harvard. Malcolm then told her that Count Basie was playing at the Roseland that weekend and asked her if she wanted to go dancing with him. Laura was very excited by Malcolm's proposal and said she had never been there but had heard so much about it. She had often imagined what it was like.

She said that she would give anything to go, but she was sure her grandmother would never allow it. Malcolm said maybe some other time.

Malcolm in zoot suit with Ella, 1941

Schomburg Center

But the day of the dance Laura came into the drugstore bursting with excitement. She had decided to go with him to the Roseland. She had never lied to her grandmother before, but today she told her grandmother that she had to attend some school function that evening. Malcolm indicated that he had to stop off at Ella's place to change clothes before they could go.

When Malcolm brought Laura home to meet Ella, her jaw dropped in amazement. She could not believe that Malcolm had finally met a well-bred Hill girl. While Ella and Laura sat and talked downstairs, Malcolm pondered whether to wear the wild sharkskin gray zoot suit that he had planned to wear or the more conservative sky-blue number he had first bought. He decided on the latter. When Malcolm came downstairs he discovered that Ella and Laura had become friends. Ella had even made tea. Although she eyed Malcolm's more "conservative" zoot suit disapprovingly, she was at least grateful that he had not worn the other one. Ella was impressed with Laura's intelligence and graceful manners and insisted that Malcolm treat her "like a lady."

At the Roseland Malcolm soon discovered that Laura was a great dancer, moving gracefully and effortlessly across the floor in perfect synchronization with him. Malcolm described her movements as so light that she felt nearly weightless, like a beautiful ballerina. Malcolm and Laura were so in sync that if he just thought about a maneuver she responded instantaneously. But as well as they danced together, Malcolm did not think Laura would have the stamina to survive a long, tough, "showtime" competition, where the very best lindyhoppers remained on the floor as long as possible to try to eliminate each other. All the other dancers formed a "U" with the big band at the open end as the greatest dancers took over the dance floor. The girls then slipped out of their heels and pumps to change into low white sneakers. As the crowd shouted for their favorites, Malcolm could hear many of them yelling, "All right now Red!" "Go get 'em Red!" (Red was Malcolm's nickname.) With Laura standing right beside him, a woman named Mamie Revels, who had danced with Malcolm in the past, ran up to him. Not knowing what to do with Laura standing right there, Malcolm hesitated before taking Mamie's hand as

Laura melted back into the crowd. Mamie, who was well-known for being a very strong, creative, and dynamic dancer (her style was described as "wild" by nearly everyone), put on quite a show with Malcolm as the crowd roared their approval.

On the way home Laura was very quiet. The next time she came into the drugstore she again said very little, obviously hurt and upset that Malcolm had chosen someone else to dance with in the competition. Malcolm did not say much in response. However, Ella let it be known that Malcolm should continue to see Laura because she was such a nice girl. Clearly, Ella had picked her out for Malcolm. This attitude bugged Malcolm, who insisted that his mind was not on Laura or any other girl, but on getting "sharp" in his zoot suit as soon as he left work and racing downtown to hang out with his friend Shorty and their hustling associates. Anything, Malcolm exclaimed, to get away from the stuck-up people on the Hill. But Laura was not yet ready to give up so quickly on Malcolm.

A couple weeks passed before Malcolm saw Laura at the drugstore again. Then one day she showed up to ask him if he would be interested in taking her to the Roseland to dance to Duke Ellington's orchestra. Laura confided to Malcolm that she felt horrible and guilt-ridden for lying to her grandmother the first time they went out, so she told her the truth about Malcolm and going out to dance. Furthermore she told her grandmother that from now on she would go out when and where she felt like it. Predictably, this statement led to a screaming match with her grandmother, with Laura even threatening that if her grandmother continued to oppose her she would just quit school, get a job, and move out. Her grandmother finally relented. When Malcolm arrived at Laura's house to pick her up for the dance, Laura's grandmother made her great displeasure known by refusing to even speak to or acknowledge him as he waited for Laura to come downstairs.

When Malcolm and Laura arrived at the ballroom, Laura let Malcolm know immediately that she intended to participate in the showtime dance contest this time and no other girl had better intervene! Despite the fact that Laura was such an outstanding dancer, both she and Malcolm knew that she could not match the veteran showtime female marathon dancers in staying power, but

Laura insisted she wanted to compete. The next thing Malcolm knew, Laura was among those girls over on the sidelines changing into sneakers. This time Malcolm shook his head "no" when a couple of the freelancing girls ran up to him to dance as Mamie had done.

As before, people were shouting "Go, Red, Go!" as Malcolm and Laura wowed the crowd by putting on a captivating display of power, grace, and finesse as Laura's gliding balletic style of lindy-hopping and Malcolm's intense, dynamic movements mesmerized the crowd. As the crowd closed in on the couple, the spotlight shone on him and Laura. As Malcolm described it: "I turned up the steam; Laura's feet were flying; I had her in the air, down, sideways, around; backwards, up again, down, whirling ...." Laura was dancing as she never had before. Malcolm was amazed not only by her feather-lightness, but also by her strength. Her hair was all over her face, and she was pouring sweat. With Ellington's legendary orchestra roaring in the background, the crowd shouted and stomped their approval. A massive wall of sound and noise surrounded Malcolm and Laura as they glided, leaped, and swayed to the music.

Then suddenly, like a weary fighter, Laura nearly collapsed from the heat and the physical effort. She was gasping for air, and Malcolm had to carry her off to the sidelines. Even some of the musicians in the band applauded as they slumped off. The crowd swarmed around the couple, pounding Malcolm on the back in appreciation and hugging the two of them for their great performance. One part of the crowd joyfully lifted Laura clear off her feet like she had just won the championship, but Malcolm's attention was drawn to an attractive blonde who was eyeing him intently across the ballroom floor.

Malcolm had never seen the blonde before among the white girls who regularly came alone to the Roseland black dances. The woman was in her early twenties, had shoulder-length hair, was well built, and was elegantly dressed. She was staring at him with such intensity that Malcolm almost completely forgot about Laura, who had moved away from the mob that had engulfed her and had rushed up to Malcolm, only to see him returning the woman's stare and asking her to dance. Once again, Malcolm's rudeness and indifference to Laura was evident.

In Malcolm's autobiography the woman is given the name of Sophia. While dancing with her, he agreed to take Laura home early from the dance and then rush back in a cab to go for a drive with Sophia in her new convertible. Quickly, and with utter insensitivity to Laura, Malcolm dropped her off at home and was back at the Roseland in an hour. Sophia then drove Malcolm beyond the city limits and pulled off into a deserted lane where they proceeded to have sex in her car. From then on they were seen everywhere together as Sophia began to pick up Malcolm downtown, and he would take her to dances, nightclubs, and bars in and around Roxbury. She would then drive him all over town. Sometimes it would be nearly daylight when she let him out in front of Ella's home.

Malcolm's sudden and cruel abandonment of Laura marked the beginning of a restless, chaotic, and ultimately self-destructive period in his life. At a mere sixteen years of age but looking and sometimes acting older, Malcolm was already becoming known as a "player." It was the beginning of a street reputation that he would openly cultivate and then become gradually consumed by in the next few years. His intense alienation from his teenaged peers and adults on the Hill; his mounting insecurities about status and money; his ambition to be someone who was tough and unrelenting, yet admired and respected; his desire to be considered hip, macho, and powerful within his chosen circle of friends and associates; and his fear, cynicism, and rage regarding racism in American society all contributed to a kind of homemade nihilism that made Malcolm pessimistic about lasting bonds and allegiances that did not involve exploitation of some kind. The notion that "life is a hustle," which Freddie advocated, had now become Malcolm's personal philosophy.

In refusing Laura and taking up with Sophia, Malcolm began to indicate that shallow liaisons based primarily on sex and money (and the admiration of others who shared those corrupt values) was preferable to any genuine commitment to someone who really

One of the consequences of Malcolm's moral decline was that Laura never again came to the Townsend Drugstore where Malcolm worked. Deeply hurt and disillusioned and alienated from her puritanical grandmother whom she began increasingly to defy, Laura started drinking and using drugs. To finance these activities, she turned to prostitution. The next time Malcolm saw her, she was a complete wreck, notorious around Roxbury, and repeatedly in and out of jail. She had finished high school, but she was headed rapidly in the wrong direction. Malcolm blamed himself for this drastic change. His ugly and inexcusable treatment of her had certainly contributed to her decline. As he sadly recalled in his autobiography two decades later, he still felt deeply ashamed of and plagued by guilt for his actions concerning Laura.

Not long after Malcolm met Sophia, Ella found out about their relationship. Not surprisingly, Ella, in Malcolm's words, "began treating me like a viper." Malcolm soon quit his job at the drugstore, and Sophia provided Malcolm with enough money to leave Ella's house and move in with Shorty. Ella, who was eager to entice Malcolm away from Sophia, found him a better-paying job with the New Haven Railroad. Malcolm did not mind because he wanted to travel, particularly to New York. Finally, he was assigned to a train that passed through New York on its way to Washington, D.C., but two and a half months later he quit.

Malcolm again had ideas about doing much better in the world. He fantasized about becoming a lawyer or maybe a dancer or perhaps an actor. It did not matter, as long as the job enabled him to make a name for himself and enough money to buy a big car. He was still oscillating between trying to go "legit" and entering the criminal underworld.

Despite his cocky exterior, Malcolm was terribly afraid of failure. He agonized over it. He was very aware that job discrimination against African Americans made economic and social success on his ambitious terms highly unlikely. It was 1941, and the most a black man (even a highly educated one) could reasonably aspire to during the 1940s and '50s was a job in the post office. All major professions were closed to blacks, and school guidance counselors (like Malcolm's English teacher in Mason, Mr. Ostrowski) were very reluctant to encourage black students to seek professional careers. Black high school graduates were also firmly locked out of the trades and the unions that protected these jobs.

Despite what Ella and Laura had said about his possible future as an attorney, Malcolm knew well that institutional racism was still a major hurdle for any African American with ambition, intelligence, and drive. Even a figure as renowned as famed black actor, singer, and political activist Paul Robeson, who graduated magna cum laude from Rutgers and then from law school at Columbia University, had been refused a job in a prestigious white law firm in the 1920s because white secretaries refused to take dictation from a "nigger."

The only work the unskilled Malcolm could find when he left the railroad in September 1941 was menial. He ran through four boring, unchallenging "slaves" in little more than three months. Malcolm worked first in a south Boston wallpaper company warehouse; he stayed a month. Then he took another dishwashing job, which he subsequently lost because he was underage. The third was in the Parker House Hotel in downtown Boston. There, instead of washing dishes, he worked in the dining room in a starched white jacket carting dirty plates on big aluminum trays, which he would take back to the dishwashers who worked in the kitchen. The dead-end nature of these jobs depressed Malcolm.

One day early in December he came to work so late that he fully expected to be fired. The entire crew at the hotel was too upset to notice, however. Japanese planes had just bombed the U.S. fleet at a place called Pearl Harbor, and the United States entered World War II.

Chapter 5

Taking a Bite of the Apple

M alcolm had always dreamed of living in Harlem in New York
City. From childhood he had been fascinated by stories his
parents had told him about Marcus Garvey and the huge, magnif-
icent rallies, demonstrations, and parades of thousands of African
Americans marching through its wide, elegant boulevards on
behalf of Garvey's movement and that of many other black radical
organizations and causes. Malcolm had heard of the legendary
Harlem Renaissance (1919–1930) that featured such extraordinary
black cultural and political figures as Langston Hughes, W.E.B.
DuBois, Zora Neale Hurston, Paul Robeson, Claude McKay, and
Countee Cullen, among many others, and was very familiar with
(and crazy about) the many great jazz musicians and singers who
made their reputations or lived in Harlem, including Duke
Ellington, Count Basie, Billie Holiday, Dizzy Gillespie, Jay
McShann, and Lester Young. Malcolm was so determined to get to
New York and to find out for himself what the "Big Apple" was all
about that he jumped at the chance to work for the railroad as a
sandwich vendor for the New Haven railroad line.

In early January 1942, an elderly Pullman porter and friend of
Ella's had recommended Malcolm for the job. He had told Ella that
the war draft was taking railroad men into military service so fast
that if Malcolm could pass for twenty-one he could get him on. By
this time the strapping six foot, four inch Malcolm looked and
sounded like an adult, so he was hired. He was promised the first

available Boston-to-New York run. For a while he worked in the Dover Street railroad yard loading food requisitions onto trains. Then he was officially listed as the "fourth cook," but that was just a glorified name for a dishwasher. Finally, he was assigned to a train that passed through New York on its way to Washington, D.C. Ella was especially happy because she wanted to get Malcolm out of Boston and away from Sophia and other people she considered undesirable.

Working on the *Yankee Clipper* train, which ran from Boston to New York, Malcolm outperformed his more experienced predecessor as a sandwich vendor. Malcolm worked so hard and efficiently that he sold much more food more quickly than the man he soon replaced, a man who was sent to another train despite his seniority. Just as in school, the detention home, and on the streets, Malcolm's ambition, initiative, and drive once again attracted the attention of others.

During his layover, Malcolm finally had an opportunity to see and experience Harlem. He jumped into his most colorful zoot suit and proceeded uptown. His first major stop along Harlem's bustling and crowded Seventh Avenue was a famous nightclub and bar called Small's Paradise, where conservatively dressed blacks quietly talked and drank in an atmosphere of sophisticated geniality. Malcolm was immediately struck by the elegance and sober style of Small's and the stylish people who inhabited it. He also got his first look at the even more famous Savoy Ballroom where, it was said, the greatest dancers in the world congregated as the finest jazz orchestras played for them. Malcolm said the Savoy made the Roseland look small and shabby by comparison. He was even more impressed with the lindyhoppers and jitterbuggers here than he had been in Boston.

Malcolm also checked out such great Harlem landmarks as the Hotel Theresa, one of the finest hotels in the city and one hotel at which blacks were allowed to stay many years before any hotels downtown would accept them. (Years later this hotel served as one of Malcolm's headquarters when he became a political activist and organizer.) During this same trip Malcolm saw the equally famous Apollo Theatre and the Braddock Hotel, which was near the

Apollo's backstage entrance. The hotel's bar was a well-known watering hole and hangout for black celebrities of the era such as Dizzy Gillespie, Billy Eckstine, Billie Holiday, Ella Fitzgerald, Duke Ellington, Sarah Vaughn, Lena Horne, and Dinah Washington. Later in his life, Malcolm personally met a number of these individuals in this hotel bar.

Malcolm as a teenager, 1940s.

Schomburg Center

Wandering the streets of Harlem after dancing at the packed Savoy, Malcolm was mesmerized by the colorful panorama of what he saw and heard along and between 125th Street, Lenox, Seventh, and Eighth Avenues. Hundreds of black soldiers and sailors gawked at and passed by the same amazing sights that Malcolm did. During the war years, Harlem was officially off limits to white servicemen. There had already been a number of racial confrontations as well as muggings, robberies, and murders of these servicemen. The police were also trying to discourage other whites from traveling to Harlem, but thousands of them came anyway, drawn by its nightspots, music, and cultural activity. Malcolm saw hustlers, pimps, prostitutes, and street vendors mingle with and try to sell their various wares to a multiracial parade of young people in search of all forms of excitement. In one night Malcolm was captivated. "This is the place for me," he thought.

On the train trip back to Boston, Malcolm reflected on all he had seen. He wished that he and Ella had been on better terms at the time so that he could try to describe to her how he felt. Although he kept his expensive wardrobe (supplied mostly by Sophia) at Ella's place and frequently slept there when the train stopped for the night in Boston, he spent most of his time at Shorty's place. He told Shorty that he should move to New York because it was the national center of the music business, and he told Sophia how fascinated he was with the "Big Apple." Sophia replied that he would never be satisfied anywhere but New York. She was right. Malcolm said that in one night New York and Harlem had "narcotized" him.

Meanwhile, Malcolm focused on his job as a sandwich vendor for the railroad. Bellowing up and down the train aisles he sold sandwiches, coffee, candy, cake, and ice cream as fast as the commissary could supply them. He found that all he had to do to get whites to buy his goods was to put on a show and entertain them. Malcolm's act was inspired by the advice Freddie had once given him about popping the shoeshine rag to make an impression. Moreover, all the dining car waiters, Pullman porters, and other black workers were engaged in this fake, Uncle Tom activity to get bigger tips. It confirmed Malcolm's cynical lessons from Freddie, Shorty, and others that "the world was a hustle" because many whites were so obsessed with their own self-importance that they paid liberally, again and again, for the impression of being catered to and entertained. Malcolm was disgusted by the exaggerated, servile behavior of himself and others, yet at the same time he viewed the white customers as "suckers" for falling for these antics. This attitude later inspired much of his involvement in crime as he raced through the rest of his adolescence during the war years.

Malcolm was also quickly becoming known among his fellow workers and customers as a "wild young man" who could not be disciplined. The white stewards resented Malcolm because he was so outspoken and independent, and they were accustomed to the black crew jumping whenever they snapped their fingers. Although Malcolm was well liked by his white supervisor, Alton "Pappy" Cousins, the *Yankee Clipper*'s chief steward, many of the passengers began to complain about Malcolm's behavior. Cousins let Malcolm slide and asked some of the older blacks working with him to try to get Malcolm to calm down. But Malcolm was having none of it.

Back home in Roxbury his fellow workers saw Malcolm parading the streets with Sophia, whom he still saw whenever the train returned to its home station. Dressed in his trademark zoot suits, Malcolm would come to work and change into his vendor uniform, talking loud and acting recklessly the entire time, half high on liquor or reefers. He would stay that way through most of the trip, jamming sandwiches and laughing in people's faces until he arrived in New York. With his fire-red conk and the flamboyant cut and drape of his zoot suits, the tall and gangly teenager would glide through the afternoon rush-hour crowd at Grand Central Station while whites would stop in their tracks to watch him pass by. Once he was in Harlem, Malcolm would spend nearly his entire paycheck drinking liquor, smoking marijuana, and painting the town red with his ever-expanding entourage. He would finally stumble home to his rooming house where he would catch a few hours of sleep before the *Yankee Clipper* rolled again.

Back on the train, Malcolm would again verbally insult passengers as he strode up and down the aisles, lugging a five-gallon coffeepot and a sandwich box, which was strapped to his shoulder. In many ways Malcolm's relationship with the passengers was even worse than the strained relationship he had had with the snooty Hill youths who had patronized the Townsend Drugstore. It was clear to Malcolm that he was soon going to be fired, so he abruptly quit in October 1942.

Angry complaints from passengers 'and conductors as well as Pappy Cousins's transfer to another train all played a part in Malcolm's decision to leave. He had been working for the railroad for only two and half months when he left, but wartime demands for labor were so great that jobs were easy to come by, even for blacks, provided they did not become too "uppity" or rebel too strenuously. By this time, however, Malcolm had decided not to continue working the way he had for the past year and to take some time off to have some fun instead. When the New Haven line paid him off, Malcolm decided it would be nice to visit his brothers and sisters in Lansing with his accumulated railroad privileges for free travel.

Malcolm Returns Home to Lansing

Seventeen and streetwise, Malcolm amazed everyone back in Lansing. Malcolm's oldest brother Wilfred was away at Wilberforce University in Ohio learning a skilled trade, but Philbert, Hilda, and Reginald were still there, as were his younger siblings, Yvonne, Wesley, and Robert. Malcolm's conk and zoot suit were a shock to everyone he encountered. His hipster lingo, reefer smoking, and wild antics floored many of the older boys and young men whom Malcolm had once envied. Many people, especially the girls, were having a hard time reconciling their memory of Malcolm as a shy, withdrawn, and often reserved youngster with the extroverted character they saw on the streets and at parties. Talking in the urban argot he had learned on the streets of Boston and New York, Malcolm confused and surprised many of the kids and adults he had known in Lansing and Mason during the 1930s. "Gimme some skin, Daddy-o!" Malcolm would exclaim as people looked in awe, disgust, or bewilderment.

As he regaled his family and friends with wild stories about his adventures getting high on reefers and dancing until dawn at the Roseland and the Savoy, some of the older kids began looking up to him, and some of the girls swooned at his highly stylish and polished dancing. He was the center of attention at the local Lincoln Center ballroom. The new city slicker had seemingly triumphed in some quarters.

Not everyone was impressed, however. Mrs. Swerlin, who ran the detention home where Malcolm had lived and had always liked him, was repulsed by Malcolm's new hipster talk and attire. She invited him in when he visited (her mouth flew open when she saw him), but she was now clearly nervous and uncomfortable in his presence. Malcolm took the cue and stayed only briefly, much to their mutual relief. Worse, when he visited his mother at the Kalamazoo hospital, she only "half-sensed" who he was. This depressed and saddened him.

Malcolm even spent two months in the neighboring city of Flint, Michigan where he proceeded to pursue a number of nice, attractive black women from both the ghetto and the upper-class elite, all of whom expressed an interest in the seemingly worldly young man. However, he ultimately remained emotionally and sexually aloof, although it was clear he was very attracted to them. Many people attributed Malcolm's tough-guy behavior around women as a cover for feeling vulnerable with them, although he never openly admitted such vulnerability. Emulating some of the behavior he saw displayed in his beloved gangster movies, and by some older men in Boston and New York, Malcolm counseled one friend, "Never wear your heart on your sleeve."

The night before he left town, a dance was given in the Lincoln School gymnasium. Malcolm had left Lansing three years earlier unable to dance and too shy to learn, but now he went around the gym floor flinging girls over his hips and shoulders, showing them his most startling and show-stopping steps. As nearly everyone left the floor to watch him fly through his various routines, their eyes became as big as saucers in amazement. That night the new prodigal hipster king of black Lansing even signed autographs using the moniker Harlem Red.

Small's Paradise

In March 1943 Malcolm returned to work at the New Haven railroad. He apparently had very mixed feelings about returning; seventeen days after he was rehired he was fired. "It was inevitable," Malcolm proclaimed. He was fired not for bad work habits but for flouting the unwritten, but highly enforced, rule forbidding the railroad's black male employees from fraternizing with the white waitresses who worked in the grill cars.

Unemployed once again, Malcolm heard from a bartender at Small's Paradise club and bar, which he often frequented, in Harlem that the club needed a waiter. Although working on the railroad was the best kind of recommendation for an aspiring waiter to receive, Malcolm was afraid that Charlie Small (brother of the club's founder, Ed) might ask some of the older railroad men who were regulars about him. Malcolm knew that Charlie would not have gone for anyone with a wild reputation. But Charlie decided on the basis of his own impression of Malcolm sitting quietly in the bar almost in awe of the people there that Malcolm would make a good employee. Charlie asked Malcolm whether he had ever been in trouble with the police, which, up to that time, he had not. Charlie then told Malcolm the house rules for all employees: no lateness, no laziness, no stealing, and no kind of hustling of any customers—particularly men in uniform, whose moral behavior off-base was carefully supervised and scrutinized by a horde of civilian and military functionaries. The hands-off-servicemen edict was observed not only by Small's, but also by every drinking establishment that wanted to keep its license.

Malcolm was so ecstatic about the opportunity to mingle with the big-timers who patronized Small's that he came to work early. Malcolm understood well how to ingratiate himself with customers by being very attentive and super-polite. Malcolm made himself so useful and accommodating that within a week, the cooks and bartenders considered him indispensable. Soon, grateful customers felt the same way.

Always present and solicitous, Malcolm became a favorite of many of the highly knowledgeable old-timers who had been in Harlem for many years and knew the history of the community going back nearly three centuries. These men taught Malcolm that African Americans had been in Harlem since 1683. He also learned first-hand about the rise and glory of such famous Harlem nightspots as The Cotton Club, which featured all-black entertainment for a whites-only audience during the 1920s, as well as the revolutionary impact of jazz and such musical pioneers as Louis Armstrong, Duke Ellington, Cab Calloway, and many others during the 1920–40 era. He also heard captivating stories about the speakeasies of the Prohibition era and the many legitimate black nightclubs that flourished in Harlem, making it a cultural mecca for the world: Connie's Inn, the Lenox Club, Barron's, The Nest Club, Jimmy's Chicken Shack, and Minton's Playhouse, where the bebop jazz style was born. Finally, Malcolm heard about the history of the glamorous Savoy, Golden Gate, and Renaissance ballrooms, which competed for the huge crowds that descended on them from all over Harlem. Malcolm soaked up this kind of scholarly and viscerally fascinating knowledge like a sponge. At Small's, Malcolm began to appreciate the power and emotional impact of oral history, which is something he would learn to master as he became older.

Soon, Malcolm was taken into the confidence of a number of former legendary figures from Harlem's criminal underworld who often congregated at Small's. They told Malcolm incredible stories about such seemingly mythological characters as the cat burglar Jumpsteady, who tiptoed from window ledge to window ledge, risking his neck to rob the wealthy occupants of elegant high-rise apartment buildings. Jumpsteady was reportedly so adept at his vocation that he even burgled when his victims were in the adjoining room. Eventually, Malcolm learned about such figures as West Indian Archie, whose infallible memory enabled him to become the perfect numbers runner. When a client placed a bet, Archie did not need to record the number on a betting slip; he just remembered it. He never put the number in writing until after he had delivered his client's money to the numbers "banker." That way, if police detectives caught him with the cash, they could not prove he had done anything illegal. Other hustlers included "Cadillac" Drake and the pickpocket named Fewclothes, who had once been one of the greatest of his trade but, whose arthritic fingers had become so deformed that people shuddered when they saw them.

What fascinated Malcolm about these and many other hustlers was that they were usually highly talented and intelligent men who had wound up using their gifts in self-destructive or antisocial ways because they felt or believed that no other viable options in the "straight world" existed for them. Ultimately, they had all been led astray by their own extreme identification with the corrupt values of the society they lived in, where greed, selfishness, and the exploitation and oppression of others for profit reflected and reinforced a larger social system of hustlers and suckers and victims and criminals. The warped quest for power and control was an essential aspect of this dialectic.

Ironically, Malcolm saw and heard many of these men, who were at this time vulnerable, aging has-beens, yet he remained open to the temptations of many others who were much younger and still very active in the underworld. Before long, Malcolm turned his back on the moral and ethical implications of the lessons learned at Small's and relearned the hard way what consequences lay in store for those who failed to heed the warning signs.

Malcolm was listening to more than just the stories of nostalgic old men. After a few drinks, some of the other customers would open up to Malcolm and tell him about the techniques of being or becoming a numbers runner, con man, dope peddler, thief, pimp, or gambler. However, Small's was not known as a refuge or nest for criminals. To the contrary, Small's was considered to be one of Harlem's most decorous and law-abiding nightspots. The New York City police department often recommended it as one of the safest places to go in Harlem. But Malcolm was attracted to criminal types, and the hustlers, in turn, took a liking to him. Knowing he was still green and inexperienced by their terms, they soon took an almost paternal interest in the sharp young man with the great curiosity about street life. Because Malcolm was already gambling all his tips on the numbers and dreaming of hitting, he was becoming increasingly well-known to this crowd.

The huge numbers industry in Harlem, in which hundreds of thousands of African Americans gambled anywhere from a penny to relatively large sums of money on the remote chance of "hitting" or duplicating a daily three-digit number, eventually became Malcolm's entry into the world of professional crime. Because hundreds of millions of dollars were being circulated in the numbers racket (odds of hitting a number were a thousand to one), young, aspiring hustlers could easily become "runners" for the organized crime syndicates who bankrolled payouts to winners as well as bribes to police officials, judges, and politicians who got a cut of the action in exchange for looking the other way as this illegal activity took place.

From being a runner, it was a small step to other forms of hustling. One of the most lucrative activities was professional thief or "booster" who would deliver in one day any kind of garment one desired. In exchange for these highly expensive stolen goods, the "customer" would pay the thief about one-third of the retail store's price. One time in Small's, a black businessman-looking individual took Malcolm's measurements and jotted the figures in his notebook. When Malcolm came to work the following afternoon, one of the bartenders handed him a package. In it was an expensive, dark blue suit. On one level, the gift was in appreciation of Malcolm's prompt service in the bar, but on another it was clearly meant to recruit him to engage in similar activities. The methods of luring young men into this line of work were often this indirect. The idea was that any truly hip person would get the message and act accordingly.

Plainclothes detectives soon were quietly identified to Malcolm by a nod or wink. Knowing who all the representatives of the law were in the area was elementary for the hustlers, and like them, Malcolm soon learned to sense and identify the presence of any police types. In late 1942, each of the military services had their civilian-dress undercover agents working to identify hustles being used to avoid the draft or hustles that were being used on servicemen.

White longshoremen or their fences also came into the Harlem bars selling guns, cameras, perfumes, watches, and other items that were stolen from the shipping docks. Merchant marine sailors often brought in foreign items, bargains, and the most potent marijuana cigarettes, which they smuggled in from ports in Africa, India, and Persia. In this atmosphere of casual criminal activity and legal intrigue, Malcolm was taught and practiced the hustling society's first rule: Never trust anyone outside of your own close-mouthed circle and take time and care to select any intimates among these people.

The bartenders let Malcolm know which regular customers were mostly "fronts" and which ones really had something going on; which ones were in the underworld with downtown police or political connections; which ones handled substantial amounts of money and which ones were merely making it from day to day; which ones were real gamblers, and which ones had just hit a little luck; and most importantly, which ones never to offend or disrespect in any way. The latter people were extremely well known in Harlem, and they were feared and respected. They were violent if disturbed, and would think nothing of cracking your head open.

Malcolm had heard stories of how the old crime heads such as Black Sammy, Bub Hulan, King Padmore, and West Indian Archie had "persuaded" people with lead pipes, wet cement, baseball bats, brass knuckles, fists, feet, and blackjacks. Nearly every one of them had done some time in prison and had come back on the scene working as top runners for the biggest numbers bankers who specialized in large bettors.

Such old-time black gangsters had worked as strong-arm men for such notorious mob figures as Dutch Schultz and Owney Madden in the 1920s and '30s, when white mobsters such as Schultz and the Mafia's Charles "Lucky" Luciano had muscled into the Harlem-run numbers industry after finding out about the huge fortunes that such legendary black crime bosses as Bumpy Johnson had made. The supreme irony that the extremely profitable numbers game that had been invented by blacks was violently taken over in the 1930s by white hoods who had previously dismissed it as "nigger pool" and "nigger pennies" was not lost on Malcolm or his confederates, all of whom now saw fleecing whites as justifiable payback for such transgressions.

During this time, Malcolm also became close friends with a man called Sammy the Pimp, who had one of the biggest stables of prostitutes in New York and lived in a palatial apartment. (Sammy later formally introduced Malcolm to selling drugs.) Malcolm was learning all about prostitution from some of the women tenants in his rooming house who were sex workers. Malcolm trusted and even confided in these women whom he saw as more honest and willing to share intimate details about sexuality than "straight" women. Though the sexual education that Malcolm received from prostitutes remained verbal, Malcolm began having sexual affairs with a number of other women in New York whom he did not care for outside of his lust for them, a feeling that the women he became involved with shared. Sometimes Sophia would visit him from Boston, and Malcolm would take her around to all the bars, speakeasies, and nightclubs in Harlem. By this time their relationship had cooled off a bit, though they remained good friends.

As he had in the past, Malcolm began to drift away from responsible behavior on the job. One spring afternoon in 1943, a black soldier came into Small's, sat down at one of Malcolm's tables, and had several drinks. He looked depressed and lonely. He had been there more than an hour and was on his fourth or fifth drink when Malcolm, who was serving him, bent over close and whispered in his ear. He asked the soldier if he wanted a woman. Although Malcolm was well aware that such solicitation of soldiers could lead to the confiscation of a bar or club's liquor license or the permanent closing of an establishment, Malcolm had grown bored with having a straight job and yearned to apply the lessons he was learning from his criminal associates. Malcolm gave the apparently thankful man the phone number of one of his best friends among the prostitutes where he lived, but he felt something was wrong. He had always been uncanny in his ability to spot the police or undercover agents before and this somehow felt like one of those times. After enough time had elapsed for the soldier to reach the house, Malcolm called the house. No soldier had been there. Malcolm's premonition had been correct. The man was a military spy.

Malcolm did not try to hide what he had done. He went straight to Charlie Small's office and confessed. When the police arrived, Malcolm was waiting for them. They took him to the station for questioning. Two things were in Malcolm's favor: He had never given the police any trouble before, and when the black "soldier" had tried to tip him, Malcolm had waved it away, telling him that he was just doing him a favor. The police agreed to just scare him and send him off with a warning. Malcolm was unaware that he was not being taken to the desk and booked. Instead, the policeman took him back inside of the precinct building into a small room. In the adjoining room, Malcolm could hear the sounds of somebody being beaten. He heard a man cry out, "Please, please! Don't beat my face, that's how I make my living!" Malcolm knew from that comment that it was some pimp.

Returning to the bar, Malcolm was fired, as he expected. He was more bitter about being barred from Small's, but he understood. Now he was not only jobless but had also lost access to his favorite club in town and the chief source of his "education." It felt like being expelled from school. Sammy the Pimp waited in the wings and was the first person to come to Malcolm's aid when he lost his job. This event marked the beginning of Malcolm's new career as a professional criminal. "Detroit Red" was born.

Chapter 6

The Rise of "Detroit Red"

By the summer of 1943, Malcolm was eighteen years old and had been around Harlem long enough to acquire a nickname that soon identified him as a rising figure on the local underground crime scene and distinguished him from two other red-conked young black men who were also well known as "Red." Malcolm had met them both and would later work with them. One, called St. Louis Red, was a professional armed robber. The other, Chicago Red, was not a criminal himself but was well known in those circles as an entertainer who worked in speakeasies. He and Malcolm became very close friends in one of them, where Malcolm worked as a waiter and Chicago Red worked as a dishwasher. (Chicago Red became famous as the stage and nightclub comedian and later, the television and movie star known as Redd Foxx. When people, knowing Malcolm was from Michigan, would ask what city he was from, Malcolm replied "Detroit" because most New Yorkers had never heard of the much smaller town of Lansing. Gradually he began to be called Detroit Red.

Sammy the Pimp (whose last name was McKnight) not only became Malcolm's mentor in crime but also guided him into what he felt should be Malcolm's first major hustle: selling marijuana. In addition to pimping, Sammy had experience at selling drugs and supplied Malcolm with some of the best "weed" he had ever smoked. Sammy convinced Malcolm that selling drugs was the best way for him to formally break into the "business." Unlike numbers running, a job which a number of people had offered Malcolm, or pimping, which Malcolm felt he had no "talent" for (Malcolm would surely have starved to death trying to recruit prostitutes), peddling reefers was a way he could make money immediately. It was also a lone-wolf operation that did not depend on others or expensive middlemen, just him and his supplier, Sammy. No real experience was necessary; all the business required was a gift for gab and a knack for meeting people. Malcolm was good at both, and his business soon thrived.

Many of Malcolm's initial contacts were jazz musicians who were known to smoke weed, and as a result, Malcolm began hanging around the big bands not only to listen to the music that he loved but also to supply a regular group of customers. In addition, Sammy and Malcolm both knew merchant seamen who could supply them with marijuana. Sammy lent Malcolm stake money so that he could purchase some weed from a supplier he knew. Later that same night, Malcolm repaid the loan by selling his supply in the form of individual cigarettes to the musicians he knew at the Braddock Hotel. Malcolm then had enough money not only to pay Sammy back, but also to be in business on his own.

As Malcolm increased his rate of profit, he also began to satisfy his own growing drug habit at little cost. Except for cocaine, which he inhaled, he took all of his drugs orally because of his great fear of hypodermic needles. He did not take heroin at all, largely because of this fear, but he was an occasional user of other strong drugs such as Nembutal, Seconal, amphetamines, and opium. However, marijuana, which was far less expensive, became his habitual drug of choice and his favorite mode of escape. Cocaine was the only other drug that he took with any frequency. Both drugs made Malcolm feel less socially alienated and estranged from others, and marijuana gave him a distorted sense of deep relaxation and contentment.

Malcolm continued to indulge his personal passion for movies, both downtown in Greenwich Village and uptown in Harlem. Often, he saw as many as five a day. Two of his favorite actors were Humphrey Bogart and James Cagney. He loved the tough guys and action films and was also an enthusiastic fan of big musicals, especially those rare few featuring all-black casts such as *Stormy Weather* and *Cabin in the Sky*. After leaving the movies, he would make his connections for his drug supply, roll his joints (marijuana cigarettes), and in early evening start making his rounds. Often his customers were also friends of his, so he would sometimes "get high on his own supply" with them.

Free now to do pretty much as he pleased, Malcolm visited Boston on impulse. He saw his sister Ella there and gave her money as a token of his appreciation for her help when he moved from Lansing. However, Ella was deeply disappointed in the course Malcolm's life had taken and was still angry with him for how he had treated Laura. Catching up on family news, Malcolm was happy to hear that his always reliable and steadfast older brother Wilfred had proven to be so good at his skilled trade that the school dean had asked him to stay on as an instructor at Wilberforce University, a fine black college located in Ohio. Ella had also received a letter from Malcolm's younger brother Reginald stating that he was now in the merchant marine.

Malcolm also tried to see Sophia again, who was now married to a former white male dance partner of hers who had been drafted for service in the military. However, Shorty quickly reminded Malcolm that, as in New York, the Boston cops used the war as an excuse to publicly harass interracial couples, stopping them on the street and grilling the black male about his draft status. Like Shorty and most of his friends, Malcolm was desperately trying to avoid the draft, so he called Sophia a cab and sent her home. Malcolm went out alone to hear Shorty's band, which was doing well playing small clubs in Boston.

Shorty had also managed to get a 4-F (ineligible for service) deferment from the army, which Malcolm especially admired. He was determined to do the same when his turn to be drafted came up, which was on the immediate horizon. Malcolm also brought Shorty up to speed on his "progress" as a hustler in New York and the new "friends" he had acquired, such as Sammy the Pimp.

Malcolm Feels the Heat

When Malcolm returned to Harlem, narcotics detectives began to take an active interest him, and it did not take them long to find out he was selling reefers. Occasionally, the police would have him followed. Malcolm knew that if evidence were found, he would go to jail. However, the law clearly specified that a person could not be convicted of a drug violation unless the incriminating evidence was found on his or her person. Malcolm devised various schemes to avoid being captured with the drugs in his possession. One method was to carry fifty joints in a small package under his armpit, inside his coat. Keeping his arm flat against his side, Malcolm would move about with his eyes open for any suspicious-looking person. Whenever he suspected that a cop was tailing him, he would quickly cross the street or turn a corner and raise his arm. The small packet of marijuana would drop unnoticed in the dark. If he decided he had been mistaken about being followed, Malcolm would go back and retrieve his joints. However, he would often lose reefers this way, which would cost him money. When he knew he had frustrated or outfoxed a detective, he took great pride in it.

The police stepped up the pressure. One day while he was out, detectives searched his room. Knowing that if the cops could not find any evidence, they often would plant some where the drug dealer would never find it and return to "discover" it, Malcolm quickly moved out and found another room to live in. He also began carrying a gun for protection.

He was now selling less marijuana because he spent so much time being careful. Justifiably paranoid about getting caught, Malcolm now moved from time to time to other rooms, telling no one but Sammy where he slept. The news was on the grapevine that the Harlem narcotics squad had Malcolm on a special list for harassment. Every other day or so, and usually in a public place, the cops would flash their badges and search him. But Malcolm would proclaim loudly enough for bystanders to hear that he had no contraband on him and that he did not want any planted. Fearing that an angry crowd would gather on Malcolm's behalf, the cops would back off.

Harlem was already very tense because of widespread racism in the city and the special problems presented by World War II. The city exploded in riotous violence in July 1943 when a white police-man shot an off-duty black soldier who had intervened when the officer tried to violently arrest a black woman for disorderly con-duct. There had been so much police brutality against black citi-zens in Harlem that this incident proved to be the last straw. As news of the shooting spread by word of mouth throughout Harlem, wild rumors began to surface that the policeman had killed the black soldier while the soldier's mother looked on helplessly. Actually, the soldier was wounded in the shoulder and hit the policeman in retaliation with the policeman's own billy club (both men were hospitalized), but the truth came out too late to quell the bottled-up rage that erupted. Within an hour angry black mobs were rampaging throughout Harlem as pitched battles went on between the police, local citizens, and the U.S. military. Neither the Mayor of New York, Fiorello LaGuardia, nor the president of the NAACP, Walter White (who went riding around the embat-tled area in a red fire truck), could convince the incensed crowd to disperse.

Finally, thousands of police and the U.S. Army had to be called in to stop what Harlemites called a massive "racial rebellion." After the looting, arson, fights, and gunplay finally subsided, Harlem looked like an invading army had attacked it. The riot was the first one in the so-called "modern era" in which blacks took the physical initiative in rioting against their oppression. A month later in August 1943, Detroit erupted in an even bigger riot that featured yet another case of racial conflict over violent police prac-tices in the black community. Clearly African Americans had had enough and were fighting back.

While all this incendiary social conflict was taking place, Malcolm was preoccupied with trying to find still more places to stash his drugs. Now afraid to carry the illegal substances with him, he hid his reefers in various places. After his clients paid him, he told them where to pick up the drugs. He would fill empty cigarette packs with joints and drop them behind garbage cans. But many of his regular customers, especially the stylish and well-known jazz musicians that he did business with, took a very dim view of such practices. They would not be seen scrounging around garbage cans, so Malcolm once again started hawking his goods directly on Harlem's streets. This practice was dangerous not only because of the many police, military, and undercover agents hovering around, but also because many addicts lacking money to buy drugs would often follow him and waylay him in dark doorways and back alleys for his supply. Not wanting to be hurt or killed for his drugs, Malcolm was forced to hand over the reefers.

Malcolm began to lose money so quickly that he was not only a marked man, but he was also in debt. Soon Malcolm found himself borrowing money from Sammy and even some of his musician friends to buy drugs. The money was often just enough to enable him to eat and to stay high himself. Clearly his new "career" was going nowhere fast. It was time to find a safer way to make a living.

Sammy suggested that Malcolm use his old railroad ID card to make a few runs until the heat cooled. Malcolm found that if he flashed his railroad card and behaved professionally, the conductor would wave him aboard the train and allow him to ride wherever the train went. Soon Malcolm began working for the New York Central Railroad while selling his reefers surreptitiously among his friends who were on tour with bands. Because he already had the New Haven ID card, Malcolm was able to work a couple of weeks for other railroads, which enabled him to acquire additional ID cards.

In New York he rolled and packed a great quantity of joints and sealed them into jars. The ID cards that Malcolm had picked up were a part of his new hustle and worked like a charm. He used them to persuade conductors that he was a fellow employee who had to go home on some family business. The conductors, thinking Malcolm was on staff, would let him on board without a second thought. Malcolm would then travel for free to various towns where his friends were playing and sell his reefers to dancers and other people who filled the auditoriums, gymnasiums, and ballrooms where the bands played. When he ran out of supplies, Malcolm returned to New York, loaded up, and then hit the road again.

To gain entry to dances and concerts in other towns and cities, Malcolm would announce at the door that he was some musician's brother. In many cases, people just assumed that he was a band member. Sometimes he stayed overnight. Sometimes he drove the band's bus to its next stop. In some of the small towns, people thought he was in the band and mobbed him for autographs. In Buffalo, New York his suit was nearly torn off by frenzied fans.

Back in New York things had cooled down. Word was around that Malcolm had left town, and the local narcotics squad was satisfied with that. Around this time, Malcolm's younger brother Reginald, who was now sixteen and a merchant marine, came to visit Malcolm. The little brother who had once followed Malcolm everywhere, trying to be just like him, was now nearly six feet tall and very self-possessed. Darker than Malcolm, he, too, had greenish eyes and dark, reddish hair. Malcolm liked him. He was impressed by his younger brother's relaxed attitude and dignified sense of self. Malcolm also felt that Reginald was a lot surer of himself than Malcolm had been at sixteen.

Checking into a hotel on Sugar Hill in Harlem, Reginald and Malcolm talked all night about the Lansing years. Malcolm told his brother things about their parents that Reginald had been too young to remember. Reginald told Malcolm about their other brothers and sisters. Yvonne, Wesley, and Robert were still in school in Lansing. Wilfred was still a teacher at Wilberforce University, and both Hilda and Philbert were considering marriage. Reginald and Malcolm also openly joked about their older brother Philbert, who had become deeply religious the last time Malcolm had seen him. Malcolm thought that was ridiculous, and he and Reginald laughed at the very image of their now sternly upright sibling.

Reginald's ship was in town for about a week getting some repairs on its engines. Pleased to be able to spend some extended time with his brother, Malcolm, who thought Reginald dressed a little too loudly, began schooling him on proper attire. He asked a reefer customer of his to get Reginald a more conservative and stylish overcoat and suit. Malcolm then told Reginald what he had learned: To get something in life, you had to look as though you already had something. Before Reginald left, Malcolm was urging him to leave the merchant marines. He told him he would help him get a job in Harlem. Despite all the many people he hung around with, Malcolm was lonely. He felt having his kid brother around would be a good thing for him. Then there would be *two* people he could trust (Sammy being the other). But unlike Malcolm at that age, who would have jumped at any chance to get to New York and Harlem, his younger brother, knowing what Malcolm's life was like, was cool and cautious. When he left, he simply said, "I'll think about it."

Malcolm Outwits the U.S. Army

Shortly after Reginald's visit in October 1943, Malcolm was fired from his job on the New York Central Railroad. It was just as well, because by then the U.S. military draft board had finally caught up with him. They had initially written him at Ella's house in Boston, and when they received no response, they notified the New York draft board. They sent the official letter to Sammy's place. Malcolm admitted he was scared. As he put it: "In those days only three things really scared me: jail, a job, and the army." He had about ten days to show up at the Manhattan army induction center or be arrested.

Malcolm, who anticipated being called ever since Shorty told him about his 4-F ineligibility status, had an elaborate plan all worked out so that he, too, could avoid service. He had no intention of submitting to military discipline in a racially segregated army for a country he and all his friends and associates considered to be oppressive and utterly indifferent to their humanity. Malcolm was also well aware of the black undercover military agents dressed in civilian clothes who hung around in Harlem with their eyes and ears open for young black men trying to avoid the draft. He knew that whatever he said in public would be immediately picked up and reported to white authorities downtown. So he started circulating the word around Harlem that he was "frantic to join ... the Japanese army!"

As part of his scheme to convince the military spies that he was unfit for service, he talked and acted high and crazy. He made a big show of reading his letter of "greetings from Uncle Sam" aloud in public places so that the spies were certain to hear who he was and when he was to report downtown. The day Malcolm reported to the induction center he went, as he stated, "costumed like an actor." He wore his wildest zoot suit with yellow knob-toe shoes, and he frizzled his hair into a bushy, reddish conk. In his autobiography, Malcolm described his exaggerated behavior: "I went in skipping and tipping, and I thrust my tattered 'greetings' notice at that reception desk's white soldier—'Crazy-o, daddy-o, get me moving. I can't wait ...."

As he was processed along with several dozen other prospective inductees, Malcolm continued to talk loudly, spewing slang and running his mouth "a mile a minute." The other, mostly white draftees looked on in shocked silence, hateful stares, or nervous amusement as Malcolm continued to act out. Most of the ten or twelve black men who were also being processed with Malcolm were amused by his antics. Stripped to his shorts after his physical examination, Malcolm made his loud eager-to-join-the-army comments in the exam room where a number of the medical staff in white coats looked at him as though he were indeed deranged. Malcolm's scam appeared to be working. Soon he was taken from the line, and one of the men in white accompanied him to an adjoining hallway. Malcolm knew he was on his way to see the Army psychiatrist. His plan was proceeding just as he hoped. He proclaimed that he was willing to "fight on all fronts" and that he would "like to be a general someday."

As the psychiatrist sat quietly doodling with a blue pencil, he let Malcolm rant on for another three or four minutes without saying a word. Then the psychiatrist began to quietly ask Malcolm a series of questions about why he had so much anxiety. Careful not to rush his attack, Malcolm began to verbally spar with the psychiatrist, feinting and parrying with him as he continued his verbal barrage, giving the psychiatrist the desired impression that he was drawing from Malcolm what the psychiatrist wanted to hear.

As Malcolm talked, he kept jerking around in his seat and looking over his shoulder in a paranoid fashion. Suddenly Malcolm sprang from his chair and stooped down and peeped under both doors in the room, as though someone might be listening. Then he bent down and whispered quickly in the psychiatrist's ear: "Daddy-o, now you and me, we're from up North here, so don't you tell nobody … I want to get sent down South. Organize them nigger soldiers, you dig? Steal us some guns and kill up crackers!"

That did it. The psychiatrist, looking alarmed, dropped his blue pencil and his calm, objective, professional demeanor. Fumbling for his red pencil, he stared at Malcolm in horror. Malcolm was secretly elated. He knew his act had succeeded. He was declared psychologically unfit for the army by his draft board. When his coveted 4-F card arrived in the mail, Malcolm knew his hustle had outwitted the U.S. military. He never heard from it again.

Malcolm Recruits His Brother into the Underworld

By early 1944, Malcolm was not only unemployed but also had to give up selling reefers because the narcotics squad was too familiar with his operation in Harlem. Living entirely by his wits on the street, he had become a real predator, willing and able to exploit anyone he could for money, especially women. Not only did Sophia, who was now married, continue to send Malcolm money and even visit from time to time, but Malcolm had also now "graduated" to armed robbery with his criminal mentor, Sammy, as his guide. During the next six to eight months, Malcolm and Sammy pulled a series of successful small-time robberies and stick-ups in nearby cities and towns.

By this time, Malcolm habitually carried all kinds of guns. For robberies he would substitute larger .32, .38, and .45 caliber guns for the smaller, .25 automatic pistol that he usually kept with him. He carried the larger guns to instill great fear in his victims and thereby ensure that he would not have to actually fire the weapons.

Following Sammy's recommendations about proper criminal procedure, Malcolm steeled himself for each "job" by sniffing cocaine. The high from cocaine made him feel exceptionally powerful and confident, and Malcolm used this cocaine-induced "courage" to make himself virtually fearless in order to react quickly in a sudden crisis and thus avoid capture by the police.

In one such episode, Malcolm and Sammy narrowly escaped arrest for a heist when they heard a police car's siren as they were fleeing the scene of the crime. They immediately stopped running and slowed to a walk. When the police saw them and slammed on the brakes to stop, Malcolm and Sammy calmly stepped into the street, flagged the car, and asked the policemen for directions. The maneuver worked. The policemen, who had apparently thought they were going to provide them with information, cursed them and sped away, unaware that they had been fooled. Once again, Malcolm's ability to use his intelligence and guile to fool someone had worked.

During this period Malcolm also became a compulsive gambler who bet large sums of cash from his criminal activity trying vainly to get a big payoff by hitting the numbers. Although he was able to hit a smaller number from time to time, he was unsuccessful in pulling off that big 600-to-1 shot that would make him wealthy. The result from all the gambling was that Malcolm was often cash-poor regardless of how much he scored with his various hustles. He was rapidly falling deeper and deeper into a trap of his own design. He temporarily found safer work as a numbers runner in the Bronx, but then Malcolm soon began to change hustles the way he had once changed jobs.

During a hold-up, Sammy was nicked by a bullet. Sammy went back to his apartment to recover, and Malcolm later joined him there. Sammy's beautiful Spanish mistress, Hortense, was so distraught over his injury that when she saw Malcolm, whom she held partly responsible for what happened, she attacked him with bared fingernails, clawing and screaming. In an attempt to fend her off, Malcolm struck her. Sammy was so angry with Malcolm for hitting her that he pulled a gun on Malcolm. Hortense screamed again and distracted him long enough to allow Malcolm to make a hasty exit through the door. Sammy chased Malcolm for a block.

Malcolm and Sammy later made up, but both knew that their friendship would never be the same again. Malcolm, who had always admired Sammy's cold, calculating way with women, now felt that showing emotion in reaction to Malcolm striking his mistress betrayed a weakness in Sammy that Malcolm, lost in his own ruthless and cold-hearted misogyny, could no longer respect. In his twisted view, Sammy had gone soft. This opinion and the fact that his friend had pulled a gun on him with every intention of using it meant that Malcolm could no longer fully trust Sammy.

Around this period Malcolm's brother Reginald once again visited while on ship leave in New York. Malcolm came to rely more and more on his younger brother Reginald as the only person in the world he could trust. Malcolm soon convinced Reginald, who was only sixteen, to quit the merchant marine and become a hustler. Clearly Malcolm had reached the point where he could not be with someone he loved without getting that person to wallow in the same corruption that was destroying his life. Soon he was schooling his brother in hustling the same way Sammy and others had schooled him.

Because Reginald now had nowhere to live, Malcolm decided to get his first actual apartment in Harlem, after a couple of years of living in rented rooms. Living right behind Malcolm and his brother in a rear basement apartment was one of Harlem's most successful narcotics dealers. With the apartment as their headquarters, Malcolm gradually introduced his brother to many of Harlem's after-hours clubs. Every morning around two o'clock Malcolm and Reginald would stand around in front of an after-hours joint, and Malcolm would teach Reginald about nightlife.

Malcolm first got his brother into a "safe" hustle that involved selling inferior goods (shirts, underwear, cheap rings, watches, and so on) for an exorbitant price. To get the goods, Malcolm first purchased a city's peddler license and then went to a manufacturer's outlet where he purchased a supply of cheap, marked-down items. Watching Malcolm pull this scam in Harlem, Reginald quickly caught on to going into barbershops, beauty parlors, and bars and acting very nervous while allowing the customers to peep into his small valise of loot. With so many other thieves around anxious to sell stolen, high-quality merchandise cheaply, many people jumped at the chance to pay higher prices for inferior goods whose sale was perfectly legitimate because they assumed from Reginald's nervous attitude that the goods had been stolen and were of high quality. Selling an entire valise of goods for at least twice what it had cost was easy to do. Then, if any cop stopped Reginald, he had in his pocket both the peddler's license and the manufacturer's outlet bills of sale. Reginald only had to make sure that none of the customers to whom he sold the cheap goods ever saw that he was legitimate.

Soon after Reginald was introduced to this sordid life, he began emulating his older brother in other ways as well. Already six feet tall, and in some ways even more mature than Malcolm, Reginald also looked and behaved older than he was. He quit his street hustle and began going out with a black woman twice his age who was a waitress in a rich, exclusive restaurant downtown. She gave him money and clothes and cooked and cleaned for him.

Malcolm, who claimed he admired and respected his younger brother for his ability to hustle and manipulate women, felt "very close" to Reginald, but his brother secretly disagreed. Despite his love for Malcolm, Reginald found he could never really get close to someone who regarded all personal questions as unwelcome intrusions. Reginald felt that he never knew what Malcolm was thinking or feeling. He was more emotionally guarded and alienated than even his brother imagined. As far as Reginald was concerned, aside from their mutual interest in hustling and superficial talk about their other siblings, he and Malcolm were never as close as he wanted to be.

Hustling had made Malcolm unable or unwilling to fully trust or respect anyone. By the fall of 1944, Malcolm was too far gone to see or feel anything that did not correspond to his now warped sense of values. He would spend almost eighteen more intense months in the criminal underworld before the law and circumstance finally caught up with him for good.

Chapter 7

Living in the Hustling World

During most of 1944, Malcolm worked various hustles that temporarily sustained him and kept him from deeper involvement in far more dangerous and high-risk criminal activities such as robbery and drug pushing. For all of his public bravado and macho posturing, Malcolm was deeply afraid of using guns, though this fear did not stop him from pulling his weapon in self-defense or in simple anger on someone when he felt the occasion called for it.

During the period he worked as a numbers runner in the Bronx, Malcolm got into some major trouble as a result of his own compulsive gambling habits. He began placing his daily bets with the legendary gambler and violent hoodlum, West Indian Archie, one of the old-timers that he had heard stories about when he was still working at Small's Paradise. Archie, who was now sixty and had done a long prison stretch at the notorious Sing Sing penitentiary before Malcolm arrived in Harlem, still had the kind of photographic memory that enabled him to recall any combination of numbers that his bettors requested. He never wrote any of the numbers down nor used betting slips, which protected him from police using such documentation as evidence in court. Because of this gift, Archie was in the elite of all numbers runners, and you crossed him only at your peril. Because he had also worked as a strong-arm enforcer in the mob when he was younger, people were extremely reluctant to question his judgment.

Just to be known as a client of Archie's was a status in itself, because he only handled the biggest bettors. He also required integrity and sound credit. His clients did not have to pay as they played; they could pay him on a weekly basis. He routinely carried a couple of thousand dollars of his own money on him. If a client came up and said he had hit for some moderate amount, such as a fifty-cent or one-dollar combination, West Indian Archie would peel off the three or six hundred dollars and collect his money later from the numbers banker. Every weekend Malcolm would pay his regular gambling bill, and when he hit the number on a couple of rare occasions, Archie would pay him from his own roll. But this arrangement came back to haunt Malcolm and got him entangled in a direct and highly dangerous confrontation with West Indian Archie.

Meanwhile, Malcolm continued to work as a runner and to brag to visitors from Michigan that he was a big-time gang leader who had six or seven felons working for him and who had bribed the police to protect his illegal operations. These lies and other exaggerations served to bolster Malcolm's sagging ego and faltering sense of self-esteem because he no longer felt he was making any real progress in his career as a gangster.

Malcolm also worked in a gambling den and then worked as a "steerer" for a Harlem brothel that catered exclusively to many of the richest and most powerful white men in New York's commercial, professional, and political establishment. A steerer was someone who worked for a madam and was responsible for picking up johns who were out looking for prostitutes and then steering them to the proper destination. Malcolm's official post for such activity was a busy area outside a major hotel in midtown Manhattan. There he would watch the moving traffic to spot a taxi, car, or limousine with an anxious white face peering out who, having been tipped off by the madam in advance, was looking for "a tall, reddish-brown-complexioned Negro" (Malcolm) wearing a dark suit or raincoat with a conspicuous white flower in his lapel. Then, unless the car had a chauffeur, Malcolm would take the wheel and drive the john to the destination. If the john was in a taxi, Malcolm would always tell the cab driver, "The Apollo Theatre in

Harlem, please", because some New York City cabs were driven by policemen. Malcolm would then get another cab driven by a black man and give him the correct address. As soon as the customer was settled, Malcolm would telephone the madam. She would have him rush by taxi right back downtown to his point of origin on 45th and Broadway at a specified time. Appointments with johns were strictly punctual. Rarely was Malcolm on the corner more than five minutes. In this way and by moving about so as not to attract attention, Malcolm was able to avoid any vice-squad plain-clothesmen or uniformed police. With very heavy tips Malcolm was often able to make more than a hundred dollars a night (a very big sum in the 1940s) steering up to ten customers per evening to their various assignations.

The great majority of these white men were wealthy, middle-aged and older, Ivy League types: society leaders, major politicians, tycoons, and government officials. There were also all kinds of professional people, Hollywood celebrities, and well-known artists, as well as racketeers. These men were willing to pay large sums of money for illicit and taboo sex with black women. Malcolm often witnessed many of these erotic spectacles and grew to despise and openly mock the moral and ethical hypocrisy of these public figures in official positions of authority, whom he had seen engaging in the most degrading behavior. He also worked as a steerer for a white madam who specialized in hiring out black male prostitutes to have sex with bored and wealthy white women from New York's ritzy Upper East Side. At nineteen, Malcolm had grown extremely jaded and cynical because of all the human exploitation he had seen, experienced, and participated in.

Despite his criminal activity, Malcolm still harbored a desire for mainstream social acceptance and respectability. Vacillating between legitimate pursuits and illegal ones, Malcolm got a job at a nightclub called the Lobster Pond where he worked as a bar entertainer in July 1944. There he used his dancing ability to good advantage and occasionally played the drums. He took the stage name of Jack Carlton, which was virtually a duplicate of the stage name that his half brother, Earl Little, Jr., used in his act (Jimmy Carlton). Malcolm was largely secretive about his desire to be an entertainer; but during a brief trip back to Michigan, he revealed his ambition to a friend. Malcolm still very much wanted to be out front, on stage, and in public entertaining audiences. He still dreamed of getting people to notice him in a positive way for his talents. It was as if he had finally realized what a dead end his life had become and was desperate to find a viable alternative. At the same time, regular menial work no longer interested him. His ego and ambition, not to mention personality, demanded more. These conflicting desires and needs were tearing him apart as he continued to drift.

Malcolm's employer at the Lobster Pond, like many of his previous employers, liked him and thought he was "a good boy," but he also felt that he was somewhat unstable and neurotic. He was pleased with Malcolm's work, but he had to let him go in September because the position of bar entertainer was seasonal employment. Malcolm then left New York and returned to Boston. In October, he once again took a regular job, becoming a packer at the Sears Roebuck warehouse in a Boston suburb. It paid only twenty-nine dollars a week. Quickly tiring of the back-breaking labor, Malcolm failed to appear for work six times in a three-week period. In November he quit. Although Malcolm had an enormous capacity for work when he was properly motivated and found employment that was compatible with his aspirations, he now felt completely alienated from the only kind of legitimate work he could get.

Back in Boston, Malcolm stayed at Ella's place, which, given his sister's severe disillusionment with him, proved to be a tense and uncomfortable situation for both of them. By now he was not the only roomer at Ella's spacious home. Their two aunts, Sarah and Grace (his father's sisters), now lived together on the ground floor. Malcolm did not get along with Aunt Grace as well as he did with Aunt Sarah, so in yet another self-destructive act, he stole Grace's fur coat in late November 1944 and pawned it for five dollars. An outraged and incensed Ella immediately called the police who took Malcolm to jail. He was given a three-month suspended sentence and placed on probation for a year. This sentence marked the first time Malcolm had ever been caught, arrested, and convicted for a criminal act. When Malcolm returned to New York, Abe Goldstein, his former employer at the Lobster Pond, put him to work at one of his nightclubs. But after Christmas, this job, which was also seasonal, ended.

Now completely adrift and wallowing in self-pity, Malcolm returned to Lansing. Dressed in conservative attire and no longer speaking in hipster slang, he looked forlorn and unhappy. Defensively lying to everyone he encountered, Malcolm tried to hide his very recent criminal past. He told one ex-classmate that he had been dancing in shows in New York. He told another old friend that he had just come from California, where he had been acting bit parts in Hollywood movies. He told a third person that he was "in business," and a fourth that he was associated with a Madison Avenue modeling agency. Gone was the familiar bounce in his step and his usual rapid gait, which resembled his father's. He now walked slowly and aimlessly.

Changing his mind yet again about working, Malcolm waited on tables for two weeks at an East Lansing nightspot called the Coral Gables. He also worked briefly as a busboy at the Mayfair Ballroom. He began stealing again. After one victim awoke and discovered Malcolm had stolen her purse, she demanded her money, which Malcolm insisted he had not taken. However, the woman cornered Malcolm in her room, and Malcolm took a swing at her. It was then that he discovered she was a professional female wrestler, and she picked him up and threw him across the floor. A dazed Malcolm staggered to his feet only to be thrown again. Landing near the door he hastily unbolted the door, fled downstairs, and half-ran, half-limped his way for about a mile and a half to his brother Philbert's house where Malcolm received help for his injured leg. He was limping because in his eagerness to hurdle a picket fence along the way, he cut his shin to the bone. The scar remained with him the rest of his life.

Malcolm moved in with a man named Jimmy Williams and robbed him at gunpoint soon after. Williams refused to press charges. When a friend of Williams found out and angrily confronted Malcolm, he pleaded with the man not to hit him. The man, who was much shorter than Malcolm but a very good fighter, was amazed at Malcolm's fear and let him go. Malcolm then went to Detroit and robbed Douglas Haynes, who had been kind enough to put him up for the night.

Taking none of the precautions that he had taken in New York to avoid arrest, Malcolm appeared to be begging to be sent to prison or even killed. His victims were all people who knew him. Douglas Haynes swore out a legal complaint against him, and the Detroit police alerted Lansing police officials, who apprehended Malcolm in March 1945.

The authorities retrieved several items Malcolm had stolen from Haynes, including a coat Malcolm had pawned. Confronted with the evidence, Malcolm still asserted his innocence. His brother Wilfred generously provided the money he needed to make bail, and after he was released on bond, Malcolm played up his bad reputation for all it was worth. He bragged that the Boston cops were still after him. He falsely boasted that he had already done time in prison. However, Malcolm tried to hide his criminal past when he was with people he respected. With a minister's daughter he had once liked, he tried to rationalize his behavior by claiming that he had to hustle in order to eat. Lost in his general moral confusion and desperately trying to impress his peers by either wildly exaggerating or suppressing his exploits to prove he was a success, Malcolm's wavering self-esteem and destructive attitude was leading him to a far different conclusion: He was a miserable failure, and he knew it. As Malcolm continued to flounder, his past began to catch up with him.

For the time being, Malcolm's trial in Detroit was postponed. Jimmy Williams, despite having been robbed by Malcolm, still refused to give up on him and found a job for him making mattresses at a bedding company in Lansing where Williams was a supervisor. Malcolm showed up only intermittently for work, and when he was there, he did not work very hard. In July 1945, he quit and took a job sweeping floors at the Reo truck factory for about five days. The following month he returned to Harlem and skipped out on his trial hearing in Detroit, which lead to a new warrant for his arrest.

Around this time he began transporting moonshine liquor for a Jewish bootlegger named Hymie. Hymie supplied many supposedly reputable New York bars and restaurants who, after saving their empty liquor bottles, would have them filled with illegal home-made rotgut liquor provided by Hymie's truckers. Malcolm was one of those who trucked the empties to Long Island where they were filled with the illegal stuff. He then redelivered the newly filled bottles to tap rooms and cocktail lounges throughout New York where they were sold to unsuspecting customers who could not tell the difference between their favorite legitimate brands and the bootleg stuff.

Hymie loved to talk and philosophize about politics and history and often gave Malcolm spirited lectures about the need for American blacks and Jews, as national minorities in a racist and anti-Semitic society, to unite. Hymie hated Jews who had assimilated to the point where they anglicized their last names, and he was contemptuous of Jews who were not openly proud of their cultural and social heritage. Hymie was impressed with Malcolm's intelligence and ability to listen and learn and paid him very well, sometimes as much as two to three hundred dollars a week. With Hymie's approval, Malcolm also made extra income on the side by supplying Harlem bars and the few remaining speakeasies with some lesser quantities of bootleg liquor.

Eventually, the State Liquor Authority caught up with Hymie's scam. One of New York State's biggest scandals of the era was the public exposure of wholesale graft and corruption in the State Liquor Authority. Apparently someone high up on the bootleg corruption food chain had been taken for a great deal of money, and rumors spread about an informant in Hymie's operation. One day Hymie did not show up where he had told Malcolm to meet him. It was clear that Hymie had been killed by the mob. As Malcolm put it rather cryptically in his autobiography: "I never heard from him again … but I did hear that he was put in the ocean, and I knew he couldn't swim."

By the fall of 1945, when Malcolm was not stalking trouble, it stalked him. One day the twenty-year-old found himself mistaken by two Mafia thugs for another light-skinned black man who had robbed some Italian racketeers in a floating crap game in the Bronx. They cornered Malcolm in a barroom phone booth. For once, Malcolm was unarmed. All he had in his pocket was a cigarette case, which he tried to pretend was a gun. The hoods called his bluff, snatched open the door of the phone booth, and told Malcolm to come outside with them. Luckily, at that very moment a policeman walked through the front door of the bar. The two thugs quietly slipped out. Malcolm remarked that he had never been so happy to see a cop in his entire life.

Malcolm was still shaking from this close brush with death when he arrived at his friend Sammy's apartment. Malcolm did not pay much attention when Sammy told him that West Indian Archie had been there looking for him. Not thinking it was anything important, Malcolm quickly forgot about it. He and Sammy then sniffed some cocaine together. Feeling no pain, they went out to a nightclub to hear Billie Holiday.

When they returned to Sammy's apartment, West Indian Archie knocked on the door and announced himself. Malcolm answered and was shocked to find a very angry Archie holding a gun on him and demanding "his money." Malcolm was not only frightened out of his wits, but also completely dumbfounded. What had happened and why was Archie mad? Stuttering, Malcolm was barely able to utter a sound as if there was a disconnection between his brain and mouth, "Man—what's the beef?" West Indian Archie told him that he thought Malcolm was trying to pull a fast one on him earlier that afternoon when Archie had paid Malcolm three hundred dollars with Malcolm's assurance that the number he had "combinated" had won. But when Archie had double-checked the betting slip, he discovered that Malcolm had "combinated" a different number.

Malcolm genuinely thought that the once infallible Archie had made a rare mistake, but working against him was Archie's experience that this would have not been the first time a young, ambitious hustler had tried to make a name for himself by conning an established hood. Both Malcolm and Archie also knew that it would not have been the first time Malcolm had attempted to outsmart an older, more experienced competitor or colleague. As

Malcolm vainly tried to talk Archie out of it by assuring him he was telling the truth about the number he hit, Archie continued to brandish the gun and issued an ultimatum to Malcolm: "I'll give you until twelve o'clock tomorrow to come up with my money." Then Archie backed out of the apartment with his gun in hand and slammed the door.

Malcolm was petrified. He knew that the real issue was not the money itself. He still had about two-thirds of it and could have easily raised the rest. This disagreement was a question of saving face for Archie. In the hustler code of the streets that demanded honor and respect, Archie could not let Malcolm get away with what he perceived to be an attempt to hype (hustle) him. Malcolm, whose street reputation was also at stake, could not cave in to Archie's threat. But as Malcolm well knew, those who defied Archie did so at their peril. Archie made certain that most people remained fearful of him. Malcolm was no exception, but he prepared himself to make the rounds of his usual hangouts. His peers would have interpreted any change in his routine as cowardice and an absolute transgression of the hustler code.

Malcolm, despite his fear, decided to let the chips fall where they may. Sammy let Malcolm have his .32 caliber pistol because Malcolm's own guns were at his apartment. Malcolm was glad that his brother Reginald was out of town. He might have tried protecting Malcolm and gotten shot by Archie. Anyway, because Malcolm could not stay out of sight, he stood on a nearby street corner trying to figure out whether he had indeed been mistaken about the number or whether Archie was pulling a hype on him to hold him up to ridicule. Either way, it did not matter. The anticipated showdown between them was already hot on the underground wire. It appeared that push would come to shove.

Later, Malcolm and his date took a cab to one of his favorite nightspots in Harlem, a bar called La Marr-Cheri. He had already sniffed the little packet of cocaine Sammy had given him earlier. Malcolm felt secure. He had his gun and the "courage" supplied by the cocaine, which made him feel invincible. There he had drinks and got so high that he asked his date to take a cab home alone, which she did. Foolishly Malcolm stayed at the bar. He sat there with his back to the door, thinking about West Indian Archie. (He later remarked that he never again sat with his back to any door.)

The next thing he knew Archie was standing over him with his gun drawn, cursing Malcolm loudly in public and threatening him. Everyone in the bar froze. Archie was also high on drugs, which Malcolm had never seen before because Archie rarely even took a drink. Malcolm thought he recognized Archie's behavior as that of a hustler keying up his nerve to do a "job." Malcolm thought he would kill Archie if he turned his back and Malcolm got the drop on him. The .32 was tucked under Malcolm's belt, beneath his coat. Suddenly Archie seemed to read Malcolm's mind and stopped cursing. Then he jarred Malcolm by saying very calmly, "You're thinking you're going to kill me first, Red. But I'm going to give you something to think about. I'm sixty. I'm an old man. I've been to Sing Sing. My life is over. You're a young man. Kill me, you're lost anyway. All you can do is go to prison."

At that point some friends of West Indian Archie eased up beside him, quietly pleading to Archie to leave. Eventually they physically maneuvered him toward the rear of the bar past Malcolm as Archie glared at him. Taking his time, Malcolm got down off the barstool, dropped a bill on the bar for his drink, and strolled out the door. For about five minutes Malcolm stood outside in full view of the bar with his hand in his pocket clutching his gun and waited for Archie to come out. When he did not, Malcolm left.

Malcolm later reflected that Archie might have been trying to scare him into running, both to save his face and life. He also insisted that, although he had never killed nor even fired a gun at anyone, he would not have hesitated to kill Archie. But unlike the gun-toting heroes of the cowboy and gangster films that Malcolm loved so much, no professional gunman in twentieth-century Harlem, or anywhere else, would ordinarily dispatch his victims in public where there were many witnesses and where the police could easily find and arrest him for the deed. The fact that Archie refrained from such an attempt on Malcolm's life did not necessarily mean that he was backing down. On the contrary, he had publicly humiliated Malcolm, who had not retaliated. It was probably more accurate to say that, in more ways than one, an absurdly reck-less Malcolm had once again dodged a bullet. Besides, Archie had still not withdrawn his ultimatum.

The next day, in a deep panic, Malcolm told himself that he had to stay high. He said that he was so jumpy that he was ready to fire his gun "if I heard a mosquito cough." He took some opium, which made him drowsy. Then he took some bennies (Benzedrine) in his bathroom to perk himself up. The combination of the two drugs had his head swimming in opposite directions at the same time. He knocked at the door of the apartment behind his. The drug dealer there let him have over a hundred joints on credit. As they rolled the joints they both smoked some.

Malcolm then stopped at Sammy's place on the way downtown. His mistress Hortense answered the door. Not only was Sammy the Pimp finally in love (Malcolm disdainfully said that he was now "weak for that woman"), but he also was now hopelessly addicted to drugs. He seemed to barely recognize Malcolm. No matter. Lying in bed he reached under and brought out his shaving mirror on which he always kept his cocaine crystals. He slowly motioned for Malcolm to sniff some. Malcolm complied.

Badly strung out on the wide array of drugs he had so recklessly consumed and still reeling with paranoia induced by his con-frontation with West Indian Archie, Malcolm somehow made it downtown. Thanks to the drugs he had taken, Malcolm had com-pletely lost all sense of reality, and luckily, when he arrived at his hotel, two women he knew saw him tottering in the hallway and helped him to a bed, which Malcolm passed out on.

He had reached the nadir of his life. Only twenty years old, he had already seen and experienced much of the worst that human existence had to offer. Yet he was not ready to find a new pathway. Rage, confusion, fear, cynicism, hurt, oppression, and grief held him in a vise, and he could not, or would not, let go. He still stub-bornly sought to test the dangerous limits of the life he had chosen for himself. Paradoxically, he lived in fear of what might happen to him at any moment.

He was awakened later that night, a half day beyond Archie's deadline. He went back uptown. News about him and Archie was already circulating on the street and in the criminal underworld. Everyone Malcolm knew was staying far away from him; no one wanted to be caught in a bloody crossfire. But nothing happened. Nor did anything occur the following day. In response Malcolm just stayed high on drugs.

As he moved about, trouble began to follow Malcolm around. In a bar, he hit a young hustler in the mouth during a fight in which the young hustler pulled a knife on Malcolm. It was not clear who had provoked the fight. However, Malcolm insisted that he would have shot and killed the youngster if bystanders had not intervened to stop him. Despite his insistence that he was always ready to use his guns to kill, Malcolm once again passed up the "opportunity" and gave his weapon to another man. That turned out to be a very smart move, because a cop came in soon after the fight and escorted Malcolm outside to the sidewalk where he and his partner frisked him. When Malcolm asked them what they were looking for, they informed him that there was a report that he had a gun. Malcolm told them that he did, but that he had thrown it in the river.

Before releasing him, the policeman who had come into the bar suggested to Malcolm that he leave town. It was sound advice. As Malcolm pointed out, "everything was closing in on me." With Archie gunning for him, the Mafia upset at him and erroneously suspecting that he had robbed some of their colleagues in a crap game, the young hustler he had hit still vowing revenge, and the police watching his every move in hopes of finally putting him away, Malcolm knew it was certainly time to leave New York. For four years Malcolm had been lucky enough (or shrewd enough) to avoid going to jail or even getting arrested in New York. For all of his criminal activity, he had never been in any serious trouble yet. But he also knew and understood that something had to give soon.

Just at this precipitous moment, Malcolm's old friend Shorty came to his rescue from Boston. Shorty had contacted Sammy, who had informed him how much trouble Malcolm was having in Harlem and that someone needed to come and get him. Shorty volunteered.

When Shorty arrived in Harlem in his car, Malcolm was elated. Malcolm no longer objected to getting out of town. As Shorty stood watch outside Malcolm's apartment, Malcolm gathered up the few things he had that he cared about and threw them into the trunk of the car. Driving without sleep for three days, Shorty took them down the highway at breakneck speed toward Boston. Malcolm, still high on drugs, babbled incoherently for the entire trip. For the time being he was safe, but a long time passed before Malcolm could admit that he had been run out of Harlem.

Chapter 8

The Defeat of "Detroit Red"

Finding himself back in Boston at Shorty's apartment, Malcolm was more isolated than he had ever been. Except for Sophia and Shorty, most people stayed away from him. Consumed by personal demons, Malcolm had deliberately alienated most of the people who really loved him. Ella, for one, was appalled by how far her brother had fallen. Devouring drugs, spewing profanity, and expressing extreme bitterness and dark cynicism about life in general, Malcolm was, in his own words, "like a predatory animal." He had never been as angry, suspicious, and sullen as he was then, and his general contempt for women had reached a point where he believed that they were nothing but a commodity to be exploited. Even Shorty was not fully prepared for how Malcolm lived and thought and, for the first time, had begun to seriously question his reckless and unpredictable behavior. Malcolm seemed to harbor a death wish.

When he first returned to town, Malcolm slept a lot. And when he was awake, he stayed high smoking reefers. Shorty was astounded by Malcolm's prodigious consumption of weed. Also, Malcolm, who in the past was nothing if not loquacious, rarely spoke. Smoking reefers and listening to his favorite jazz records all day filled the majority of his waking hours. Enjoying hours of floating and daydreaming while on drugs, Malcolm carried on imaginary conversations with his beloved New York musician friends. Within two weeks, he had slept more than during any two months in Harlem hustling all day and night.

After this relaxing hiatus Malcolm was once again ready to return to Roxbury's streets. But first he had to locate a peddler of "snow" (street parlance for cocaine) and get his "courage" back. Only when he had the old, familiar, and illusory feeling of supreme self-confidence and exaggerated well-being brought on by cocaine did Malcolm begin to open up and want to talk again and throw his weight around.

Shorty's band was playing around town three or four nights a week, and after he left for work Sophia would come over. She and Malcolm would talk at length about his renewed plans for the future. She would return to her husband before Shorty returned from work, after which Malcolm would proceed to bend Shorty's ear until daybreak. Although Sophia's husband had gotten out of the military and lived in Boston, he was a salesman who spent a great deal of time out of town and knew nothing of the ongoing relationship between his wife and Malcolm. Sophia would often reveal that they were not doing too well as a couple despite their highly comfortable financial status. Malcolm, of course, did not care one way or the other. As long as Sophia continued to give him money (and by this time he was demanding more from her all the time), Malcolm was more than happy to continue exploiting her as she became increasingly dependent on Malcolm for both sex and friendship. In some ways, Sophia's sexual addiction to Malcolm had begun to mirror the dependency he had on drugs.

The relationship also began to become physically abusive. Malcolm increasingly gave Sophia a hard time "just to keep her in line," and he began to beat her periodically. Sophia would always cry, curse Malcolm, and swear she was never coming back, but she always did, as Malcolm knew she would. The sadomasochistic nature of their relationship had always been a subconscious aspect of their intense sexual and racial attraction to each other, and it clarified for Malcolm just how sick, destructive, and degraded the exploitation of the categories of race, gender, and sex had become in the deeply racist and sexist society he was living in.

Soon, Sophia began bringing her equally attractive seventeen-year-old sister Joyce around to visit Shorty and Malcolm, and the four of them began to haunt the bars, restaurants, ballrooms, and clubs in Roxbury. Shorty, who was now thirty years old, became obsessed with Sophia's sister, which both amused and irritated Malcolm. He knew that the teenager was hung up on Shorty as an older, experienced black hipster and musician, which, in her idol-atrous view, gave him a special sexual aura. What he could not quite understand was why Shorty, who had a great deal of experience with women, was so fascinated by a kid, no matter how she looked.

Seeing Shorty behave this way made Malcolm feel vaguely disappointed with his mentor. But, by this time, Malcolm was no longer hung up on hero-worshipping as he had been in the past. From now on, he vowed, *he* would be the man in every situation. Malcolm felt like the time had come for him to assert himself as a leader in his chosen circle. Besides, no one could deny that despite his recklessness he still had a great deal of charm, charisma, street smarts, and shrewdness to augment his native intelligence. He started dressing in an elegantly expensive and conservative manner; he gave up the zoot suits and lindyhopping and was even wearing "banker's shoes." He yearned to be taken more seriously by his older colleagues. However, the question remained: Could he harness enough of his intense energy and discipline to become a force in the underworld? Events soon revealed that he was not only unready, but he also was very lucky to have survived his attempts at leadership at all.

Creating a Gangster Persona

After about a month of "laying dead" (being inactive) Malcolm was anxious to get a new hustle going. Broke and essentially alone whenever Shorty was out playing music, Malcolm called on Sophia to give him enough money as a stake to enter a big-time stud poker game at a well-known gambling house run by a cardsharp named John Hughes. Hughes had been a big gambler who, in the past, would not have even spoken to someone like Malcolm. But during the war, the word had gone out in Roxbury that Malcolm had run a few hustles in Harlem, so he now had a reputation. Being known in New York made it easier to be accepted in other hustlers' circles throughout the country and gave Malcolm a prestige and special cachet that he otherwise would not have had.

Hughes had become very successful as a gambler during the war years and now had enough money to open a gambling house that catered to big-time gamblers all over the East Coast. One night in a high-stakes game Malcolm successfully betted and bluffed his way to winning a big pot of money. Hughes, who was the last gambler to stay in the game before finally quitting, was a very experienced and clever player who was highly impressed with Malcolm's skill. He told his house aide, "Anytime Red comes in here and wants anything, let him have it." Hughes also offered Malcolm a job dealing cards for the house, but Malcolm declined, preferring to continue to take his chances gambling. Hughes kept his word: On several occasions he lent Malcolm money to play with. Malcolm seemed poised and mature to Hughes; he believed that Malcolm was a full ten years older than he was.

One night, however, Hughes refused to give Malcolm any more money, apparently because Malcolm had lost too much. Malcolm exploded in anger. He leaped up from the card table, and as he had seen Bogart, Cagney, and George Raft do in the movies, placed his hand on the pistol inside his suit pocket, threw his weapon on the table, took a step back, and declared, "If I ain't gonna gamble tonight, nobody's gonna gamble!" Then he calmly withdrew another .32 revolver from his shoulder holster, tossed it on the table, and dared anyone to reach for it. No one knew whether he was toting a third gun or not. Of course, no one wanted to find out. The players all quickly scattered, much to Hughes's dismay. This incident was especially distressing for Hughes because he had a standing rule that anyone who came into his place to gamble had to check his guns at the door if he had any. Malcolm, who fancied himself a real gunslinger at this point (though he still had never fired a weapon), always checked two guns. Then one night when another gambler tried, in Malcolm's words, "to pull something slick," Malcolm drew a third gun from his shoulder holster. This kind of grandstanding added to his rapidly growing reputation of being trigger-happy and crazy.

Playing the tough guy appealed to Malcolm; he cultivated this image. He swaggered when he walked and told Shorty that the scar on his shin (which he had received running from the lady wrestler in Lansing) had been caused by a gunshot wound. When two white sailors attacked Shorty, Malcolm volunteered to help track them down. For three weeks he and Shorty went in and out of every bar downtown on Massachusetts Avenue in Boston, looking for them. Malcolm also flashed his guns at every opportunity. He would pull back his suit coat so that his shoulder holster lay exposed. In bars, he would "accidentally" drop a pistol, sending patrons scurrying in all directions. Then he would nonchalantly reach down, retrieve it, and return to his drink as if nothing had happened. This kind of macho role-playing only further alienated him from former friends and colleagues who thought he was asking for a bad end.

Once when a merchant marine seaman Malcolm knew tried to sell him a stolen machine gun, Malcolm asked the seaman, "How do I know it works?" The seaman loaded the weapon with a cartridge clip and told Malcolm all he had to do was squeeze the trigger. Malcolm took the gun, examined it, and then pointed it at the seaman and threatened to "blow him wide open." Malcolm asserted that "he knew I was crazy enough to kill him," but in reality Malcolm's behavior was a carefully calculated craziness, the same kind he had employed in his encounter with the army psychiatrist. Malcolm kept the machine gun for a month at Shorty's place before selling it. Such potentially dangerous games had their desired effect: People grew very reluctant to cross him. Looking back on such behavior years later, Malcolm openly acknowledged that he had deliberately risked death more willingly than he had risked failure.

Malcolm had one more major incident involving the potential use of violence, but this incident showed that Malcolm was still capable of acting on behalf of someone else without regard for his own safety or expecting anything in return. A side of the anti-hero aspired to heroism. The incident was also an eerie foreshadowing of his later future as a political leader.

Malcolm was talking with Shorty and another friend in a Roxbury bar when someone summoned a policeman and asked him to evict an inebriated black woman who was creating a disturbance. The woman resisted. When the white police officer began yanking her out of the building, she stumbled and fell. The policeman then reached down and grabbed her by the hair, and just as he was about to drag her out the door caveman style, Malcolm confronted the police officer and said, "Take your hands off that woman. If she were your mother or your sister, you wouldn't manhandle her like that." The cop, now finding himself surrounded by an angry crowd, retreated to a call box for help and backup. Quickly, Malcolm put the woman in a cab. He flipped the driver five dollars and then got away clean.

In defending a stranger against abusive treatment, the twenty-year-old showed that he could be fearless in a manner that was not merely reckless or self-aggrandizing. He was still visibly angered by racial injustice, although he was engaging in behavior that deprived others of their rights and property. Malcolm was still not prepared to face this stark contradiction in his life. It was going to take the armed intervention of authorities and forces that he despised to stop him. But, by now, Malcolm preferred it that way. In his view, they were as illegitimate and criminal as he was.

One Last Big Hustle

By the end of 1945, World War II had ended, and African Americans hoped that their supreme human sacrifice in the war (more than one million blacks served in a completely segregated military that systematically discriminated against and exploited them) would compel the nation to finally acknowledge their great debt to them and provide the black population with the first-class citizenship that had always been denied them. African Americans, particularly the returning soldiers, were determined to fight for their social, economic, and political freedom despite the widespread white opposition and resistance to their organized efforts.

Malcolm was getting organized, too, although his motivation was money and his criminal reputation instead of social justice. Malcolm had virtually nothing to show for all the many hustles, scams, and criminal activity he had engaged in for the past year. Despite the many thousands of dollars he had personally handled and spent, Malcolm was still living like the working chumps and squares he had so much contempt for. In addition, he now had a twenty-dollar-a-day cocaine habit to support and was chain-smoking four packs of cigarettes a day. Still looking for a hustle that would finally put him in the driver's seat financially and cement his reputation as a successful criminal, Malcolm felt strongly that whatever he pursued this time had to include a much larger group than himself. It would also have to fulfill one of his often-mentioned dreams: to be a gang leader beholden to no one, yet followed and respected by all.

Malcolm decided that he would recruit Shorty first, who as a working musician was not making a great deal of money and who was often just breaking even after paying for rent, food, and other expenses. As glamorous as the gig seemed to people on the outside, the average black jazz musician, like African Americans everywhere, were as subject to the vagaries of racial, employment, and wage discrimination as anyone. Shorty was living proof, as Malcolm pointed out to him, that "only squares kept on believing they could ever get anything in life by slaving." Having very little to show for all the years of sacrifice and struggle, Shorty was ready to take a very risky chance on Malcolm's typically wild idea: house burglary. The fact that Shorty had absolutely no experience in burglary made the idea even more ludicrous, but an absurdly optimistic Malcolm pressed on.

In early December 1945, Shorty introduced Malcolm to a man named Rudy who was half black and half Italian. Rudy worked for an employment agency that sent him to wait on tables at exclusive parties for wealthy whites in Boston. He was ideal for what Malcolm had in mind. As a trusted servant Rudy had physical access to many homes in the area where he worked. In professional burglary parlance, this access enabled him to function as both a *finder* (one who locates lucrative places to rob) and as one who could *case* the physical layouts of these places to determine the means of entry, the best getaway routes, and so forth. The white coat of a waiter was also a perfect cover should anyone question his movements when he "sized up the loot and cased the joint."

Rudy so deeply resented how he was treated on the job that he was eager to join Malcolm's "gang" when the idea was proposed to him. With both Shorty and Rudy in his corner, Malcolm was almost ready to proceed with his plans. He knew that burglary, if properly executed, offered the maximum chances of success with the minimum risk. If the job were planned carefully so as to avoid encountering any of the victims, there would be no eyewitnesses. And most importantly, the likelihood that one would have to maim or kill anyone would be minimal.

Malcolm was also aware that selecting a specific area of burglary and sticking to that area was crucial. Professional burglars were specialists. Some worked apartments only; others worked houses only. Still others worked only stores or warehouses, and others focused solely on safes and strongboxes. As far as residences were concerned, there were further specialty distinctions. Day burglars, dinnertime and theater-time burglars, and the night burglars all had their own specific targets and agendas. As far as Malcolm was concerned, he had a very practical reason for never working during the daytime: his distinctive physical appearance. As he put it, "I could just hear people [potential witnesses] talking: 'A reddish-brown Negro over six feet tall.'" One glance would be enough to sink him.

Despite this knowledge and an atypically cautious attitude, Malcolm still insisted on including rank amateurs on the operation: Sophia and her sister, Joyce. Malcolm wanted the white women involved for two reasons: They could much more easily scout white Boston suburbs for appropriate targets in places Rudy would not or could not be, and they could case rich, white residential areas by pretending to be pollsters, vendors, or college girls doing a survey. In this way, they could gain easy access to and be able to describe the layout of targeted homes without arousing suspicion.

Although Malcolm disliked the idea of having too many people involved for fear of betrayal, he was certain that his closeness to Shorty, Sophia, and her sister assured that no one would squeal. Everyone, including Rudy, would be sharing the same risk. In Malcolm's words they would "be like a family unit." Malcolm decided that the group needed a base of operations outside of Roxbury. He had Sophia and Joyce rent an apartment in Harvard Square, where, unlike the blacks, the white girls could freely go shopping for the locales and physical situations that Malcolm wanted. The apartment was on the ground floor where, under the cover of darkness late at night, everyone could come and go as they pleased without arousing suspicion or attracting notice.

To assert his authority in the group, Malcolm used fear as a twisted kind of psychological advantage. A bizarre example of this is an incident where Malcolm played the dangerous game of Russian Roulette. He took out his .32 pistol, emptied the chamber of bullets, reinserted one cartridge, and rotated the cylinder. Then he pointed the gun at his head, grinned, and squeezed the trigger. As everyone gasped in horror, the gun clicked. Nothing happened. Then Malcolm pulled the trigger a second time. At this point Sophia and Joyce frantically pleaded with Malcolm to stop. Once again the gun clicked, and everyone was crying out, begging him to stop. Malcolm was undaunted. "I'm doing this to show you that I'm not afraid to die," he told them. "Never cross a man not afraid to die ... now let's get to work." His cohorts, who were unaware that Malcolm had conned them by palming the bullet he had pretended to put into the gun's chamber, took him at his word. Sophia and Joyce were awestruck, and Shorty and Rudy thought he was crazy and were afraid of him. After that, no one in the group ever questioned his authority again.

One night, Malcolm and the others, plus a tough twenty-three-year-old ex-con named Francis "Sonny" Brown were cruising around Arlington, a posh Boston suburb. Suddenly, Malcolm and Sonny decided to break into an expensive-looking home, and the deed was done before the women had any idea what the two men were doing. Malcolm knew that Sophia, whose intense fascination with him seemed to increase with each reckless foray, would do whatever he told her to do, including keeping her mouth shut. Her sister Joyce would then follow Sophia's example. Besides if he were caught, he could count on Sophia and Joyce, who had money and connections, to supply the necessary lawyers that would enable him to get off easy. Malcolm and Sonny also roped Shorty into their premature act in much the same way that they roped in the women. One night Malcolm and Sonny began filling Shorty's car with loot before he knew what was happening. Shorty protested to no avail. "If I ever get caught," Malcolm told him, "I'll tell the police you were with me."

Despite Malcolm's preoccupation with advance planning and organized precision, the burglaries turned out to be anything but professional. In mid-December 1945 during the height of the Christmas season, the burglary ring went on a stealing binge. The procedure varied but usually it involved the young burglars driving around their targeted area until they located an unlighted home. Sophia and Joyce knew many wealthy people who were away on vacation. One of them rang the doorbell. If no one answered, one or two of the men would sneak in the back door, smash the lock with a hammer, or open a window with a screwdriver or crowbar while one of the others kept watch. Malcolm always wore gloves on these operations to eliminate the possibility of fingerprints, but he inexplicably removed the gloves during one or two of the burglaries. The police reportedly found his prints on a windowsill. They may have also obtained his fingerprints from the flashlight he left behind in one victim's home or from the batteries that he had inserted into the flashlight shortly before the break-in.

Many of the hauls that Malcolm and his makeshift gang made were from very wealthy whites, such as the people who manufactured the famous Eberhardt fountain pen. So the loot that they took—especially jewels, oriental rugs, antiques, and the like—was very appealing to their fence, who would then turn a far bigger profit on the goods than the thieves themselves. As Malcolm pointed out, "Every burglar knew that fences robbed the burglars worse than the burglars robbed their victims." Nevertheless, the burglary ring was quite successful.

The only close brush with the law came once when they were making their getaway with three of the gang in the front seat of their car and the backseat loaded with stolen goods. Suddenly they saw a cruising police car around the corner coming toward them. As it passed them, everyone drew a sigh of relief. But then the police car made a quick U-turn to follow them, and Malcolm knew the police would flash them to stop. The police had spotted them and knew that blacks had no business in an all-white area late at night. But once again Malcolm was able to think quickly in a dangerous situation. He told Rudy to stop the car before the squad car started flashing its light. As he had done once before with

Sammy in a very similar situation, Malcolm got out of the car and flagged the officers down to stop as he walked toward them. Pretending he was lost, Malcolm played dumb and asked the officers for directions back to Roxbury. The police complied and did not pursue the getaway car.

After a number of successful heists, Malcolm and the gang decided to lay low for a while. They had made a good pile, and they drove to New York to live it up in style for a week. As their two cars sped south along the Merritt Parkway, Malcolm, caught up in the blind euphoria of the moment and feeling recklessly carefree, yanked out a pistol from his jacket, leaned out the window of Sophia's convertible, and fired a couple of shots in the direction of Shorty's black 1938 Buick, which was in the lead. Laughing, Malcolm later told Shorty, "I could have hit your tires if I had wanted to." This kind of wildly erratic behavior only cemented Shorty's conviction that Malcolm was now out of control and on the verge of completely losing it.

Two days before Christmas they all returned to Boston. Celebrating the holiday, Malcolm took Sophia and Joyce out to nightclubs where Shorty played and to many other places as well, spending money like it was going out of style. The girls dressed in highly expensive jewelry and furs they had selected from the gang's heists. No one in town knew exactly what their hustle was, but everyone could see from their ostentatious, public displays that they were doing quite well. On other occasions, Sophia and Joyce would meet Malcolm and Shorty at Shorty's place in Roxbury or in their Harvard Square digs in neighboring Cambridge, where they would all smoke reefers, have sex, and play music until the early dawn.

After surviving a near confrontation in a local nightclub with a black police officer who despised him, Malcolm continued to act recklessly in public. Pumped up with drugs, Malcolm was once again taking a cavalier approach to life. Marijuana and cocaine had become, in his words, the center of his life. The drugs made him feel as though he were beyond any personal worries or stress. If any worry did manage to assert itself in his consciousness, Malcolm would suppress it with even more drugs and pretend that all was well. However, whereas before he had always been able to consume as many drugs as he wanted and have the overt effects rarely show, taking drugs was no longer that easy. He was becoming deeply addicted, which caused him to take more unnecessary and foolish risks than ever before.

A major example of this risk-taking behavior was an incident in which Malcolm, high as usual, came into a club and saw Sophia and her sister having a drink with a white man. For all he knew the man could have been Sophia's husband, whom he had never seen before. Under ordinary circumstances he would have avoided going over to Sophia's table and risking a confrontation, but the cocaine in Malcolm's system was making him feel far more macho and overconfident than usual. He marched right up to Sophia's table. When Sophia saw him, her face went pale with fear. Malcolm was so far gone that he did not care who the white guy was.

As it turned out, the other man was the best friend of Sophia's husband. They had served in the war together. With Sophia's husband out of town, the man had asked Sophia and Joyce out to dinner. While driving around town after dinner, the man had suddenly suggested that they go over to the black ghetto for drinks. The women, who by now were well known in Roxbury, tried to change the man's mind, but he had insisted. So holding their breaths, they walked in, stiffly flashing signals to the bartenders and waiters they knew to not reveal their knowledge of them. The blacks working in the bar caught their message and pretended that they had never seen the women before. But Malcolm went up to his long-time secret lover and called her "baby." As the white man's face turned red, Sophia and Joyce vainly pretended that they had never seen the flirtatious black man before. Malcolm was not yet aware of it, but in his subconscious desire to be caught, Detroit Red's days were numbered. Malcolm and his brash alter ego had finally run out of luck.

Another careless act sealed Malcolm's fate. He knew very well that the majority of burglars were not apprehended at the scene of the crime, but while trying to market and sell their stolen goods. He was also aware of the need to remove all identifying marks and serial numbers from each stolen item, yet he pawned a wedding band that was clearly stamped with its owner's initials. He also gave the proprietor of the jewelry shop where he had pawned the ring a stolen watch to repair. The watch was very expensive, so all the jewelers in Boston, not to mention the police, had been alerted. Malcolm foolishly supplied the jeweler with his real name and Ella's address and promised to return for the diamond-studded man's watch.

Detective Stephen Slack, who served the wealthy white suburban community of Milton, Massachusetts, where the wedding band had been stolen, periodically drove into Boston to check the daily reports that each jeweler filed with the city police department. His cousin, Stanley Slack, was a Boston police officer who staked out the shop where Malcolm had left the watch for repair. Two days later, on January 12, 1946, Malcolm returned to the jewelry store. The proprietor of the store waited until Malcolm paid him before he laid the watch on the counter. He then gave a signal to Detective Slack, who suddenly emerged from hiding in the rear of the store. Malcolm immediately knew he was a cop. "Step into the back," the officer told Malcolm.

Just then another black man, who was completely innocent, walked into the store. The detective, erroneously thinking he was with Malcolm, turned to confront him. Now his back was to Malcolm, who was armed and had a fully loaded .32 caliber pistol in his shoulder holster. But once again Malcolm, who had always falsely portrayed himself as a man who would kill without compunction, did not draw his gun and shoot the detective. Instead, he surrendered and told the detective to take his gun. This very wise decision, as Malcolm later acknowledged, saved his life. If he had tried to use the gun, he would have been immediately shot and killed by two other armed detectives who had been hiding with Detective Slack in the back of the store. Malcolm's arrest took place just five days before he was scheduled to appear in court in Michigan on his old Detroit robbery case from a year earlier.

If Malcolm had not been arrested at that time, he could have easily wound up being killed by Sophia's husband, whose friend had told him about Malcolm's long-term affair with his wife. The enraged husband had gone to Malcolm's apartment that morning with a gun, looking for him. Somehow, Malcolm had narrowly escaped death twice that day; some of his luck was still with him. Malcolm later soberly reflected "a thousand times" in prison that Allah (God) was with him "even then."

When the police interrogated Malcolm, he admitted his role in the burglaries and break-ins. He implicated his fellow burglars in return for his jailer's promise to persuade the judge in his case to give him a suspended sentence for the gun-carrying charge that also had been filed against him. Soon after Sophia and Joyce were picked up by the police, the two quickly implicated Sonny Brown, whom the police never caught. Rudy also disappeared. Shorty was not so lucky; he, too, was arrested. The Boston police turned Malcolm over to the Milton, Massachusetts authorities. The Boston police found the Harvard Square apartment loaded with evidence, including jewelry, fur coats, clothes, cash, lock picks, fake keys, pencil-beam flashlights, and Malcolm's small arsenal of guns.

Malcolm and Shorty were immediately exposed to the blatant racism and double standards of the criminal justice system. The women were released on very low bail, but Malcolm's and Shorty's bails were set at ten thousand dollars each, which was completely beyond their capacity to pay. In addition, the main obsession of the authorities was the racial/sexual taboo of white women involved with black men. They wanted to know why "decent, well-to-do, upper middle-class white women were involved with niggers." This intimate association bothered the assigned social workers and the police far more than the crimes the two men were arrested for. They demanded to know how, when, and where had Malcolm and Shorty met the women? Did they sleep with them? Did they coerce them into joining their gang? Nobody wanted to know anything about the robberies, Malcolm discovered. Disgusted, he just looked at the social workers and asked, "Now, what do you think?" Even the court clerks and bailiffs joined in on the attack: "Nice white girls ... goddamn niggers!"

Chapter 9

"Satan" on Lockdown

The trial was held during the last week of February 1946. Sophia and Joyce sat at the defense table while Malcolm and Shorty were locked in a courtroom cage that was reserved for prisoners who were unable to make bail. As white spectators stared at the two men with seething hatred, openly calling them "black bastards" and "dirty niggers" in the courtroom, the judge nonchalantly called for order. One of the spectators even sidled up to the bars of the cage and snarled, "If we had you down south, you'd been strung up by now!"

The white, court-appointed defense lawyers were equally upset with them. Before the judge entered, Malcolm told one of the defense lawyers, "We seem to be getting sentenced because of those girls." The attorney turned red with anger as he shuffled his papers and shouted, "You had no business with white girls!" The moment Judge Allen Buttrick strode into the courtroom, Malcolm and Shorty knew they were done for. The judge's face was a "mask of stone."

Because some of the burglary victims were in the courtroom, the prosecution went all-out in its vigorous indictment of the defendants. The prosecutor even tried to pin a number of unrelated, unsolved burglaries on them. But Shorty's personal lawyer was able to successfully defend his client of these charges. The other defense attorneys appeared far less committed to a proper defense of their clients. Malcolm had no lawyer of his own. Ella refused to provide him with legal assistance because she was very angry with him. Years later, she openly acknowledged that she wanted Malcolm to spend some time in prison. She felt and hoped that a year or two in jail would finally straighten him out. She was even thankful that her beloved brother had finally been caught and arrested because she had long feared that, barring police custody, Malcolm would eventually be killed in the streets.

Sophia, dressed primly and demurely in black, turned state's evidence and falsely testified that Malcolm had forced her and her sister to participate in the burglaries. She also lied that he threatened to kill them unless they continued to cooperate. "We lived in constant fear," she asserted. For her testimony she received a light suspended sentence of six months; her younger sister received a mere two months of probation. The racial divide-and-conquer strategy of the police and the prosecutor had worked like a charm.

Sophia, who had been so obsessed with Malcolm that she willingly became a criminal and even risked the destruction of her own marriage, dramatically confirmed Malcolm's fundamental distrust and cynicism regarding whites in general. When he heard Sophia's testimony, he was not surprised. Yet some small part of him naively believed that Sophia would eventually come to his aid. In any event, Malcolm knew from personal experience that both racism and his own criminal behavior were responsible for his present situation. He would take this particularly harsh and bitter lesson into the prison walls with him. Malcolm did not testify on his own behalf. In fact, he put up no defense at all. Any defense would have been futile anyway. All that remained was for him and Shorty to be sentenced.

Judge Buttrick called the opposing attorneys to the bar. After extensive discussion, a defense lawyer finally walked over to Shorty and advised him to change his plea to guilty. "It'll go easier if you do," he told him. "The judge wants to avoid the time and expense of jury deliberation. Anyway, they've got you dead to rights." Shorty reluctantly pleaded guilty. Malcolm, who had formerly pleaded not guilty despite his earlier confession to the police, followed suit. They quickly discovered that the judge's conception of leniency was far different from their own. Malcolm and Shorty thought they would get the minimum sentence of two years, which was the normal time for first offenders in burglary cases, but the judge, who made it known in the courtroom during his sentencing that he also firmly disapproved of black men who slept with white women, threw the book at them.

The judge gave Malcolm and Shorty the maximum sentence of eight to ten years at hard labor on each of the fourteen counts against them. He also decreed that the punishment for each count was to be run "concurrently." However, Shorty did not know what the word *concurrently* meant. As the judge bellowed, "Count one, eight to ten years at hard labor … Count two, eight to ten years at hard labor … Count three …," Shorty was erroneously counting in his head more than one hundred years of prison time. Sweating profusely, he temporarily lost control, cried out, and slumped in despair. The bailiffs had to catch and support him to keep him from collapsing altogether.

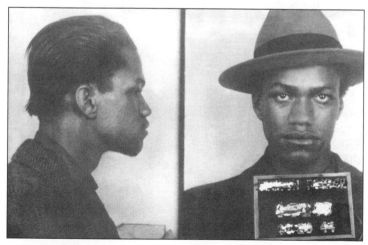

Malcolm's mug shot, 1944.

Malcolm received the same sentence, but he showed no emotion at all. Attributing the length of the sentence merely to the judge's obvious bigotry, Malcolm refused to properly acknowledge his two previous arrests and suspended sentences in Detroit and Boston, not to mention his other criminal acts which remained undetected. Even Ella, who was in the courtroom, was completely unaware of his Michigan arrest. Feeling somewhat unjustly responsible for the severity of Malcolm's sentence because she had him arrested for the theft of their aunt's coat a year before, Ella had also thought the judge would not give him such a long sentence. Faced with her own miscalculation, she leaped to her feet in great anguish and nearly started a riot in the courtroom when the sentences were read. But none of this was her fault. Malcolm had thwarted and ultimately exhausted all of her efforts to get him to live a different life. Malcolm did not really care about anything anymore. He did not protest or curse his fate when the judge read the sentence; he just sat in his cage and flashed a sardonic smile.

Malcolm and Shorty were handcuffed together and taken to the Charlestown State Prison. Malcolm was three months shy of his twenty-first birthday. As he later put it, "I had not even started shaving yet." When he arrived at the prison, Malcolm was given prisoner number 22843, and as he posed for his first mug shot, he wore the same cynical smile he had worn in the courtroom after being sentenced.

The penitentiary was in the southwestern part of Charlestown, across the Charles River from Boston. Thomas Jefferson was president when the prison opened its doors to its first contingent of inmates in 1805. When Malcolm entered Charlestown in February 1946, conditions were not much better than they had been in Jefferson's day. The seven- and eight-foot long cells were barely enough to accommodate a sleeping man. There was no running water or toilets; prisoners had to urinate and defecate in wooden buckets. The excrement was emptied daily, and the pails disinfected and scoured. But the awful stench remained. Though rats were a problem, the lice that bred in the mildew and the dampness were far more troublesome.

In accordance with Judge Buttrick's sentence, Malcolm spent his first day in solitary confinement. New inmates, called *fish*, customarily spent their first twenty-four hours there, presumably to learn what to expect if they tried to abuse the comparative "freedom" of ordinary prison life. The day in solitary was especially hard on Shorty, who was placed in a windowless cubicle next to Malcolm's. The only time he saw any light at all was when the guard cracked open the solid metal door to deliver some bread and water. After their solitary time elapsed, he and Malcolm were finally allowed to join the rest of the general prison population.

Malcolm's first visitor in prison was his ever-loyal sister Ella. The sight of her younger brother in his faded prison uniform was very upsetting for her. She tried to smile and lift his spirits, but neither one of them could find much to say to each other. A pall quickly fell over them, and Malcolm wished she had not come at all. Ella was equally upset with Malcolm's generally unrepentant and cocky attitude during her visit. She noted that he showed no remorse for his actions, nor was he concerned about family anxiety regarding his arrest and imprisonment. Ella pointed out that Malcolm foolishly believed that his only real problem was being caught, and that the next time he would be a "smarter hustler." When she left after the visit she was as upset with Malcolm as she had ever been.

Prison psychiatrists tried to interview Malcolm about his family on more than one occasion. He told fellow inmates that he deeply resented their probing questions, particularly those about his mother. He called one psychologist every filthy name he could think of and was even more verbally abusive toward the prison chaplain. Malcolm was a fierce atheist and hated anyone trying to use religion on his behalf. When he received his first letter from his devoutly religious brother Philbert in Detroit, who told Malcolm his church was going to pray for him, Malcolm wrote a furious, profane reply that Malcolm later acknowledged he was "ashamed to think of."

As the prison authorities continued inquiring about Malcolm's past, he began lying to them, making up wild, exaggerated stories about himself and his family. He held them in contempt and shrewdly observed that their real motivation was not to help him but to determine why he was so rebellious. He even denied that he had ever been dependent on drugs and falsely asserted that he had left New York a number of times to dissociate himself from companions who had been addicted.

Malcolm was not truthful with his fellow prisoners either. He boasted about what a big-time hood he had been and how many women he had conquered. The veteran inmates did not believe any of Malcolm's wild stories, but they did enjoy his highly entertaining exaggerations. Malcolm still knew a little something about pleasing a crowd. Malcolm also tried to impress his fellow inmates with his knowledge, which even he knew was limited. He was so full of endless instructions about how to do things that Shorty eventually nicknamed him "Mr. Know-How." He also called him the "Green-Eyed Monster." But Malcolm's intense hostility toward religion prompted most of the men in his cellblock to call him "Satan." Malcolm seemed to relish his devilish image, which attracted attention and enhanced his status in the "joint" the way his outlaw image had enhanced his status on the streets.

While Malcolm was at Charlestown, he got high on nutmeg. Malcolm's cellmate was one of many nutmeg peddlers who, for money or cigarettes, bought penny matchboxes full of stolen nutmeg from inmates who worked in the kitchen. Stirred into a glass of cold water, a penny matchbox full of nutmeg had the kick of three or four reefers. Malcolm greedily grabbed a box as though it were a pound of heavy drugs. After receiving some money from Ella, Malcolm spent it to buy real drugs from prison guards, who smuggled the stuff into the prison to sell to the inmates. Malcolm received marijuana, Nembutal, and Benzedrine from the guards, who sold drugs as a sideline to supplement their small wages. For many guards, drug smuggling and dealing was how they made most of their income.

Malcolm asserted that he cursed guards while he was at the Charlestown prison and refused to answer when his number was called. He also claimed that he would intentionally drop his tray in the dining hall and throw things out of his cell and that he spent considerable time in solitary confinement. But some of Malcolm's prison claims seemed to be taken from his favorite vintage James Cagney movies. Charlestown had no dining hall; every inmate ate alone in his cell. His prison record contains no evidence that he spent more than his first day in solitary confinement, nor do any of the officers and guards who were interviewed about his prison record recall Malcolm being a real troublemaker while in their prison.

Most of Malcolm's disciplinary infractions were too minor to warrant severe disciplinary action. He did regularly violate rules regarding smoking in prohibited areas and often flashed hateful stares at the guards. He was also very insolent toward them and all other prison authorities. In the various prison workshops Malcolm employed the same kind of passive resistance he had used so effectively against authority figures at home and school and even among some colleagues on the street. He often refused to work, for example. But in general he was not considered a major problem or troublemaker. One fellow inmate characterized him as a "defiant kid."

Meanwhile, Malcolm remained strangely optimistic that he would be sprung from jail eventually with the help of Sophia's money and family connections. He refused to believe that Sophia, whom Malcolm firmly believed was crazy about him, would willingly testify against him. He felt that she had certainly demonstrated her undying loyalty to him in the past no matter what was happening between them. Once she almost shot a policeman Malcolm had an intense dislike for because he told her to hold his gun secretly under a table and to use it if the cop "tried anything." Thus, he continued to insist that the district attorney had forced her to cooperate with him.

Sophia, however, had other ideas. Initially she had been sentenced to five years in prison, but her high-priced attorneys very quickly plea-bargained that sentence down to an indefinite sentence in an appellate court. Thanks to her attorney, she was able to win a quick parole, and she went free after serving a mere seven months in a college dorm-like women's reformatory. In addition, her sister Joyce spent no time in jail at all and was given probation for two years. A white real estate operator who had received some of their stolen goods was also put on probation. Clearly, even when Malcolm's past record is taken into consideration, the standard of justice for well-to-do whites was (and remains) quite different from the one applied to poor blacks, especially those like Malcolm and Shorty, who flouted the societal taboo against interracial sex.

As time went on, Malcolm began to realize that his faith in Sophia was misplaced. His involvement with her had earned him a heavier sentence, not a lighter one. And she clearly had no intention of coming to his aid. Malcolm's situation confirmed Ella's long-held contention that black males who were involved with white women in a racist society were doomed to a bad or destructive end. Later, an embittered Malcolm blamed his imprisonment on Sophia, claiming to other inmates that she had turned him in to the police.

Malcolm's last meeting with Sophia occurred in April 1946 at his second burglary trial. The first trial, which had taken place in Middlesex County Courthouse, had involved five burglaries he had committed in the white suburbs of Arlington, Belmont, and Newton, which lie west of Boston. The second trial, which was held in Norfolk County Superior Court, dealt with four burglaries he had committed in Milton, Brookline (the birthplace of President John F. Kennedy), and Walpole, which lie south of Boston.

> *The proceedings of Malcolm's second trial were held in the same Dedham, Massachusetts courthouse that had housed the infamous Sacco-Vanzetti murder trial twenty-five years earlier. Nicola Sacco and Bartolomeo Vanzetti were political radicals who were convicted of (many felt unjustly) and ultimately executed for the murders of two shoe factory employees.*

By the time the second burglary trial began, Sophia had mastered the deceptive role of the reluctant burglar. With the prosecutor coaxing her with leading questions, such as "The real reason you participated was ...," she insisted that she had never loved Malcolm and that she had taken part in the burglaries only under severe duress. At that, Malcolm exploded. "I might have known you would brainwash her!" he screamed at the district attorney. Each time Sophia started to tell another lie, Malcolm would beat her to the punch with the truth. "If you didn't want to take part, why did you tell us what families were out of town?" "Why did you rent the [Harvard Square] apartment?" "If you didn't love me, why did you come to my place alone? Why did you bring your clothes? I didn't hold a gun on you then." Malcolm raged on and on. "You stole money for me from your own father. You said you knew ways to get more." Malcolm then stood up and pointed his finger at Sophia's wealthy father, who was sitting in the courtroom. "You told me you hated your father and mother and wanted nothing to do with them anymore!" None of Malcolm's protestations made any difference with the judge, who promptly sentenced both Malcolm and Shorty to six to eight years in prison, which were meaningless sentences because they ran concurrently with those that had already been meted out by Judge Buttrick in Malcolm's first trial.

Back in prison, Malcolm hardly spoke to his old friend Shorty at all. Shorty had cold-shouldered him since his arrest. Although outwardly he laughed off the rebuff, inside the ever-sensitive Malcolm was hurt and resentful.

Malcolm began to seek out other friendships. The first prisoner Malcolm met who made any positive impression on him at all was an inmate named John Elton Bembry, called "Bimbi" in Malcolm's autobiography. They met at Charlestown in 1947. He was, in Malcolm's words, a "light, kind of red-complexioned Negro, as I was, about my height and he had freckles." He was a veteran burglar who had been in many prisons. He was also a legendary guru-like figure in the state prison system and possessed an extraordinary intellect. He operated the machine that stamped out numbers on the license plates in the prison license plate shop where Malcolm was on the paint crew.

Bimbi was the first black convict Malcolm had known who did not respond to "What'cha know, Daddy?" or any other shallow or insincere attempts to get to know him. After work, both black and white prisoners and guards would gather around Bimbi and listen to him expound brilliantly on a wide range of topics and areas of knowledge, such as history, science, psychology, literature, philosophy, theology, and other subjects. Everyone was riveted by Bimbi's astounding command of the science of human behavior. He would often quip that the only real difference between the inmates and the people outside prison is that the inmates had been caught. He especially liked to talk about historical events and their meaning. As Malcolm so eloquently put it,

> When he talked about the history of Concord, where I
> was to be transferred later, you would have thought he
> was hired by the Chamber of Commerce, and I wasn't the
> first inmate who had never heard of Thoreau until Bimbi
> expounded upon him. Bimbi was known as the library's
> best customer. What fascinated me with him most of all
> was that he was the first man I had ever seen command
> total respect with his words.

Initially, Bimbi seldom said much to Malcolm, as he was often gruff with individuals, but Malcolm sought out a friendship with him. What made Malcolm seek out Bimbi was his discussions of religion. As a man who considered himself an atheist, Malcolm wanted to understand what Bimbi saw in the concept of God. But instead Bimbi put the atheist philosophy in a rational context and made Malcolm understand for the first time how a critical interpretation and use of ideas worked better than a blindly emotional approach to reality. That discussion ended Malcolm's vicious and rage-filled cursing attacks whenever the subject of religion came up. Bimbi's approach to ideas and emotions sounded so much stronger than his own, and Bimbi never used a foul word.

Gradually the two men became friends. One day Bimbi bluntly told Malcolm that he had brains and should start using them. Although Malcolm did want his friendship, he did not want this kind of advice. He had heard it before from Ella and Laura, Sophia, Shorty, Sammy, Mrs. Swerlin, and even Mr. Ostrowski, among others. And where had any of it ever got him? Malcolm even reflected that he might have cursed out another convict for such unsolicited advice but *nobody* cursed Bimbi, not even Malcolm. For the first time in years, Malcolm listened to someone who encouraged his intelligence in a productive way. Bimbi then told him that he should take advantage of the prison correspondence courses and the library.

As he had with his older brother Philbert, and later with both Shorty and Sammy, Malcolm began following Bimbi around, asking him questions about everything under the sun. He also began reading books in the prison library. Because he had not been reading since he dropped out of school some six years earlier and because the streets had erased nearly everything he had ever learned in school, his vocabulary was limited and reading was not an easy task at first. As Malcolm put it, he "didn't know a verb from a house." The experience of studying for the sheer personal value and pleasure of it was also something that Malcolm had not experienced since he became a hustler.

Malcolm was also encouraged by a letter from his older sister Hilda who had written him with the suggestion that he study English and penmanship because she had barely been able to read a couple of scrawled postcards Malcolm had sent her when he was selling reefers on the road. So Malcolm began a correspondence course in English. As time went on, Malcolm's characteristic discipline and diligence kicked in, and through the correspondence course lessons and exercises, the mechanics of grammar gradually began to return to him from his experience in school. It took Malcolm only two days to finish lessons in his English course that took other inmates ten days to complete. Within a year Malcolm could write what he called a "decent and legible letter." In truth he was far too modest.

For now, Malcolm was content to use Bimbi's dictionary to improve his reading ability. He borrowed the dictionary so often that Bimbi finally gave it to him. Malcolm began studying the dictionary systematically by using it as an encyclopedic source, as well as a vocabulary-building device, as he scrutinized the definitions and derivations of every single word on each page. This intense interest in words and their meanings eventually led Malcolm to becoming a world-class etymologist who actively studied and mastered philology. Soon Malcolm was taking another correspondence course, this time in Latin because of Bimbi's influence; Malcolm had often heard Bimbi explain the derivations of words in his lectures.

Malcolm was quickly gaining a reputation as an intellectual in the state prison system. "When I get out of this place," he told Bimbi, "I'm going to be a bad nigger, but I'm going to be a *smart*, bad nigger." When a mimeographed listing of available books was passed from cell to cell, Malcolm would put his number next to titles that appealed to him, if they were not already taken. Within months Malcolm was reading everything he could get his hands on. Bimbi recommended such literary classics as *Moby Dick* by Herman Melville and the complete collection of Shakespeare's plays, which Malcolm loved (he quickly became a genuine scholar of world literature).

One of Malcolm's favorite books was *Aesop's Fables*, with its didactic and allegorical parables about wily foxes, hungry wolves, and other fascinating creatures who looked like animals but acted like human beings. Years later, Malcolm would become renowned in his political speeches for his brilliant oratorical use of metaphors that often used animals as symbolic figures. He was particularly fond of the tale about the old lion who was too weak to hunt for food and pretended to be ill, devouring whomever went into his lair to wish him well. A fox, who saw through the ruse, inquired from a distance how he was feeling. "Bad," answered the enfeebled king of the beasts, who asked why the fox did not visit his cave. "I would have," replied the fox. "But I saw a lot of tracks going in, and none coming out." Years later Shorty even pointed out to an interviewer that in order to fully understand Malcolm, one should visualize him as the fox in each of *Aesop's Fables*.

Because Malcolm was now intent on pursuing knowledge for its own sake, it was only a matter of time before his perception about who he was and where his life was headed also began to undergo fundamental changes. So although Malcolm became his cellblock's bookie, he became its bookworm as well, with his primary focus on the latter role.

Still, he was not completely finished hustling yet. For a while he walked around the prison yard with pad and pencil taking bets on ballgames, horse races, and boxing matches. He also became so adept at playing dominoes, a favorite prison pastime, that he began to beat everyone at the game. Because the major currency for betting in prison was packs of cigarettes, Malcolm soon acquired several cartons. By booking cigarette and cash bets, Malcolm became a popular figure at Charlestown.

In January 1947, Malcolm was transferred to Concord Reformatory. Malcolm complained to Ella that, "They treat you like a baby here." But Concord was a definite upgrade from Charlestown as far as facilities went. It even had toilets and a dining hall. Yet Concord was tougher than Charlestown in some ways. Fights broke out frequently. The perpetrators were usually hot-headed and perversely ambitious young hoods trying to emulate the behavior of older, hardened Charlestown inmates and aspiring to "big-house" status. Malcolm observed these activities with a jaundiced and ironic eye; after all he had very recently been just like these young men. By now, however, Malcolm was only interested in protecting himself from harm, doing his time without too much trouble, and getting released. Most other inmates sensed that Malcolm was not to be trifled with, and they left him alone, which suited Malcolm just fine. No longer looking for trouble, Malcolm had decided to bide his time and try to stay ahead of the game.

One way of staying out of trouble while in prison was to become much more involved in following sports. As he mentions in his autobiography, he never forgot the prison sensation created on April 15, 1947, when Jackie Robinson was finally brought up from the minor leagues to play with the Brooklyn Dodgers. As the first African American ever allowed to play professional baseball in the notoriously racist major leagues, Robinson was an immediate national hero, not only to blacks, but to all Americans who believed in justice and equal rights. He also quickly became a hero for Malcolm, who described himself as Robinson's "most fanatic fan." Even though Malcolm had pretty much abandoned interest in sports when he was an adolescent, Malcolm had his ear glued to the radio whenever Robinson played, listening for the latest exploits of this elegant and courageous man.

> Jackie Robinson had been an intercollegiate sports hero and had gradu-
> ated from UCLA. While serving in World War II as a lieutenant in the
> army, he was court-martialed for refusing to sit in the back of a bus in the
> deep South.

For thirteen months Malcolm worked in Concord's furniture shop. The guard in charge, Arthur Roach, was kinder than most of his colleagues. He kidded the one he called "Little Malcolm," who immediately retorted, "There's no joking between me and you." Malcolm had no use at all for the prison officers, most of whom were as cruel and calloused as the convicts they were supposedly helping to reform.

At Concord, as at Charlestown, Malcolm contented himself with committing only petty offenses, such as refusing to do his chores. Sometimes he would sneak to the front of the line of inmates who were patiently waiting to take their weekly shower. But that was about as bad he got. Malcolm knew that the physical and psychological price of real defiance in prison was very severe, and for once he tried to "play it straight." But this did not mean he would take any overt abuse from anyone, inmate or guard, who tried to give him a hard time. Malcolm was no one's chump. In fact, it was in prison that Malcolm began to demonstrate the leadership qualities that he would later become renowned for.

Malcolm was beginning to make a real name for himself among his peers in prison. Still, there was no getting around the fact that he was imprisoned, and he desperately longed to get out. In the spring of 1948, Malcolm was introduced to the Nation of Islam (NOI). It would prove not only to be his ticket out of prison, but also the start of a completely new life.

Chapter 10

Malcolm Discovers the Nation of Islam

Malcolm's older brother, and former sibling rival, Philbert wrote to Malcolm and told him that he had discovered the "natural religion for the black man." Philbert, whom Malcolm then described as "forever joining something," was more devout and committed to religion than ever. An intense disciple of one religious group after another since early adolescence, Philbert now excitedly told his atheist younger brother that he, along with Wilfred, Hilda, and Reginald, had all joined a rapidly growing black sect called the Nation of Islam (NOI). Among other things, NOI advocated the establishment of an independent and separate nation for African Americans within the United States, a homeland where they would be masters of their own land, culture, and economy and would be free from the political, social, cultural, and economic control and domination of their white oppressors.

The NOI, like Marcus Garvey's UNIA before it, envisioned a world where members of the African diaspora in the West would ultimately join in a worldwide movement for complete separation from white American and European hegemony. Its leaders and followers fervently believed that Allah (God in Islamic doctrine) would eventually deliver blacks from bondage in an Armageddon that would subdue the whites who were known as "devils" in the NOI. Philbert told Malcolm that he should "pray to Allah for deliverance" and join the sect. If he did, he, too, would soon be released from bondage, Philbert said.

This advice struck the militantly antireligious Malcolm as absurd and delusional. He wrote back to Philbert in very strong and dismissive language that he was not interested in his crazy religious notions. Malcolm's command of English had improved considerably since he last wrote to his brother, but he was still as disdainful of Philbert's latest attempts to save him as he was when Philbert still belonged to the Holiness Christian church and asked the congregation to pray for Malcolm. When the members of the Little family received Malcolm's caustic reply to Philbert's letter they enlisted Reginald to write to him, knowing that Malcolm felt closest to his younger brother and would be more inclined to listen to him.

When the letter from Reginald arrived Malcolm was not aware that it was the result of a family decision and that the letter from Philbert was merely the first attempt to recruit him. Malcolm did know that Reginald had given up the hustler life and was now spending a great deal of time in Detroit with Wilfred, Hilda, and Philbert. Reginald's letter was much more relaxed and informal than the intensely self-righteous letter of their straight-arrow brother Philbert, and Malcolm was immediately responsive to Reginald's more newsy and friendly banter. The end of Reginald's letter really intrigued Malcolm. Reginald told his older brother, "Don't eat any more pork, and don't smoke any more cigarettes. I'll show you how to get out of prison."

Malcolm assumed that his brother had come upon some scheme to work a hustler-like scam on the penal authorities. Still thinking in the limited terms of the street, Malcolm went to sleep and woke up trying to figure out what kind of hustle it could possibly be. Was it something psychological, like the hustle that Malcolm successfully worked on the New York Draft Board back in 1943? Could he, after going without pork and cigarettes for a while, claim some physical malady that could bring about his release? The magic phrase "get out of prison" danced around Malcolm's skull and hung in the air taunting him. He wanted out so badly. He wanted to confide in his prison mentor Bimbi about it but decided not to. Something this big, he thought, you revealed to no one.

Quitting cigarettes was not too difficult for Malcolm despite the fact that he had been chain-smoking anywhere from two to four packs a day since he was sixteen years old. Once again displaying the extraordinary discipline that became his trademark, Malcolm finished the pack he had before reading the letter and went cold turkey. He never smoked another cigarette the rest of his life after he received Reginald's letter in 1948! Now it was time to find out if he could stop eating pork, which, Malcolm recalled, his mother had admonished her children against eating in the first place.

Philbert, Wesley, Wilfred, Reginald, 1949

Schomburg Center

The opportunity to test his will came about three or four days later when pork was served for the noon meal. When the meat platter was passed to him, Malcolm hesitated with the platter in mid-air and then passed it along to the inmate waiting next to him. The next inmate began serving himself and then stopped abruptly. He turned to Malcolm looking surprised. Malcolm said to him, "I don't eat pork." The platter was then passed along to the next man. Malcolm was amused by the general response of his fellow inmates who were fascinated by his refusal. As Malcolm pointed out, in prison where little breaks the dull monotony of the daily routine, the smallest thing causes a commotion and gossip. By nightfall his entire cellblock was talking about the fact that "Satan doesn't eat pork." This attention made him feel very proud. In refusing the pork he felt he was also attacking the racial stereotype that blacks could not do without pork in their diet. Malcolm was especially happy to see that his not eating it startled the white convicts. When Malcolm later studied and committed himself to Islam, he recalled that the act of refusing the pork was his first experience of the ancient Muslim teaching in the Qur'an that "If you will take one step toward Allah—Allah will take two steps toward you."

A Prison Paradise

Malcolm requested a transfer to the Norfolk Prison Colony, an experimental rehabilitation jail. This state penal institution accepted only the best-behaved prisoners. Convicts often said that, barring a recommendation from someone in an administrative capacity in the prison system, such as a warden, only those with the right money or political connections could get transferred to Norfolk. The penal policies there were by far the most progressive and humane in the entire system. For Malcolm and other prisoners, Norfolk's policies were considered too good to be true.

Malcolm, however, was lucky to have the tremendous support of his loyal sister Ella in his corner. When she found out that Malcolm was now serious about changing his behavior and preparing for his future, she tirelessly lobbied the prison authorities on Malcolm's behalf. She enlisted the necessary assistance of a local black politician and white judge, both of whom she knew. Because of the pervasive corruption and graft of the criminal justice system, she had to pay for their "services." Her money and her prodigious efforts at using her good name and standing in the community as collateral (they were as impressed with her as Malcolm and many others had always been) finally persuaded the authorities to transfer Malcolm to Norfolk in the fall of 1948. Of course Malcolm, now twenty-three years old, was elated at the news.

Compared to Concord and Charlestown, Norfolk was paradise. It had flushing toilets, dining halls, and extensive recreation facilities. It had no cells or iron bars, only walls, and within those walls, prisoners had a lot more freedom. The housing was built like a dormitory. Each man had his own room, with a door allowing privacy, except for a small window that enabled the guards to peer inside from the corridor. There was also plenty of fresh air to breathe because the prison was not located in a city. The basement of each of the six-story dormitories had a recreation room containing a ping-pong table. Next to the recreation room was a common room with a radio (television was still in its infancy in 1948). Each of the upper floors had a shower room where the inmates could shower as often as they chose, unlike all other prisons where showers were often allowed only once or twice a week. There was a baseball field for those interested in sports and garden plots for those who liked to grow their own vegetables.

Except for those who were locked up for violating prison discipline, the inmates could move freely within the space provided, except after dusk when no prisoners were allowed outdoors. Norfolk was also far less crowded than most other prisons. It contained 1200 inmates, of which 15 percent were African Americans. However, just to remind everyone that Norfolk was still a prison and not summer camp, there were also twenty-foot-high walls that were manned by guards armed with rifles, shotguns, submachine guns, and hand grenades.

Free to wander around inside the dorms and engage in a wide variety of activities, including reading, Malcolm thrived. Norfolk was one of the few prisons in the United States where the emphasis really was on rehabilitation and reform, instead of exclusively on punishment. The prison's outstanding library had been willed to the Commonwealth of Massachusetts by State Senator Lewis Parkhurst, who had devoted his career to penal reform. There were so many books that the shelves could not hold them all. In this library, Malcolm eventually pored through many books on

Buddhism, Hinduism, Islam, and Christianity. Malcolm's new-found scholarly interest in religious philosophy and theological doctrine, along with his incredibly extensive studies of history (his favorite subject), philosophy, mathematics, literature, philology, etymology, political science, and biology soon led him to seek out others in the prison who were interested in education and advanced intellectual pursuits.

The Colony, as it was known, certainly was the most enlightened prison that Malcolm had ever heard of or experienced. He remarked on the fact that unlike other prisons where a tense, oppressive atmosphere of "malicious gossip, perversion, grafting, hateful guards, and general corruption" prevailed, Norfolk contained more relative culture than other prisons. A high percentage of inmates there were very active in group discussions, debates, and the communication of ideas. Instructors for the various educational rehabilitation programs came from nearby educational institutions such as Harvard, Boston University, Emerson College, and M.I.T.

Reginald Recruits Malcolm

Malcolm soon heard from his brother Reginald, who wrote him that he was coming to Norfolk to visit. Malcolm was still avoiding cigarettes and pork as his brother suggested. By the time Reginald arrived, Malcolm was aching to find out what scheme his brother had in mind to get him released from jail. Unlike his older brothers, Reginald was well aware of how Malcolm's street-hustler mentality operated, which is why his approach was so effective. Well dressed and carefully groomed, Reginald, who gave up his own short-lived street hustling to join the NOI, understood that Malcolm was full of anxiety and high expectations about how giving up smoking and pork could free him. So, like always, Reginald played it cool.

Reginald talked about everything except the riddle of cigarettes and pork. This tactic, of course, only increased Malcolm's interest in what he had to say. Reginald beat around the bush for a while talking about the family, what was happening in Detroit, and the last time he was in Harlem. Malcolm, who was nothing if not direct, did not push him to get to the point but waited patiently, certain that something momentous was about to go down. When they were running the streets in Harlem Reginald had often liked to talk about things in just such an indirect matter. It used to bug Malcolm sometimes in the past, but this time he just listened.

Then in a very off-hand manner Reginald said, as if it had just occurred to him, "Malcolm, if a man knew every imaginable thing that there is to know, who would he be?" Malcolm looked at him hard and said, "Well, he would have to be some kind of god." Reginald replied, "There's a man who knows everything." When Malcolm asked him who that was, Reginald responded, "God is a man, and his real name is Allah." The word *Allah* rang a bell with Malcolm because he remembered the name being mentioned in Philbert's earlier letter. Malcolm wondered where this conversation was going. Was Reginald going off the deep end of religion as well? But Reginald went on to talk about Islam and "the Nation," as it was known to its adherents, in a calm but intense tone. He explained that God had 360 degrees of knowledge and that this "represented the sum total of knowledge on earth."

As Malcolm later pointed out, to say he was confused was a great understatement. But he continued listening to Reginald, knowing that his brother was just taking his time in revealing something that would actually help his big brother. Reginald continued to talk about many arcane and esoteric things related to his newly adopted religion, and then he dropped a bombshell on Malcolm. This stark and bizarre revelation had a profound impact on how Malcolm viewed reality and his identity within it for many years to come.

Reginald told him that God had come to America and he had made himself known to a man named Elijah, who was "a black man just like us." This God had let Elijah know, Reginald said, that the devil's "time was up." Malcolm still did not know what to think. He just listened. Then his brother said, "the devil is also a man." Malcolm asked him what he meant. With a slight movement of his head, Reginald indicated some white inmates and their visitors talking across the room. "Them," he said. "The white man is the devil." He then told Malcolm that all whites knew they were devils, "especially Masons." At this point Malcolm's mind began to race, flashing across the "entire spectrum of white people he had ever known." Then he asked his brother, "Without exception?" "Without any exceptions," Reginald replied.

After Reginald left Malcolm once again thought long and hard about all the whites he had ever known from the start of his life. He began to make a huge catalogue of them in his mind's eye: The Ku Klux Klan. The state welfare workers who were always harassing his mother and calling her crazy in front of her children. The white neighbors who threw stones at him and his family demanding that they leave when they moved into "their" lily-white neighborhood. The whites who had allegedly burned their house down. The white supremacist Black Legion vigilantes who stalked and harassed his father and whom his mother and others always insisted had murdered him. The white farmer who had sold land to his father and then sued to take the property unjustly away from him. The white widow who lied to his parents about the tax lien on half of the land that she had sold to them, that they then had to pay. The openly racist collusion of judges, bankers, real estate developers, and police that not only denied them justice in the legal system, but also made sure that his family was left holding the huge burden of court costs in judgments that were fixed against them. The callous, cruel, and indifferent white people who ran the Michigan State Mental Asylum in Kalamazoo. The white judge and state agencies that split up his family and sent him and his siblings to the homes of others. The white classmates and teachers who routinely taunted and bullied him and his siblings and called him "nigger" and many other derogatory names in every school he had ever attended. The white teacher he trusted and respected who told him in the eighth grade that he could never become a lawyer because he was a "nigger" and should become a carpenter instead. The whites in Boston, Lansing, and New York who went to their "white-only" dances six days a week while blacks were allowed only one night a week at places like the Roseland Ballroom. The white customers whose shoes he shined for tips and who gave him hostile comments and condescending pats on the head. The whites who jeered, taunted, and openly laughed in his face as he took their dirty plates back to the kitchen in the Parker House Hotel in Boston. The endless hateful stares and routinely disrespectful attitudes of white railroad crewmen and passengers on the trains where he served them meals and desserts. The violently racist white cops and criminals he dealt with in New York. The hundreds of whites who piled into the black speakeasies, night-clubs, bars, and dancehalls searching for taboo sexual liaisons with black women and men and then hypocritically denied in public that they were ever into that sort of thing. The wealthy white men he had steered to the black "specialty sex" they wanted and the bored, rich white women who secretly pursued their lust for black men. The even more racist and violent Boston cops. Sophia, her sister Joyce, and the friend of Sophia's husband. The social workers and psychologists who endlessly questioned him and Shorty about "defiling respectable white women" such as Sophia and Joyce and denounced their "typical predatory black sexual behavior." The casual way that even the Swerlins called black people "niggers" in front of him. The mascot-like treatment he received from teachers and classmates in Mason, Michigan—the litany went on and on.

Malcolm's head was swimming as he reflected on the horrible combination of tragedy, grief, hatred, indifference, violence, anger, destruction, cruelty, oppression, discrimination, and exploitation that white American racism had wreaked on him and everyone he had ever known. He was astonished that for all of his street-wise experience, book-learning, and support from friends and family that he had never had a relationship with a white person or social insti-tution since early childhood that was not fraught with pain, decep-tion, dishonesty, conflict, fear, injustice, greed, and hatred. It unnerved him that he had never thought about the profound impli-cations of all this for his own behavior as an individual black man who had wound up being complicit in much of this oppression by cynically, fatalistically, and ignorantly ignoring the obvious signs and misdirecting his rage and fear of racism at himself or other black people. Now he began to think that he should focus his atten-tion, intensity, and rage on an actual social target for once. Malcolm also began to rethink his previous dismissal of all religions from a new intellectual perspective of gauging and assessing the ethical and moral limitations of society, and then proposing changes in philosophy and behavior that would challenge the society to grow beyond those limitations. In this specific context, the study and practice of Islam began to make sense to him.

When Reginald made a return visit to Norfolk, Malcolm was open and receptive to him. He now listened enraptured as Reginald, only twenty-one years old at the time, spoke for two hours in spellbinding rhetoric about how slavery and its legacy had deprived them of their cultural roots and left African Americans "mentally dead." He went on to talk at length about the history of the "devilish white man" and the "brainwashed black man." At the end of his oration, Reginald was very pleased to note that Malcolm's general attitude had changed; Reginald's impassioned proselytizing was having a definite effect on him.

After this visit, Malcolm's other brothers and sisters who had joined the NOI bombarded Malcolm with letters urging him to turn to Allah and join the organization. Malcolm was left to ponder some of the first serious political thoughts he had ever had in his life: The white man was quickly losing his power to oppress and exploit the so-called "Third World" (those societies and cultures of African, Asian, and Latin American ancestry); this world was starting to rise to destroy colonialism and its vestiges throughout the globe; the "white world was on the way down and on its way out."

Malcolm also thought a great deal about how white racism had concealed the fact that Africans, and thus African Americans, were the descendants of highly advanced ancient civilizations that were rich in culture, history, knowledge, and political and economic power. He especially focused on Reginald's comment that the black man had been "cut off from all true knowledge of his own kind." Finally, Malcolm reflected on the rhetoric in Reginald's statements that African Americans were the victims of the evil of devilish white men ever since the Atlantic slave trade stole black people from their native land and severed their spiritual and material ties to their societies, cultures, and ancestors.

Soon Malcolm began receiving at least two letters every day from his siblings in Detroit. Both his eldest brother Wilfred and his first wife Bertha wrote, as well as Philbert and his eldest sister, Hilda. The family then scraped together enough money to send Hilda to visit Malcolm. When she arrived she immediately took up where Reginald had left off. She told Malcolm that the holy city of Mecca had been founded by Africans. She then went on to tell Malcolm about some of the extraordinarily complex and racially-based origin myths, demonology, and allegories that the NOI indoctrinated all of its members with.

Hilda's visit had a decisive impact on Malcolm. She and his brothers all told him about the Muslims, who were followers of a black man they called "The Honorable Elijah Muhammad." He was described as a small, gentle man whom they sometimes referred to as "The Messenger of Allah." He had been born October 7, 1897, on a farm in Georgia. He had moved his family to Detroit in the 1920s, and in 1930 he had met a mysterious man there named Wallace D. Fard, who Muhammad said was "God in person." It was he who had given Allah's message to Elijah Muhammad to educate and lead the black people who were, in his words, "the Lost-Found Nation of Islam here in the wilderness of North America."

Fard taught that the "original man" was black and that all whites were devils who had distorted the truths of holy texts, such as the Bible and the Qur'an, and brainwashed the descendants of the "original man" in Africa and its diaspora in the West into believing that they were inferior and deserving to be oppressed and enslaved. Fard's anointment of Elijah Muhammad as Allah's Messenger in 1931 was the capstone of the rise and eventual domination of the Islamic faith over and against Christianity, which Fard and his followers viewed as a religion that had become corrupted by whites. (He also believed and taught that the Holy Bible had been rewritten to change and distort the historically central role that Africans and their descendants had played in the development and evolution of world religions.) Fard predicted as early as 1930 that Islam would supplant Christianity as the predominant faith of African Americans, This prediction seemed impossible at the time but not today: Some four million African Americans have converted to Islam in the past forty years alone.

As Malcolm's family urged him to accept the teachings of Muhammad, Reginald finally explained that pork was not eaten by those who worshipped in the religion of Islam, and not smoking cigarettes was a rule adhered to by the followers of the Honorable Elijah Muhammad because the faith did not allow its members to take "injurious things such as narcotics, tobacco, or liquor into their bodies." Malcolm was also introduced to what was called "the true knowledge of the black man," which the faithful followers of the Honorable Elijah Muhammad were said to possess. Malcolm also learned that the key to a real Muslim is complete spiritual submission, the attunement of one toward Allah. These concepts and assertions were given intellectual shape and content for Malcolm in his siblings' lengthy letters and the NOI literature that they sent to him.

At his sister Hilda's suggestion, Malcolm wrote a long letter to the NOI's leader, Elijah Muhammad in late 1948. Before mailing it Malcolm rewrote it about two dozen times, because he wanted to be clear and he did not want to embarrass either himself or "the Messenger" with stupid or shallow questions. Malcolm anxiously awaited Muhammad's reply to his painstakingly written letter. He had not yet officially embraced Islam and the NOI, but he was definitely on the verge. All that was left for Malcolm to do was to finally receive the words and blessings of Elijah Muhammad. Then, Malcolm said, he would become a member and commit to Islam and the NOI.

Malcolm Submits to Allah and Joins the Nation of Islam

In early 1949, Malcolm received a reply from Elijah Muhammad. Muhammad's letter was accompanied by a gift of money and was probably similar to the many letters that he sent to hundreds of other convicts. These letters were primarily designed to alleviate the convicts' guilt and to tell them what they must now do to make amends. Malcolm had used his time in prison to seriously reflect on his crimes, and he had finally admitted a great sense of guilt, remorse, and shame for his past criminal activity. He begged the Messenger to forgive him. Muhammad told Malcolm that the real criminal was not the black lawbreaker but the whites who had made him turn to crime. The black prisoner, he said, symbolized white society's crime of keeping black men oppressed and deprived and unable to get decent jobs, thus turning them into criminals.

However, Malcolm would have to personally atone for his crimes and misdeeds not only by renouncing his past, but also by humbly bowing in prayer to the supreme power of Allah and making a spiritual promise not to ever engage in any evil or destructive behavior again. The NOI promoted and practiced an austere moral code that had been successful in rehabilitating thousands of ex-cons and others by offering them the respect, dignity, pride, and acceptance that many men and women like Malcolm had outwardly scorned, but secretly craved and needed. The price for such acceptance and spiritual renewal, Muhammad sternly insisted, was complete and utter submission and obedience to Allah (as well as unswerving loyalty to his Messenger). Discipline, humility, and the full practice of the religion of Islam were absolute prerequisites to becoming a member of the NOI.

Could Malcolm find it within himself to submit? Despite Malcolm's apparent leap of faith, submission to Allah was by no means an easy task for him to complete. Malcolm had always been rebellious and deeply skeptical. He had become accustomed to critically, even cynically, questioning and challenging the beliefs, values, and moral codes of others. His previous deep distrust of religion was based on his refusal to submit to anyone else's doctrine about how he should live or behave. For Malcolm, his submission was not achieved without great internal conflict. This conflict was so intense that it took him a week to finally bend his knees and pray for forgiveness. As he poignantly notes in his autobiography, every time he began to prostrate himself, something made him get back up. But his great need for personal atonement drove him back down on his knees. The Messenger then welcomed him into the Nation with open arms. Finally, his brothers and sisters all agreed, Malcolm was truly saved.

By this point, Malcolm had concluded that "Satan" was the last thing he wanted to be called. He was on a feverish quest for his real name, his "original name" as the NOI members called it. Muhammad told Malcolm that a NOI member's last name was temporarily replaced with an X until such time as his or her "original name" was bestowed upon the new member. But that member would first have to serve a period of apprenticeship in the organization before the X was granted. The apprenticeship was designed to make certain that the new recruit was sincere in his or her verbal commitment to the NOI by testing that commitment through assigned tasks over an unspecified period of time. During a subsequent waiting period, the X would be given to the individual. As it did in algebra, the X represented the unknown. Not until Elijah Muhammad himself substituted a Black Muslim's "slave" surname (all Africans brought to the Americas were initially given the last name of the slaveholder who "owned" them) with an Arabic one did a person truly become a complete and full-fledged member of the Islamic faith as defined by the NOI.

By the spring of 1949, Malcolm's conversion had led him to drastically change his life in a number of ways. He was surprised how rapidly he made the transformation from a tough criminal to a deeply religious person. It was as though his former identity had been someone else. His outward appearance also began to change. In accordance with the NOI's custom requiring new male members to cut any long hair, Malcolm had the barber completely shave his head. The fire-red conk that he had carefully pampered and taken care of for almost a decade was now a relic of the past. Instead, he grew a beard and a moustache that curved downward at the corners of his mouth. His house officer in the Colony instructed him to shave off the beard, but Malcolm refused on the grounds of "freedom of religion." To be deprived of one's hair against one's will, he told Shorty, made a man lose his strength. He then cited the biblical example of Samson and Delilah as proof.

By this time, Malcolm had become a voracious reader in the excellent prison library and wrote daily to his siblings in Detroit, where his eldest brother Wilfred, who was the first to join the NOI in 1947, was the leading minister in the Detroit Temple (the NOI's houses of worship were called both temples and mosques). Malcolm sent them a barrage of letters quoting scholarly texts that proved the "evilness of the white man" and corroborated Muhammad's views on theology, history, and science.

Initially, everyone who had joined the NOI (which now included everyone in Malcolm's family except his youngest brother Robert and his half sister Ella) was very receptive to Malcolm's lecture-like letters. But by the fall of 1949, his beloved brother Reginald, who had done so much to convince Malcolm to join the sect, began arguing with him about the validity of the teachings of Elijah Muhammad. Reginald had changed his mind about Muhammad's self-proclaimed divinity. Muhammad, he told Malcolm, was no Messenger of Allah. He said he even had evidence that Muhammad was a false prophet. In subsequent visits to the prison, Reginald would continue to talk disparagingly of Elijah Muhammad, implying that Muhammad had treated him unfairly for breaking rules that Muhammad himself had violated.

Deeply shaken by Reginald's accusations, Malcolm wrote to his brother Wilfred about it. When Wilfred visited him weeks later, Malcolm discovered that Reginald had been suspended from the Black Muslims (the popular name for the NOI) for committing adultery. Wilfred and Malcolm's other siblings believed Reginald was now making his "wild, unfounded charges" about Elijah Muhammad only because he had been excommunicated from the NOI. The excommunication meant that no members of the NOI could speak to, write, or associate with Reginald. The stress caused by his brother's plight made it nearly impossible for Malcolm to sleep. Lying on his bed in semidarkness, reading the Bible well into the night, Malcolm searched for some story or parable that he could cite in letters to Muhammad as grounds for saving Reginald.

Almost daily for the next several weeks, Malcolm wrote letters to Elijah Muhammad asking him to reinstate his brother. Malcolm was concerned that the excommunication would eventually ruin his brother's mental health. Malcolm was always apprehensive about these matters in his family because his mother was in a mental hospital. In the late fall of 1949, Reginald suffered a nervous breakdown, just as Malcolm had feared. Though Malcolm's other siblings, disobeying the strict rules of isolation, secretly tried to nurse Reginald through his emotional and psychological crisis, he began experiencing acute paranoia and delusions of grandeur (he believed he was more powerful than God), and he had to be hospitalized.

Shutting Reginald out of his life hurt Malcolm deeply, but as the weeks passed, he was able to suppress his anguish over Muhammad's punishment of Reginald and press on with his vision of the role he imagined himself playing in the rapid rise of the Nation of Islam. These events and Malcolm's response to them would, years later, play an eerie and in many ways prophetic role in his eventual conflict with Elijah and the NOI over both the form and content of his new spiritual mentor's message, and his and others' methods of transmitting and delivering that message to both the faithful within the organization and the much wider world of Islam and the international revolutionary movement of the African diaspora and the African continent itself for freedom, justice, and independence. But, in 1949 all that was still more than a decade away.

From the stark vantage point of Malcolm's third full year in prison, Elijah Muhammad, the NOI, and the intellectual world of books and scholarship were his salvation, and nothing, not even the disillusionment and subsequent breakdown of a loved one, was going to keep the highly determined and ambitious new convert from his destiny. Malcolm felt that his emotional struggle with Reginald's situation was part of the personal sacrifice that he had to make to acquire his X and thus discover the "true knowledge of the black man." From here on, Malcolm told himself, his life belonged to Islam, the Nation, and the Honorable Elijah Muhammad. For the next fifteen years, in good times and bad, he honored that pledge until new realities, circumstances, and truths compelled him to do otherwise.

Chapter 11

The True Knowledge of the Black Man

The post-World War II period of the late 1940s that Malcolm spent in prison was an era in which a number of rapid and fundamental changes took place in both the United States and the rest of the world. By 1947, the Soviet Union (former wartime ally of the United States, Britain, and France against fascism) was locked in a fierce global struggle with the United States for political, ideological, and economic domination. This struggle, dubbed the "Cold War" (so named because the battle was now primarily one of competing ideologies and political and economic systems instead of physical combat), had quickly led to major domestic strife in America between the right-wing forces of political conservatism and those who represented a far more progressive and radical political perspective in American life. Among this latter group were not only liberals but also independents as well as traditionally affiliated socialists and communists who were often vilified and denounced by these highly conservative elements.

The fallout from this major conflict was the brutal and reactionary political hysteria of what became known popularly as "McCarthyism." Named after Senator Joseph McCarthy, a Republican from Wisconsin, McCarthyism was a label that encompassed a massive array of loosely affiliated groups and individuals who were vehemently opposed to communism, socialism, anarchism, and even many more conventional liberal political and philosophical ideas and practices in the United States. Led by the demagogic, media-savvy, and shrewdly manipulative senator, the McCarthy movement accused thousands of American citizens of being communists, an accusation that applied not only to the then legally sanctioned, card-carrying members of the Communist Party of the United States (CPUSA) but to virtually anyone who publicly fought for civil rights, women's rights, economic democracy, and leftist political reform.

In the poisoned and polarized political and ideological atmosphere of the Cold War, the very use of the word *communism* in the United States became suspect; to be accused of being one was tantamount to being called a dangerous heretic or traitor to one's country. Thousands of people lost their jobs, reputations, and even lives as the right-wingers attacked, hounded, and harassed teachers, professors, political and social activists, union workers, government officials, writers, actors, directors, artists, farmers, and anyone else who spoke out forcefully against the pervasiveness of racism, anti-Semitism, sexism, political corruption, and economic exploitation in American society.

Such famed and internationally esteemed African American intellectuals and leaders as W.E.B. DuBois and Paul Robeson were, like many others, blacklisted and arrested and had their passports seized or revoked by the government. W.E.B. DuBois (1868–1963) was a Harvard Ph.D., co-founder in 1909 of the NAACP, founder and editor of that organization's *Crisis* magazine for over twenty-five years, and an esteemed author of over thirty books on American and world history, sociology, literature, and politics. Paul Robeson (1898–1976) was an actor, singer, cultural critic, scholar, and political activist. In April 1949, Robeson and DuBois were villified by the U.S. media and the federal government for attending and making pro-socialist statements at the World Peace Conference in Paris, France.

In July 1949, along with many other fervent supporters of Brooklyn Dodger Jackie Robinson, Malcolm was shocked and bitterly disappointed when his favorite athlete was called by the notorious witch-hunting congressional body known as the House

Un-American Activities Committee (HUAC) and agreed to testify against Paul Robeson as a so-called test of African Americans' loyalty to the nation. Robeson, who was also a great political hero to Malcolm as well as many other black and white Americans, was now perceived and treated as an "enemy of the state" for his fearless and eloquently outspoken views on racism and capitalism in the United States. As a result of this virulent public campaign against him by the federal government and the national media, Robeson's passport was confiscated by the U.S. State Department from 1950–58, which put him under virtual house arrest in his own country.

On August 27, 1949, a huge white mob of KKK members, assorted extremist right-wing groups, and private citizens rioted and physically attacked and assaulted hundreds of African Americans, Jews, and others attending an outdoor concert given by Robeson in Peekskill, New York. Overturning cars and setting them on fire, the hysterical mob (armed with guns, sticks, baseball bats, rocks, guns, and other weapons) smashed the stage, torched the camp chairs set up around it, and put over a dozen Robeson concertgoers and supporters in the hospital. They also hung Robeson in effigy.

Just one week later on September 4, determined not to be intimidated by hundreds of death threats, Robeson gave another outdoor concert as hundreds of former GIs, union members, assorted radicals, and ordinary supporters and fans of Robeson formed a massive protective cordon around the singer. As he defiantly sang in the open air for a supportive but tense crowd of thousands, several white men with guns on the ridge surrounding the area where the concert took place menaced the crowd. During the concert Robeson's security men flushed out two potential assassins who were carrying high-powered rifles and hiding in a hill overlooking the hollow where the event was taking place.

In 1951, at the age of 83, DuBois was arrested, handcuffed, booked, and indicted for (of all absurd charges) sedition and not registering his international lobbying organization, the Peace Information Center, as "an agent of a foreign power" (allegedly because of its various radical affiliations). He was subsequently

acquitted of all charges, but not before he unjustly served three
months in jail for his political beliefs.

Malcolm, 1950s

Schomburg Center

During this highly charged and dangerous social and racial time, Malcolm plunged into a ferociously intense and astonishingly comprehensive study of history, politics, economics, and philosophy. Malcolm also began consuming academic, literary, and political books, magazines, newspapers, and journals at a phenomenal rate. To Malcolm, this whirlwind of intellectual activity was merely making up for lost time. He had always been interested in and fascinated by ideas and theories, but he had never before possessed the proper discipline, dedication, or concentrated time to pursue these interests. For the first time since middle school in 1940–41, Malcolm was seriously involved in keeping abreast of national and world events. Malcolm knew that his studies were absolutely crucial to fully grasping what the Honorable Elijah Muhammad and the NOI meant by the phrase "the true knowledge of the black man." Toward that end, Malcolm immersed himself in a highly organized learning plan.

While other inmates spent their free time playing ball, gossiping, or attending bad movies, Malcolm holed up in his room and absorbed entire books the way other people devoured food. He characterized his devouring of books as "intellectual vitamins for his hunger-stricken soul." On weekends, during which time most inmates were given a break from work, he studied twelve to fifteen hours a day. If someone made the mistake of knocking on his door while he was engrossed in a book, he was greeted stonily or with outright hostility. What could anyone possibly want with him while he was trying to acquire knowledge of himself and the world? Malcolm thought. He preferred the hermit-like existence such a regimen imposed on him, because it enabled him to make constructive and productive use of his penchant for emotional withdrawal while in prison.

Malcolm systematically read and studied as much or more than any advanced post-graduate student at an Ivy League institution. He read major texts by historians such as Will Durant and H.G. Wells. He read the works of W.E.B. DuBois, Carter G. Woodson, J.A. Rogers, and Arnold Toynbee among many other highly prominent historians, black and white. He read dense and informative historical texts on the ancient civilizations and cultures of Egypt,

Ethiopia, Greece, Rome, and China. He read deeply about the unspeakable horrors and brutalities of the Atlantic slave trade and the social, political, and economic institution of slavery as practiced in the United States and throughout the Western hemisphere for nearly three centuries. He read books about such important figures as Herodotus, "the father of history," and Aesop, the African philosopher and writer of Malcolm's beloved fables. He read the works of Plato, Socrates, Aristotle, Kant, Hegel, Spinoza, Nietzsche, Marx, and Schopenhauer. He read Mahatma Gandhi's accounts of the anticolonial struggle to drive the British out of India. He read an extensive collection of books and pamphlets by the Abolitionist Anti-Slavery Society of New England that vividly documented the pervasive atrocities committed by white slaveholders throughout the United States. He read books about biology, chemistry, mathematics, and still more books about anthropology, philology, etymology, and of course, history. As a great student of politics and one who was subconsciously training himself for a position of leadership, biographies of major political figures from the entire ideological spectrum were also a great source of knowledge and fascination for Malcolm. He read books about Hannibal, Haile Selassie, Karl Marx, V.I. Lenin, Josef Stalin, Adolf Hitler, Gandhi, Rommel, Patrick Henry, and John Brown, among others.

Malcolm was so involved in his reading that when the prison lights were turned off every night at ten, he was outraged. Fortunately, he was able to use a small corridor light right outside his door that cast a glow into his room. The glow was just bright enough for him to continue reading, once his eyes adjusted to it (because he read so much by poor light, Malcolm believed that is why he eventually needed glasses). The night guards would pace past every room at one-hour intervals. As soon as Malcolm heard approaching footsteps he would jump into bed and feign sleep. When the guard passed, Malcolm got back out of bed onto the floor near the dim corridor light where he would proceed to read for another hour before the guard approached again. He continued this ritual every night until three or four in the morning. Sleeping only three or four hours a night was no big deal for Malcolm who had often slept less than that when he was hustling on the streets, and reading was far more important than any of that.

Malcolm began attending, and eventually giving, prison lectures. Many of the lectures he attended were by teachers from major universities in Massachusetts and Connecticut. He joined Norfolk's debating team and loved matching wits and knowledge with the teams that came to the prison from schools such as Harvard, M.I.T., and Yale. He was quickly becoming an outstanding debater and orator, with a razor-sharp delivery, a devastating use of irony and deadpan humor, a scholar's mastery of logic, and an encyclopedic command of facts. Many of the subjects the prison team debated with the white academics were crucial issues of the day, in which Malcolm excelled. Malcolm became such an accomplished debater that the answers that he, Shorty, and other team members had carefully researched and discovered formed on his tongue as quickly as his adversaries raised their questions. Though sometimes he lost his temper, he never lost his poise or ability to convey knowledge and insights in a particularly striking and dynamic manner.

He informed one friend that he fully intended to put his expertise in public speaking to practical use when he left prison. He promised his siblings and Elijah Muhammad that all of his skills would be harnessed and used for organizing others to embrace Islam and the NOI "in the name of the Messenger" and that he would find an effective method for conveying the "true knowledge of the black man" to everyone he encountered. By now, Malcolm was writing daily letters to Muhammad, as well as his family. He was determined, he said, to introduce the power, beauty, and truth of his new faith to his fellow inmates and ask them to humble themselves to the divine majesty and spirituality of Allah. His brothers and sisters told him it was important to practice *Salat*, holy prayer, six times daily while physically facing east and to continue his disciplined regimen of eating properly and meditating. Elijah Muhammad continued to send both letters and literature about Islam and the NOI and encouraged Malcolm in his proselytizing efforts.

The prison authorities at the Colony now began to view Malcolm as a far different kind of threat than one who merely engaged in physical violence or petty crime within the prison and were becoming increasingly unhappy with the overtly political way in which Malcolm recruited other inmates as he spoke about Islam and his involvement in the teachings of the NOI. After writing a series of very critical letters to various national government officials, including then President Truman, Malcolm was put under secret surveillance by the FBI and other national security organizations who were deeply concerned with the rapidly growing membership and influence of the Honorable Elijah Muhammad and the Nation of Islam, both in the African American community at large and among black prison inmates.

FBI Director J. Edgar Hoover and others in the U.S. intelligence community had historically attacked and attempted to destroy politically independent African American organizations, activists, and artists since the 1920s (among the people they went after were Marcus Garvey, W.E.B. DuBois, A. Philip Randolph, Langston Hughes, and Paul Robeson), and this effort continued into the late 1960s and early 1970s. Although Malcolm was not yet aware of such surveillance he was, as always, very conscious of being watched carefully by prison authorities. This convinced him even more that he was on the right track.

> One of the largest and most notorious dossiers that the virulently racist and reactionary FBI Director J. Edgar Hoover amassed, outside of the ones on Malcolm, Elijah Muhammad, the NOI, and the Black Panther Party, was on Dr. Martin Luther King Jr.

On March 23, 1950, at the height of the Cold War and with U.S. military involvement in the Korean War just a few months away, Malcolm was suddenly transferred from the Colony back to Charlestown Prison. It was clear that prison authorities at Norfolk were deeply concerned about Malcolm's success at recruiting and converting a number of black inmates to Islam as an organizer for the NOI. The prison censors were also closely monitoring, reporting on, and in some instances even confiscating his mail.

The official reason given for Malcolm's transfer back to the more conventional prison was that Malcolm had refused to take mandatory typhoid inoculation shots (Norfolk's well water was chemically untreated and susceptible to contamination by sewage). Malcolm understood the real reason, however. He told prison authorities that he did not mind being transferred because wherever he went he would continue to work on behalf of Islam, Elijah Muhammad, and the NOI.

Nevertheless, Malcolm was concerned and worried that his activism might adversely affect his chances for parole, for which he would soon be eligible. But he also reasoned that the members of his parole board might look at his organizing and advocacy for Islam in another way. Instead of keeping him in prison, they might want to make sure he got out, so they could eliminate what they perceived as a problem. In any case, Malcolm knew he had been a model prisoner in terms of personal behavior, so any delays in parole would have to be because of his "spreading Islam" the way his father had spread the philosophy of Garveyism and the UNIA twenty years earlier.

Less than a month after Malcolm returned to Charlestown, he, Shorty, and another former Norfolk inmate who followed Malcolm named Osborne Thaxton demanded prison cells that faced eastward so that they could pray toward Mecca during their *Salat*. Not surprisingly, Warden John O' Brien thought the three Islamic convicts were out of their minds and said he "wasn't sure he could comply immediately" with the request. Malcolm then threatened to appeal to the Egyptian consulate in Washington, D.C. "He'll appreciate our position," he said. "Our religious freedom is being infringed." At Norfolk, Malcolm had steeped himself in constitutional law, using the relevant law books in Parkhurst Library (he was finally getting an opportunity to work as an attorney, after all). The books, however, subsequently vanished. Reading material that Ella had mailed Malcolm also disappeared. Clearly powerful forces within the prison system did not want Malcolm's ideas and methods to spread further.

The threat of outside intervention worked. Apparently the prison authorities feared a public controversy. Malcolm, Shorty, and Thaxton were transferred to new cells, and the story made the *Boston Post* newspaper. However, Malcolm failed to win any more concessions from the prison administration, which turned down his requests for a nonpork diet and time off from work on Islamic holidays. Nor did the warden accord official recognition to the prison's Islamic minority, despite the fact that in his annual reports to his superiors, he always made careful note of the number of Christians and Jews who were in the prison population and the institutional obligation to protect, respect, and honor their right to worship in any manner they chose. By not officially recognizing their existence, the prison administration and the state system in general could prevent Muslims from worshipping communally and receiving religious instruction from outside. The authorities also feared that the antiwhite doctrines of the Nation of Islam would breed internal dissension and racial violence within the prison system.

Charlestown's strict regime made it much harder for Malcolm to recruit converts than it had been for him at Norfolk. Yet he sought out his fellow inmates in the small prison yard, where prisoners congregated after work before picking up their dinner trays and carrying them to their cramped and smelly cells, which were locked until the following morning. Somehow Malcolm managed to get a transfer from the license plate fabricating shop to the prison laundry, which regularly issued clean clothes to each inmate. Malcolm took full advantage of the opportunity to court potential recruits and converts there.

One time he was so busy trying to interest a fellow black inmate in Islam and the NOI that he let the white convict standing next in line for clothes wait too long. The convict complained to a guard who snarled, "Any time someone comes here for clothing, black or white, you give it to him right away, or you'll end up in seclusion, you black bastard." Malcolm did not say a word in response but stared the guard down with his blazing eyes. All followers of Elijah Muhammad were instructed to behave respectfully and with dignity toward authority, even white authority, both as a means of protecting themselves and to demonstrate that they were equals and deserved the same respect. Consequently,

Malcolm limited his Islamic-inspired rebellion to the applicable rules and regulations, which he knew as well or better than any of the prison officials did.

Highly disciplined and yet uncompromising in his actions and behavior, Malcolm did not allow the prison authorities to provoke him in any way they could use against him. Clearly, the twenty-five-year-old firebrand was maturing. When prison officials tried to make him shorten his six-, eight-, and ten-page letters to the outside world, which were apparently driving the censors crazy, Malcolm refused on the grounds that they had no authority to order him to do so. The officials retaliated by refusing to mail his letters. When Malcolm again threatened to have outside allies intercede, the authorities relented and, for the time being, backed off from any further confrontations. The authorities also tried to induce Malcolm to stop recruiting and soliciting converts. He refused, but he promised that there would be no trouble. He was already exhibiting an uncanny ability to survive in a hostile political and social environment without losing his highly disciplined control of either his devoted followers or himself.

By deftly preaching the faith and providing his fellow converts with the "true knowledge of the black man as taught by the Honorable Elijah Muhammad and the religion of Islam," Malcolm was quickly and unmistakably becoming the leader that he had always fervently hoped he would be. That he was now accomplishing his goals through the commanding use of words, moral authority, and intellectual prowess dramatically confirmed what Bimbi, Ella, Laura, his parents, numerous books, and his other siblings had always tried to teach him: Knowledge was power, and once you attained it, no one could take it away. Malcolm was more determined than ever to use his new acknowledgement of this ancient truth to free himself and his people from bondage.

In the summer of 1950, Charlestown Prison heard the news that war had erupted in a distant Asian nation called Korea. For draft-eligible inmates who expected or hoped, like Malcolm, to be released soon, the news was ominous. Prison was preferable to warfare for many of the younger inmates. Two days after President Truman dispatched American troops to Pusan, where U.S. military power intervened to prevent the fall of the entire Korean peninsula to the communists, Malcolm calmly predicted that the government would promptly begin drafting huge numbers of men.

In a letter to a friend, Malcolm said he was not personally concerned about a draft; even if he enlisted voluntarily, the armed forces would not induct him. "I've always been a communist," Malcolm asserted (a private statement that the FBI, who along with the prison censors was reading his mail, immediately submitted to Malcolm's ever-expanding file). He also said he was *persona non grata* to the American military because of his 4-F status during World War II and his faked attempts to join the Japanese army. He concluded the letter by admitting that he was feigning madness, as he had done during his 1943 encounter with the army psychiatrist. Of course the prison censors, among others, were dutifully documenting remarks from his letters, a fact that Malcolm was well aware of. Despite this, Malcolm kept up his intense letter-writing campaign. Authorities did not take kindly to Malcolm's fiery words, but his letters were shrewdly constructed in such a way that authorities could not ascertain whether he was really crazy or not. He emphasized to all that he had no intention of joining the military or donning any kind of uniform except perhaps for an organized crusade against whites and their racism.

A vivid example of Malcolm's militancy on behalf of his new religious beliefs and black people's historical place in them was when Malcolm went to a popular prison Bible class at Charlestown that many black inmates regularly attended. Hoping to find new converts there by intellectually confronting the white Harvard Seminary student who ran the class, Malcolm listened patiently as the "tall, blond, blue-eyed devil" (as he put it) lectured and then opened up the discussion to a spirited question-and-answer session. Malcolm grudgingly admitted that the seminary student knew his stuff. He was not sure whether he or the Harvard-trained teacher had read the Bible more, but Malcolm quickly acknowledged that he was "really heavy on his religion" and that he "puzzled for a way to upset him [the Harvard teacher] and to give those Negroes present something to think and talk about, and circulate."

Finally Malcolm put up his hand, and the teacher nodded. The theme of his talk had been Paul, one of Jesus Christ's major disciples. Malcolm stood up and confidently asked, "What color was Paul?" Continuing to talk and pausing between phrases, Malcolm said, "He had to be black ... because he was a Hebrew ... and the original Hebrews were black ... weren't they?" The teacher, now uneasy and flushing red, replied, "Yes." Having put the class in a bit of an uproar with his remarks, Malcolm continued to challenge the white historical record of the racial identity of the prophets and leaders of Christianity. He then asked, "What color was Jesus? ... He was Hebrew, too, ... wasn't he?"

The black and white convicts alike sat bolt upright in their chairs, eagerly anticipating the teacher's response. As Malcolm pointed out, the convicts, having been taught their entire lives, like every other Christian in the United States, that Jesus was white were not prepared to hear that he was not. The instructor walked around with a severe look of consternation on his face. Finally he said, "Jesus was brown." Malcolm stated that he "let him get away with that compromise." But his dramatic point had been made. He was triumphant, and the entire prison buzzed as Charlestown's inmates, white and black, began spreading the story throughout the prison of Malcolm's extraordinary challenge to Christian religious orthodoxy.

In the eyes of many black inmates Malcolm was now a hero. Wherever he went on the prison grounds they nodded at him in approval. This approval opened up a huge opportunity for him to recruit and convert still more black men to Islam and the NOI. Anytime he had a chance to exchange words with a fellow black prisoner, he would exclaim, "My man! You ever heard about somebody named Mr. Elijah Muhammad?"

Although this new development greatly pleased Malcolm and his new mentor, Elijah Muhammad, prison officials (and Malcolm's parole board) were far less happy about it. When Shorty and Malcolm became eligible for parole in the summer of 1951, the board paroled Shorty, but not Malcolm. This decision was made despite Malcolm's numerous letters to the board and warden indicating that he had seen the error of his ways and was prepared to cared about him. Malcolm saw Sophia as a showpiece that he could parade around the ghetto as an example of both a sexual and racial conquest. The status accorded a white female with money in the underground subculture that Malcolm inhabited gave an illusory authority to any black male who was able to "win" her. Shorty, whom Malcolm now saw less of, called Sophia a "Beacon Hill chick (referring to a wealthy white area in Boston)." Because Shorty had "schooled" Malcolm in the street life that he now embraced, the fact that Malcolm hung out with and was "kept" by Sophia gave Shorty even more status among his peers.

This exploitation was mutual, of course. Sophia saw Malcolm as a black stud who could satisfy her insatiable sexual desires while confirming her pathetic belief in the racist mythology of superior black sexual prowess. Bored, restless, and alienated from her own community, Sophia had once told a friend of hers that a woman who had never slept with a "nigger" had never experienced sexual release. Thus, in this particular relationship, one form of racial pathology reinforced another. She also told Malcolm that she would also occasionally date white men "just to keep up appearances" so as not to have her secret desires exposed.

Malcolm seemed to enjoy the role of stud. Neither he nor Sophia saw their sexual encounters as either an act of love or intimacy but rather as payment for payment: Sophia continually gave Malcolm money and bought him clothes and other gifts in exchange for his attentions. Other black hustlers viewed Malcolm enviously; these conmen, pimps, club managers, gamblers, and numbers bankers were pounding Malcolm on the back, setting up drinks at special tables for him and Sophia, and calling him "Red" as though they were all old pals. Sophia's voluptuous blond attractiveness and her bankrolling of Malcolm at bars, clubs, and other public places now led the people that Malcolm admired to see him as more than just another hustler "wannabe" or conked and zoot-suited youngster. Malcolm surmised that one of reasons they began to view and treat him differently is that many of them coveted Sophia for themselves. At last, Malcolm felt like one of the "cats." Of course, he had not seriously considered the steep price of this reputation.

re-enter society as a responsible and reliable citizen. The prison authorities still questioned Malcolm's sincerity and were not yet thoroughly convinced that his religious and political activity on the part of the NOI and Islam was not representative of his ongoing "rebellious attitude." He also lacked an official sponsor for his parole that the parole board would accept.

Malcolm's loyal and reliable older brother Wilfred came through and agreed to be personally responsible for his parole. Wilfred also advised Malcolm to tell the parole board, without irony or condescension, what it wanted to hear: He had seen the futility of his former behavior and was now ready to live a different life. This advice was very sound. Malcolm, weary of prison life and eager to begin work as a formal member of and organizer for the Nation of Islam, finally complied. At long last the board accepted Malcolm's entreaties, and he was paroled on August 7, 1952, in his eldest brother's custody.

Coming home to Detroit where Temple Number One of the NOI was located (so named because it was the first one that had been established by Elijah Muhammad in 1931), Malcolm was gratified to be with his family again. He was also extremely happy being a part of a genuine community again, after so many years in environments where human trust, respect, love, and support were in very short supply. For Malcolm, this new community was not merely that of his African American family and neighborhood, but the entire Nation of Islam. Malcolm felt that this social and cultural base of discipline, goodwill, unity, and order would provide his entry into a society where black people could fight for and communally develop independent systems of political, economic, and social freedom. For Malcolm this fundamental infrastructure would come from the teachings and wisdom of the Honorable Elijah Muhammad, his ministers, and followers in the faith of Islam.

For once, Malcolm was absolutely sure of his path in life. By organizing "in the name of the Messenger" Malcolm was convinced that he would finally find what he had been fitfully and desperately searching for all along: a place where he could truly belong and be respected, encouraged, and nurtured by family, friends, and loved ones. He could also be free to give the very best that he had to offer. At age twenty-seven, following many personal trials and tribulations, Malcolm finally felt at home. As he walked out of state prison for good after six years of imprisonment, he could not know that his extraordinary quest had just begun.

Chapter 12

Organizing in the Name of the Messenger

When Malcolm was released Wilfred got him a job at a furniture store that he managed in Detroit. All his siblings agreed that the best place for Malcolm to make a new start was Detroit and not Boston or Harlem, where he might run into his former criminal associates or local police who had it in for him. Big sister Ella also agreed, adding that her major consideration was for his personal welfare and not that of the Muslims, for whom Ella had no use.

Despite Hilda's and Reginald's repeated attempts to recruit her, Ella's strong will and legendary sense of independence prevailed. She neither accepted Elijah Muhammad as a prophet nor the racial doctrine of the NOI. As for the religion of Islam itself, Ella stated categorically to Malcolm and the rest of the family that she felt strongly that anyone could be whatever he or she wanted to be: Holy Roller, Baptist, Catholic, Seventh-Day Adventist, Jehovah's Witness, or even an agnostic (she did not believe in atheism), but personally she "wasn't going to become any Muslim." After the official expulsion of Reginald from the NOI in 1949, five Little siblings remained members of the Nation: Wilfred, Philbert, Hilda, Wesley, and Malcolm. (Yvonne and Robert were still too young to join.)

Hilda insisted that Malcolm still had much to learn about Islam and Elijah Muhammad's teachings and that he ought to come to Detroit and become an active member in a temple of practicing

Muslims. Wilfred and his wife Ruth graciously invited Malcolm to share their home, and he gratefully accepted. The serenity, generosity, and peaceful environment that Malcolm found in his brother and sister-in-law's home starkly contrasted with the general chaos, distrust, and tension Malcolm had become accustomed to in prison and on the streets. Wilfred gently and patiently explained the daily routine and ritual of living in a home that practiced Islamic principles, and Malcolm was deeply and sincerely moved.

The tranquility and orderliness of prayer, civility, and respect for others that Wilfred and his family practiced was something that Malcolm saw expressed and shared throughout the community of members of the NOI. All members were required to address each other with the pleasant and gentle greetings of *As-Salaam-Alaikum* (Arabic for "Peace be unto you") and the reply *Wa-alaikum-Salaam* (and unto you peace). These greetings gave Malcolm a general feeling of well-being and relaxation that far surpassed the ephemeral pleasures of marijuana. The discipline of regular prayer, meditation, and study both at home and work as well as the quiet, tasteful, and dignified dress of fellow Muslims greatly impressed Malcolm.

Malcolm was also impressed by the gracious manners, attitudes, and civility of the children in the NOI toward their elders and each other, which had been taught them from birth. He was "thrilled" at how the Muslim men used both hands to grasp a black brother's hands while voicing their joy and happiness to see and meet him again. Malcolm was especially touched and gratified to see the honor and respect accorded to the Muslim women and expressed how wonderful it felt to him. The salutations which the group exchanged were always warm, and also filled with mutual respect and dignity; they called each other "Brother" and "Sir" or "Sister" and "Ma'am." As Malcolm exclaimed, "Even children speaking to other children used these terms—beautiful!"

An atmosphere of great pride leavened with humility and respect pervaded the services and meetings of the then relatively small Detroit Temple Number One, which were held on

Wednesdays, Fridays, and Sundays of each week. The storefront that served as the temple was immaculate and beautifully decorated, despite its small size.

Caught up in the rapture of his new life and eager to recruit new members, Malcolm thought it was outrageous that the temple still had some empty seats. He complained to his brother Wilfred, who was chief minister of the temple, that all the seats should be filled, especially considering that the surrounding area was filled with so many "brainwashed black brothers and sisters" who like himself at one time "were drinking, fighting, cursing, and using drugs. These [behaviors] were the very things that Mr. Muhammad taught were helping the black man to stay under the heel of the white man here in America."

Malcolm was determined to bring more black people into the fold both by adopting a proactive stance on recruitment and by aggressively propagating the faith. He felt very strongly that the attitude toward recruitment of new members at the temple was passive and therefore ultimately self-defeating because it was based on an assumption that Allah would bring more Muslims to the movement. Malcolm, however, was an excellent organizer, and he knew the African Americans who lived in the ghettoes because he had lived that way for years. He was deeply familiar with their disillusionment, fear, anger, cynicism, rage, unhappiness, isolation, poverty, and desperation, especially as it related to the pervasive and destructive force of white racism on their lives. He had been just like many of them until he found the Nation. Thus, he advocated that members of the temple go out into the streets directly to recruit new members.

Although Wilfred understood Malcolm's impatience and eagerness to be an activist, he counseled Malcolm to be patient. Soon, Wilfred told him, he would see and perhaps even meet the man who was called "the Messenger." Because of the intense anticipation of finally meeting Elijah Muhammad in the flesh, Malcolm followed Wilfred's advice.

In the meantime, Malcolm paid close attention to the regular lectures of Lemuel Hassan, a leading minister at Temple Number One. Minister Lemuel Hassan lectured about Elijah Muhammad's teachings for more than an hour at a time and frequently illustrated points by chalking key words or phrases on the blackboard. Malcolm sat transfixed, absorbing Hassan's every "syllable and gesture."

Malcolm Meets the Messenger

On the day before Labor Day in 1952 the members of the temple formed a caravan of ten automobiles to visit Chicago Temple Number Two to hear the Honorable Elijah Muhammad. Malcolm was ecstatic. After four years of writing letters to and receiving letters from a man that he and the other members of the NOI spoke of in hushed and reverent tones as "divine," Malcolm was finally going to hear and see Elijah Muhammad speak in person.

Elijah Muhammad appeared almost tiny in comparison to the tall, strapping, Fruit of Islam (a paramilitary wing within the NOI) bodyguards who encircled him as he strode to the platform to give his speech. The Messenger had a gentle-looking and sensitive face and demeanor that hid an ironclad will and self-righteous ego that could at times be ruthless. Dressed in immaculate dark suits, crisp white shirts, and bow ties (official uniforms for which NOI ministers would quickly become legendary throughout the national black community of the United States), Elijah Muhammad and the Fruit of Islam guards calmly eyed the assembled crowd from the Detroit and Chicago temples. The Messenger wore a gold-embroidered fez.

As Malcolm stared in awe at Muhammad, Malcolm thought back to this "great man who had taken the time to write to me when I was a convict whom he knew nothing about." This man had spent over twenty years of his life trying to, in his words, "lead the black people to freedom from bondage and give life to them, and put them on the same level with all other civilized and independent nations and peoples of this planet earth." Spellbound, Malcolm sat and listened to the frail, five-and-a-half-foot tall man speak in a low-key voice. Muhammad spoke of how in the "wilderness of North America" the "blue-eyed devil white man" had for centuries brainwashed the "so-called Negro." He spoke of how the black man was Original Man, who had been kidnapped from his homeland and stripped of his language, culture, family structure, and family name until the black man in America did not even realize who he was. Muhammad went on to say that his teachings of the "true knowledge of black people" would lift up the black man from the bottom of the white man's society and place him where he belonged and where he had begun: at the very pinnacle of civilization.

As he concluded his talk he called Malcolm's name and asked him to stand. This first public recognition of him by Muhammad, Malcolm later recounted, felt "like an electrical shock." Muhammad told the crowd that Malcolm was just out of prison and remarked on how strong he had been while there. "Every day," Muhammad told the congregation, "for years, Brother Malcolm has written a letter from prison to me. And I have written to him as often as I could." While standing there feeling the eyes and rapt attention of two hundred Muslims upon him, Malcolm heard the Messenger make a supportive parable about him. "When God bragged about how faithful Job was," said Elijah Muhammad, "the devil said only God's hedge around Job kept Job so faithful. Remove that protective hedge, the devil told God, and I will make Job curse you to your face." Muhammad went on to point out that the devil could claim that, hedged in prison, Malcolm had just used Islam for protection. But the devil would say that now that Malcolm was out of prison he would return to drinking, smoking, drugs, and a life of crime. "Well, now, our good brother Malcolm's hedge is removed, and we will see how he does," Muhammad said. "I believe he is going to remain faithful."

After the lecture and meeting, Muhammad invited the entire Detroit group to dinner at his newly purchased eighteen-room house on the south side of Chicago. At dinner he encouraged the Detroit group to talk as he listened. Malcolm, who was never shy about letting his ideas and opinions be known, spoke up about the problem of bringing more converts into the temple and said that waiting for Allah or divine intervention to bring this about was not sufficient. Malcolm further remarked that millions of African Americans all over the United States had never heard of the teachings and wisdom of Elijah Muhammad and the NOI.

Malcolm was convinced that with the proper organizing and recruitment efforts that many more black people would be stirred and moved to join their organization. As the Messenger listened intently, Malcolm fervently maintained that only Elijah Muhammad was capable of waking and "resurrecting" the black man from his slumber.

Then Malcolm asked Muhammad a point-blank question: "How many Muslims are supposed to be in Temple Number One in Detroit?" Muhammad replied, "There are supposed to be thousands." Malcolm then asked, "Sir, what is your opinion of the best way of getting thousands there?" "Go after the young people," Muhammad told him. "Once you get them, the older ones will follow through shame." Malcolm made up his mind immediately that he was going to follow this advice.

Back in Detroit, Malcolm spoke with Wilfred and offered his services to the temple's head minister, Lemuel Hassan. He shared his determination with his brother and Hassan that they should all apply Muhammad's formula in a new recruitment drive. They responded enthusiastically to Malcolm's ideas. Every evening immediately after an exhausting eight-hour day at the furniture store, the tireless Malcolm would go out into the streets doing what the Muslims called *fishing* (finding new converts). It was amusingly ironic to Malcolm that in prison new inmates were also called fish. Only this time, he thought, the fish were being recruited to act on behalf of good instead of evil.

Malcolm was a huge success from the very beginning of the organizing drive. As he pointed out many times, he knew and understood both the thinking and the language of the streets. He started conversations with potential recruits by saying something like, "My man, let me pull your coat to something ...." People readily responded to him because he was never pompous, stiff, self-righteous, humorless, coercive, or patronizing in his manner or tone. Because Malcolm genuinely respected the people that he talked to on the streets, they responded warmly to, or at least with curiosity about, what he had to say.

During this time, Malcolm's application for his official name change was made and accepted from the NOI headquarters in

Chicago. He was now known both inside and outside the NOI only as Malcolm X. Malcolm's X replaced the slave name of Little, which some white man whose surname was Little, had imposed upon his paternal forebears. Malcolm pointed out that the X was to be kept until Allah "gave us a holy name from his own mouth" (or until Elijah Muhammad, acting as Allah's surrogate, bestowed an Arabic name on the convert).

Secure now as an active member of the NOI and buoyed by Elijah Muhammad's continued support and praise of his activity, Malcolm intensified his recruitment efforts. Organizing in local Detroit ghetto bars, poolrooms, clubs, and on street corners, Malcolm began to find that many black people were, in his view, "too ignorant, brainwashed, and morally, spiritually, and mentally deaf, dumb, and blind" to respond to his attempts to convert them. It angered him that recruiting was becoming increasingly difficult, especially the "hard nut" cases who were either turned off by religious proselytizing or were not interested in joining any organization, let alone one that promised them "social and spiritual salvation." Even after seeing and hearing Elijah Muhammad in person, only a few of the interested visitors would apply by formal letter to Muhammad to be accepted for NOI membership. His wise, older brother Wilfred gently reminded Malcolm that he had once been one of those brothers who had been so opposed to being recruited on behalf of the movement. Malcolm smiled and acknowledged the truth of Wilfred's statement.

However, the dogged determination and hard work by Malcolm and others in the temple finally began to pay off. Each month a few more automobiles joined their caravans to Temple Number Two in Chicago. His perseverance and his considerable knowledge of the psychology of his converts enabled Malcolm to help the temple triple its membership rolls in only six months. This growth so deeply pleased Muhammad that he paid the Detroit ministry a personal visit. The Messenger praised Malcolm warmly when Minister Hassan told him how hard Malcolm had worked in the cause of Islam. This special demonstration of support for Malcolm by his esteemed spiritual mentor encouraged Malcolm to work even harder on behalf of the NOI.

By 1953, the Messenger was very interested in Malcolm's potential as a leader in the organization and began to take Malcolm into his confidence. This encouragement increased Malcolm's worship of Muhammad and convinced him even further that the best and last hope for the survival and prosperity of black people lay with the Nation of Islam.

In January 1953, Malcolm left the furniture store to take a better-paying job working at the Gar Wood automobile factory in Detroit, which made big garbage truck bodies. Though the work was hard, monotonous, dirty, and mindlessly repetitive, Malcolm persevered, but he reserved his enthusiasm for his work at the temple. Minister Hassan, at Muhammad's behest, encouraged Malcolm to address the congregation. Muhammad also insisted that more temples be established in other cities and suggested that Malcolm and others help in this national effort. Although Malcolm insisted that it had never occurred to him that he might become a minister and thus work in an official capacity as a public representative of the Messenger, the NOI hierarchy was clearly grooming him for just such a responsibility. Malcolm's natural ambition for leadership and his proven ability to deliver the goods was evident to everyone in the Detroit and Chicago temples and was especially apparent to Elijah Muhammad.

Although Muhammad possessed only a fourth-grade education (like Malcolm's father Earl had done, Muhammad left school early to work on his father's sharecropping farm at the age of nine in 1906), Muhammad was a self-taught man whose extensive knowledge of history, science, mathematics, theology, and philosophy often astounded others who initially assumed he was illiterate or semiliterate because of his lack of formal schooling. Muhammad clearly saw something of himself in Malcolm, who had only an eighth-grade education but who had proven that sustained and disciplined study could more than compensate for a lack of official educational credentials.

Despite the similarity between Malcolm and Muhammad, they were different in many key ways. Malcolm was a phenomenally quick study and an academically gifted student whose oratorical and debating abilities were exceptional. Muhammad was more of a slow plodder intellectually and far more didactic and doctrinal in his approach to learning and teaching. Moreover, Muhammad was a relatively poor public speaker who was not known for great or mellifluous oratory. His ability to mesmerize his listeners relied far more on his deified stature as the "Messenger of Allah" and as the fatherly founder of the NOI than on any overt physical or expressive allure. He was also not particularly charismatic whereas Malcolm possessed charisma in abundance.

Muhammad understood that some of his followers and ministers were better speakers and more charismatic than he, but rather than feeling inadequate (although this attitude was to change significantly over the years), he openly encouraged his ministers to represent the Nation on his behalf at public events. The Messenger began to cut back on his own public speaking schedule and began to rely increasingly on his national ministers to do much of this organizing work. Muhammad also enjoyed playing the role of the wily, older mentor and backstage manipulator.

Malcolm Becomes a Minister in the NOI

In the spring of 1953, Malcolm began speaking to the faithful of the Detroit temple on behalf of the Messenger. Malcolm did not know whether Minister Lemuel Hassan had suggested that he begin speaking or Muhammad had. Either way, Malcolm felt humbled and blessed to be given the opportunity, and he did not disappoint. He electrified the congregation by immediately testifying what the "grace, love, and majesty" of the Honorable Elijah Muhammad had done to save and preserve his life. "Brothers and sisters," he intoned, "if I told you the life I have lived, you would find it hard to believe me ... When I say something about the white man, I am not talking about someone I don't know ..."

Minister Hassan urged Malcolm to address the assembled group with an extemporaneous lecture. Though he was initially uncertain and even hesitant about it, Malcolm complied. The experience and expertise in debating that Malcolm had acquired and developed in prison stood him in very good stead as he spoke. His subject for this first lecture was the hypocrisy of Christianity and its historical role in the horrors of slavery, which Malcolm felt particularly well equipped to speak about from so much reading and study of the subject in prison.

As a result of Malcolm's success as an organizer and teacher, Muhammad rewarded him the position of assistant minister in June 1953. Although Malcolm continued to sing Hassan's praises by remarking how he was such a "wonderful minister," it was becoming increasingly clear that Muhammad now saw Malcolm himself as a potential national minister. Muhammad encouraged Malcolm to come to Chicago as often as he could and began openly grooming him to become a leader within the organization. For hours at a time the twenty-nine year old Malcolm listened to the older man, whom Malcolm characterized as Allah's "seventh and last prophet," with a rapt attention that far surpassed what he gave his teachers and mentors in school and on the streets. Malcolm saw himself as a uniquely blessed and humble servant of Muhammad and hung on to the Messenger's instructions, observations, pronouncements, and commands as though they were gold. He began to accompany Muhammad everywhere as he toured the many small stores that the NOI owned and managed on the south side of Chicago.

Muhammad and Malcolm developed an especially close bond that became far more like that of father and son than that of professional colleagues. As time went on, Muhammad actually started referring to Malcolm within the organization as his "son" and was often more attentive and fatherly to him than he was to his own six sons. (He and his wife of twenty-five years, Clara Muhammad, had eight children, all of whom worked in and for the NOI.)

By 1954, Malcolm felt like he had a new father and another wonderful reason for living. He was well on his way to becoming the Messenger's right-hand man, and he felt certain that they were going to change the world together. Malcolm's destiny, and more importantly that of his people, lay just around the corner. Malcolm could see and sense it in the booming membership rolls in Detroit and Chicago. Black people everywhere were on the move for massive social change. The modern Civil Rights movement was on the verge of erupting, and an obscure twenty-five-year-old minister (and Ph.D. in philosophy and theology) from the black bourgeoisie of Atlanta named Martin Luther King Jr. would be world-famous within a year. The entire country would soon become aware of the NOI's existence as well.

The next stop in Malcolm's sojourn was Boston, his old stomping grounds. At nearly thirty years old, Malcolm X had come full circle. But a decidedly different man was coming to town this time around. Malcolm Little, Detroit Red, and Satan no longer existed; the Messenger of Allah, the Nation of Islam, and Malcolm X himself had seen to that. The prodigal nature of his new assignment was not lost on Malcolm, who paid very close attention to these kinds of serendipitous occurrences.

Muhammad, along with Minister Hassan, had recommended that Malcolm be sent to the East Coast to find and organize more converts. By this time, Malcolm had fulfilled his parole obligation and was free to leave Michigan and his boring factory job. The NOI had been struggling to establish a new temple in Boston, and Muhammad envisioned Malcolm building a formidable presence covering the entire East Coast as a precursor to a fully national program and identity for the NOI.

The Messenger's intuition proved accurate again. Malcolm worked extremely hard to build a new temple in Boston. He sought out people he had known when he was still running the streets. Although he neither mentioned Islam nor talked to them directly about his work as an activist for the NOI, he did invite nearly all of them to hear him speak at the many meetings he held in private homes on behalf of the organization. (Malcolm was reminded of his father Earl organizing for Garvey's UNIA over twenty-five years earlier.)

Malcolm had a great reunion with his old friend Shorty, who still had a small band and was working as a musician. Shorty was initially wary and uncertain when told about Malcolm's religious and political conversions. The street grapevine had informed Shorty that Malcolm was in town and "on a new religious kick." Shorty did not know whether Malcolm was serious or just another of the hustling "jack-leg" preacher-pimps found in every ghetto who used religion to fleece the flock in their little storefront churches and to exploit the faith, trust, and loneliness of primarily hardworking, older women who kept their pretty-boy preacher types dressed in sharp clothes and driving a fancy car in exchange for spiritual and sexual "guidance." Despite their mutual conversion to Islam in prison years earlier, Shorty was not too keen on joining any particular church or organization to validate his personal spiritual values. Shorty had always been suspicious of Elijah Muhammad and the NOI, especially after Malcolm had introduced him to the Messenger for possible membership and Shorty and Muhammad disagreed on Islamic doctrine. Malcolm let Shorty know in no uncertain terms how deeply serious and committed he was about Islam. After that revelation, they both relaxed with each other and began talking in the old street vernacular that they loved. Malcolm was then able to quickly put his former mentor and partner-in-crime at ease.

Malcolm told Shorty just enough about Islam and the Nation to see from Shorty's indifferent reaction that he did not want to hear it. Malcolm was not judgmental about his old friend, however. He knew, perhaps more than many others, that people make major decisions about the course or direction of their lives in their own way and time. He knew that most of his old friends and associates were still "brainwashed," and he recognized that merely because he had seen the light did not mean that others could always go along with him on his quest.

Malcolm even tried to convert his Aunt Sassie and his other relatives in the Little clan. One of them was his cousin Clara who bluntly told him that she was not interested. Malcolm just smiled. He also insisted that Ella's continued refusal to join did not bother him, either. However, he now had a tendency to keep all evidence of anger inside for fear of alienating others or taking his frustrations out on loved ones. He later acknowledged that such rebuffs caused anger, not only at the people who rejected his overtures, but also at himself for failing to win them over. Fortunately his activism and speechmaking provided a viable outlet for the disciplined public expression of anger in his eloquent, incendiary, and controversial statements denouncing racism, injustice, and other forms of exploitation and oppression in the black community.

Malcolm had begun his trip to Boston by telling everyone within earshot that he was "going to build a temple." He kept his word. Within a mere three months he had attracted enough people to open a new makeshift mosque in Roxbury. Once he got it up and running, Malcolm served only briefly in Boston as Temple Number Eleven's minister. As soon as the temple was properly organized in March 1954, Malcolm left Minister Ulysses X in charge and was sent by Muhammad to organize, teach, and recruit new members in Philadelphia.

Philadelphia (or as the white city fathers called it "The City of Brotherly Love") was notorious for some of the worst and most widespread racism in the entire country. Consequently Philly's sizeable black community responded even more strongly and enthusiastically to Malcolm's message about "the truth about the white man and black liberation" than the equally oppressed black citizens in Boston had. By May 1954, Philadelphia's Temple Number Twelve of the rapidly expanding NOI was established. Malcolm X was quickly on his way to great prestige and even a kind of sober stardom in the national ranks of the NOI as Elijah Muhammad, now very impressed with Malcolm's successes in Boston and Philadelphia, appointed him to the highly coveted position of Minister of Temple Number Seven in Harlem in June 1954.

Fame, tremendous successes, and crushing failures awaited in New York as Malcolm contemplated an even bigger and newer campaign to build Islam and the NOI as a powerhouse in the lives of African Americans. There was no better place than Harlem and New York's five boroughs to begin the process. After all, these areas contained over a million black people. The dream that Elijah Muhammad had nurtured and pushed for over twenty-five years was finally coming true. And the efforts of his "son" Malcolm were a major factor in the realization of the dream. But there was still much work to be done.

Chapter 13

Building the Nation

Home to nearly a million African Americans, Harlem still had a legendary reputation as a cultural and social mecca for many of the most talented and accomplished black writers, artists, musicians, intellectuals, businessmen, political leaders, and professionals in the country. Since the turn of the century, a small black elite, who represented what W.E.B. DuBois later dubbed the "talented tenth" of the national black population, had been living in the uptown section of Manhattan and had purchased large, elegant homes there, such as those situated on 139th Street between Seventh and Eighth Avenues. Some wealthy blacks were even attended to and chauffeured about by white servants. In the early 1900s through the 1920s, Harlem was a place where African Americans with ambition, drive, vision, and talent dreamed of living. But when Malcolm arrived in Harlem in the summer of 1954 it was in a state of extensive economic and social decline.

A Bit of Harlem History

Until the last quarter of the nineteenth century Harlem was mostly an unsettled, bucolic playground for the rich who went there for Sunday country jaunts and rode their horses through Central Park. But Manhattan's industrial, commercial, and demographic growth and the massive construction of rapid transit facilities and subways from downtown New York to Harlem caused a building boom that transformed Harlem. The marshes were filled in, and apartment houses and brownstones replaced the shanties of poor German and Irish immigrants. Electric lights and later telephone lines were installed. Speculators made fortunes buying and reselling Harlem land that twenty years before had not been worth paying taxes on. By the 1890s Harlem was widely considered one of the most elegant places in all of New York, of which it had become an integral part. Rents ranged from eight to fourteen times what working-class families typically paid their landlords.

Consequently, many people with wealth moved to Harlem. They included prominent businessmen, federal judges, and politicians (including more than one former mayor). All forms of cultural activity flourished, such as the Harlem Opera House (founded by famed composer Oscar Hammerstein I), the Harlem Literary Society, and the Harlem Philharmonic Orchestra. Land values skyrocketed as wealthy speculators competed with each other to buy property along the subway routes that had been or were being constructed. The real estate fever also took firm hold among the Jewish tradesmen and garment workers who left rotting lower East Side tenements in search of better housing in Lower Harlem, part of which became known as "Little Russia." This migration, as well the subsequent black one, was adamantly opposed by existing residents, who charged that the neighborhood was deteriorating.

The economic bust came in 1904–05, when it became evident that Harlem had been overbuilt. White landlords frantically competed with each other to reduce rents and attract new tenants. As a result, apartment owners began opening the doors to "colored" occupants. These renters were not poor or working-class tenants but those who could afford the now somewhat lower rents: lawyers, real estate agents, morticians, entertainers, and insurance managers.

Malcolm at a microphone, 1950.

(Corbis)

A number of racial and economic factors undermined Harlem's economic and social development. A steady influx of nearly indigent southern blacks had migrated north because of Jim Crow segregation, lynch law, and economic peonage brought on by disastrous sharecropping failures. They also came because of a severe labor shortage precipitated by the drafting of millions of young white men to military service during World War I, which had made it possible for them to find work in northern industrial cities. To fulfill this shortage, labor agents were sent South by major corporations to recruit cheap black labor.

Whites attempted to stem what they called an "invasion" through such tactics as buying back properties occupied by blacks and then evicting them and putting pressure on financial and loan companies to refuse mortgage money to blacks or to people who rented to them (a practice that is still widespread today). However, the organized efforts of white property owners to halt black residential settlements were undermined by *blockbusters*, opportunistic real estate speculators who purposely placed black families on previously all-white blocks. When the white owners fled these neighborhoods, these same speculators bought up nearby properties for a fraction of the original price. Then they leased or sold the cheaply acquired properties to blacks for whatever price they could command, or they sold them to panic-stricken white neighbors who were then willing to pay nearly anything to preserve the "racial purity" of their immediate surroundings. When it became apparent that such practices would not stem the influx of African Americans, the panic selling of racist whites increased to epidemic proportions. Within a few years, Harlem was predominately black.

During the 1920s, while much of the rest of New York and white America prospered, Harlem began to decay. Landlords, which included some of Harlem's most prominent black churches, subdivided spacious, multistory houses into undersized apartments to increase the number of rental units. White property owners, including such large corporate institutions as Columbia University and some of the largest insurance companies and banks, proceeded to do the same in order to maximize their income. This devastating collusion of racism and capitalism was so pervasive in Harlem that one government investigator discovered seven children on pallets on the floor of one tiny, two-room apartment. Deteriorating, unsafe, vermin-infested, and filthy living conditions were widespread. Consequently Harlem's Seventh District Court saw more disputes between landlords and tenants than any municipal court in New York's five boroughs. Occasionally, some judges inspected the hovels themselves. Nearly always, what they saw horrified them. One official found few buildings that were even fit for habitation. Another described the majority of available housing as diseased.

Unfortunately, little had changed by the Great Depression in the 1930s. Indicative of Harlem's plight, and that of Black America in general, were the armies of African American women who lined up every morning in the "Slave Market" in the nearby Bronx, where white housewives bid for their services. The going rate for domestics during the Great Depression was between ten and fifteen cents an hour. The cost of lunch was usually deducted from their take-home pay.

The cumulative effects of economic depression, racial oppression, and social neglect created by World War II became increasingly evident in Harlem by the late 1940s and early 1950s. The economic recession of 1953–54 did further damage. National politics were also corrupted by the pervasive control of racist Southern politicians who wielded a great deal of power in Congress and the Senate where filibustering proved to be a major obstacle to the passage of legislative sanctions against the prevalence of racial discrimination and exploitation in every area of American life. Despite the Fourteenth and Fifteenth Amendments to the Constitution, southern blacks were completely disenfranchised by gerrymandering, lynch law, poll taxes, voter qualifications' tests, and similar racist devices.

Throughout the country, but especially below the Mason-Dixon line, African Americans were excluded from white-run hotels, restaurants, churches, and clubs. In Washington D.C., the nation's capital, Jim Crow was in full effect. Black firemen were prohibited from joining white fire companies, and blacks were banned from almost all public facilities of any kind. No American president would sign or even support antilynching legislation while civil rights leaders such as Florida's NAACP chairman Harry T. Moore were publicly assassinated (Moore was murdered by the KKK in 1951). In May 1954, the U.S. Supreme Court finally declared that "separate-but-equal" educational policies were unconstitutional, but most African Americans were skeptical that the Supreme Court's decision and other reform measures against segregation would ever be effectively implemented given the incredible racial tensions of the era.

In this smoldering social context of hate, resentment, fear, repression, and the national emergence of a massive social movement for justice, equality, and political liberation among African Americans, Malcolm X, just one month past his twenty-ninth birthday, assumed command of the largest temple of the Nation of Islam and the flashpoint of Elijah Muhammad's growing empire. The national black community was demanding powerful leadership, and Malcolm was determined, with the spiritual assistance of Allah and the mentorship of Elijah Muhammad, to provide it.

Malcolm X Builds Temple Number Seven

Before Malcolm began in earnest in his quest to make Harlem's temple the most dynamic, well-organized, and effective in the NOI, he sought out an old friend and adversary: West Indian Archie. Nearly a decade had elapsed since their showdown in the Harlem underworld, and Malcolm wanted to let him know that all was forgiven and that they should be brothers instead of enemies. He also wanted to introduce Archie to his new way of life and encourage him to embrace a new and different path. Mostly, though, he just wanted to see him again to find out how he was doing and to show him respect for the financial and emotional support that Archie gave him when he was a hustler and a down-and-out gambler. He searched all his old haunts and asked his old friends and contacts about him.

While Malcolm searched, he heard some bad news about the one other person he was most interested in seeing, his old criminal mentor, Sammy the Pimp. Sammy had quit pimping and was doing well in the numbers racket. He had even settled down and married.

But shortly after his wedding he was found dead lying across his bed. The news about Sammy was heartbreaking for Malcolm. He fervently hoped that the same fate had not befallen Archie.

Initially, no one seemed to know where Archie was. Many of the slick men Malcolm had run with in the street years before were now desperately trying to scavenge up enough money for room, rent, and food. Some now eked out a marginal existence working downtown as messengers and janitors. It was horrifying and sobering for Malcolm to consider that this existence would have most likely been his eventual fate had he not found Islam.

Eventually, Malcolm learned that West Indian Archie was sick and living in a rented room in the Bronx. When West Indian Archie answered the door, it took a few seconds to fix Malcolm in his memory. Malcolm no longer had a bright-red conk, his hair was cut very short, and he wore glasses. He was also conservatively dressed. When he finally recognized him, Archie exclaimed, "Red! I'm so glad to see you!" The feeling was mutual. They were both so happy to see each other that it surprised even Malcolm.

Malcolm assisted the now-tottering old man back to his bed and told Archie that by forcing Malcolm out of Harlem, Archie had saved his life by turning him in the direction of Islam. "I always liked you, Red," Archie said. He also told Malcolm that he had never really wanted to kill him. They both wondered if they had been mistaken about the number Malcolm had "combinated" in their dispute. Finally they both agreed that it was not worth talking about, it meant nothing, and it was certainly not something they should have wanted to kill each other over.

Malcolm proceeded to talk a little about the NOI and Elijah Muhammad's teachings. He told Archie how he had learned that those who worked the streets as hustlers were victims of a corrupt white society. He also told Archie that he had often thought about him in prison, and the profound contributions his computer-like mastery of numbers might have made to mathematics and science. It was a tragedy, he continued, that so many talented, gifted individuals like himself were wasted working the con. "Red, that sure is something to think about," Malcolm remembered Archie saying.

Malcolm sensed that Archie did not have long to live. Malcolm was so disturbed and moved by his old friend's plight and the stark contrast between the man he had known and the one who now sat wearily beside him that he could not stay any longer. Malcolm did not have much money, but he insisted that Archie take what he had. It was the last time he ever saw Archie.

When Malcolm took over Temple Seven it was a small store-front, and membership was miniscule. The great majority of black people Malcolm encountered knew very little if anything about Islam, and nothing at all about Muslims or their movement in the United States. Virtually no one in America (except a handful of white policemen or FBI agents who worked in undercover surveillance) even knew the NOI existed. Malcolm changed all that. He knew that the NOI had to compete with a wide array of other political and religious groups in a community as big and complicated as Harlem and that if the NOI hoped to recruit any new members, it would have to engage these various civic, ideological, and protest groups in direct competition on the streets. Malcolm put his plans to compete into action.

Rather than attacking the other nationalist groups that were engaging in street-corner oratory and promoting various "Buy Black" campaigns, Malcolm strategically chose to attack the religious and political adversaries of black nationalists, primarily the Christian church and those forces advocating racial integration and U.S.-styled "democracy." The NOI was not against any organization or program that promoted independence and unity among black people, but it was determined to get its own voices, and most importantly that of Elijah Muhammad's, heard in the general clamor of activity.

Malcolm had some leaflets printed, and he took a small army of Muslims out into the streets and began fishing on the fringes of the crowds that attended the gatherings of the numerous black nationalist groups scattered throughout Harlem. Fishing at a nationalist meeting was a lot easier because the people attending their meetings were already interested and predisposed to talk about revolution and freedom for black people. Thrusting their leaflets and handbills into people's hands, Malcolm and the NOI members cried, "Come to hear us, too, brother!" "The Honorable Elijah Muhammad teaches us how to cure the black man's spiritual, mental, moral, economic, and political sicknesses …," Malcolm intoned.

In addition to fishing at other black nationalist gatherings, Malcolm made certain that his group hit every block and proselytized and cajoled people on every available street corner. Characteristically, Malcolm's approach was aggressive, bold, and forthright. He and the other organizers would "step right in front of a walking black man or woman so that they had to accept our leaflet, and if they hesitated one second, they had to hear us saying some catchy thing such as, 'Hear how the white man kidnapped and robbed and raped our black race.'"

These same daring tactics were employed outside the many storefront Christian churches, mostly Baptist, that blacks attended. Each Sunday afternoon, as hundreds of worshippers filed out of the churches into the streets, Malcolm and his lieutenants would be there to challenge them and their ministers. Pointing to the church minister, Malcolm would shout, "He represents the white man's God; I represent the black man's God." Malcolm quickly discovered that the best fishing audience, by far, was the Christian churches, especially the smaller working-class ones. The members of these poorer churches were more dissatisfied and less caught up in the pretense, status-seeking, and values of the bigger churches. The working-class members were more attentive and receptive to the shock of what Malcolm said was happening to them by worshipping a "blond, blue-eyed God." He thus tailored his message to those Christians who were becoming disillusioned with, or at least skeptical of, conventional religious mythology.

Malcolm had mastered the techniques and nuances of rhythmic phrase-making and dialectical thinking in his public orations. He coupled these techniques with a dynamic, fluid delivery and a highly creative and imaginative use of irony, humor, wit, repetition, and the black oratorical tradition called *signifying*. In addition, Malcolm successfully used street vernacular, popular cultural references, and highly polemical interpretations of American and religious history to challenge and persuade his audience to rethink their ingrained notions of the world and the value systems that constituted the ideological scaffolding of the reality they had been taught.

His public speeches had a powerful effect on his audiences, who were quickly becoming weary of being told to wait for freedom, wait for justice, wait for respect, and wait for equality. Black people were sick of waiting after nearly 350 years of some of the most heinous, brutal, and sustained oppression in world history, and Malcolm understood well this rapidly growing impatience with the status quo among the masses of African Americans. He often remarked during this period that the psychology of the people he was trying to lead was that of human beings who were simply tired of always being expected to work and sacrifice for the gain of others (while being abused and exploited in the process) but never for themselves.

Before long his fishing expeditions throughout Harlem began to pay off. Soon Malcolm saw many new faces at Temple Seven meetings, and the temple began to experience a slow, but very definite growth in membership. But this rate of growth was not enough for Malcolm. So he redoubled his already considerable efforts by recruiting, teaching, and lecturing out of town on behalf of the NOI. In a mind-boggling regular schedule of sixteen- to eighteen-hour days, seven days a week, Malcolm pushed on with his exhaustive routine of meetings, sermons, speeches, street organizing, and classes.

Malcolm taught history, philosophy, and theology each Wednesday at Philadelphia's Temple Number Twelve (which he established). He went to Springfield, Massachusetts to build and organize a new temple, which was designated Temple Number Thirteen by Muhammad after Malcolm and Osborne Thaxton, a man Malcolm had met and converted to Islam in prison, set up shop there. A black woman visiting a Springfield meeting asked Malcolm if he would come to her hometown of Hartford, Connecticut on the following Thursday and said she would bring some friends. Thus, Malcolm began teaching and lecturing in Hartford every Thursday evening and began fishing for new members of what became known as Temple Number Fourteen.

As it turned out, the woman from Hartford knew about fifteen maids, cooks, chauffeurs, housemen, and other domestic servants in her housing project in Hartford who worked for wealthy whites and hated every minute of it. As Malcolm pointed out, black people who waited on rich whites hand-and-foot, but were treated with condescension and disdainful attitudes for their efforts opened their eyes a lot quicker than other black people. They joined and recruited many other members for the Hartford temple.

Memberships continued to expand and grow at a steady, consistent rate in New York, Philadelphia, Boston, Hartford, and Springfield. But despite the rising success of the NOI and its higher visibility in black communities throughout the country, Malcolm was not satisfied. He was never a man to rest on his laurels, and whenever he went to meet with Elijah Muhammad in Chicago, Malcolm had to be gently chastised to be patient and not move too quickly in his quest to put the organization on the American map and to make the NOI a major contender for the loyalty and commitment of African Americans. Muhammad, for his part, was very pleased with the great progress Malcolm had made and the expansion of his empire. Malcolm always felt humble and grateful in Muhammad's presence, and the older man had a salutary effect on Malcolm's attitude and general approach to resolving problems.

In the past, Muhammad had also given Malcolm invaluable advice in preparing and giving his public speeches. He would listen to Malcolm deliver a sermon and then offer constructive criticism. In his early speeches, for example, Malcolm would begin by castigating white people without taking the time to lay a logical foundation for his assertions. Muhammad told Malcolm to give his audience examples of the bad behavior of white people before condemning them as devils. That way, the audience had a frame of reference and would be more inclined to agree with him. Secondly, the Messenger urged him to curtail severe criticism of black behavior. He should lay the ultimate blame for any objectionable behavior by blacks (such as smoking, drinking, and gambling) at the white man's door and attack the general corrupt values of the entire society. Then he should insist that any reform or rehabilitation of negative black behavior be undertaken by them through embracing Islam and the moral and social guidance of the NOI's strict program.

Just as Muhammad had counseled Malcolm to use criticism and analysis as weapons to transform the lives of African Americans through the advocacy of Islam, he now told Malcolm that no "true leader" ever burdened his followers with a greater load than they could carry and that no leader sets too fast a pace for his followers to keep up. He gave his advice to Malcolm in the form of parables, proverbs, epigrams, and metaphors: "Most people seeing an old man in an old touring car going real slow think the man doesn't want to go fast. But the man knows that to drive any faster would destroy his old car. When he gets a fast car, then he will drive at a fast speed."

Elijah Muhammad sent Malcolm on his first major trip south in late January 1955 to recruit members and organize a new temple in Atlanta, Georgia. Atlanta's Temple Number Fifteen marked the NOI's first major success in a southern city. On May 1, 1955, almost three weeks before his thirtieth birthday, Malcolm X was back in Lansing, Michigan, the city of his childhood, where his father once headed the local chapter of Marcus Garvey's Universal Negro Improvement Association. There, Malcolm officially opened the NOI's Temple Number Sixteen. After two weeks in Lansing, Malcolm quickly moved on to Joliet, Illinois, then Cleveland and Dayton, Ohio, and from there to Camden, Paterson, Atlantic City, Newark and Jersey City, New Jersey. He opened a temple at each stop. By the end of 1955, Malcolm X had increased the number of NOI temples to twenty-seven when the number had been a barely functional and understaffed seven temples when he emerged from prison just three years earlier. This remarkable achievement was a testament to his incredible work ethic, discipline, and devotion to duty and Elijah Muhammad.

By now the FBI's interest in investigating (and undermining) the organization had risen significantly. Malcolm had first brought the FBI's role to the attention of Muhammad in November of 1954 when he and others told the Messenger that FBI agents were tailing them constantly. The FBI interviewed Muslims in their homes and at work. They also interviewed their neighbors and supervisors at work, which seriously jeopardized their livelihoods. FBI agents told white employers that NOI members were Communists, a charge that often resulted in the accused being fired, blacklisted from further employment, arrested, or harassed by other governmental agencies and the police.

As the FBI's interest in (and surveillance and harassment of) the NOI escalated, the New York Police Department's Bureau of Special Services (also called BOSS and BOSSI) assigned its own undercover agents to investigate leaders of the Harlem Temple, including Malcolm X. During the 1960s BOSSI agents infiltrated the NOI, the OAAU (Malcolm's political organization), and the Black Panther Party, among many other groups.

However, none of the surveillance and harassment deterred Malcolm from pursuing and carrying out his responsibilities in New York. In addition to establishing branches of Harlem's Temple Number Seven in Brooklyn and Queens, he launched a huge building fund drive for the construction of a new Harlem temple. He also encouraged each male member to contribute fifty cents per week to finance the work of his ministry in other cities. This amount was above and beyond the required tithe of 3 percent (later 10 percent) of every member's annual earnings, which everyone in the NOI was required to make to help finance their various programs and activities. Shortly after imposing this new weekly fee (which was called the "Laborer's Travel Expense" fee or L.T.E. assessment), Malcolm, whom Muhammad now praised as his "hardest-working minister," toured the country to promote Muhammad's One Million Dollar fundraising campaign. The slogan Malcolm coined for the campaign was "You can't advance without finance!"

Now, Malcolm was not only Muhammad's chief minister and principal troubleshooter, he was also officially billed as Muhammad's chief fund-raiser. Each temple under his administrative control (his far-flung jurisdiction extended from Boston to San Diego) had to submit weekly and monthly financial reports to him, as well as to the organization's Chicago headquarters. The NOI thrived under his strong leadership, and his mentor and father figure Muhammad was immensely pleased with his work.

"Thank Allah for my brother minister Malcolm," the Messenger publicly proclaimed.

Chapter 14

Spreading the Message to a Wider Audience

Under Malcolm X's dynamic leadership, not only was membership expanding at a phenomenal rate, but the quality, expertise, and commitment of the rank and file of the movement also was
improving dramatically. For the first time in the twenty-five-year
history of the organization, the sect was attracting followers who
reflected the entire spectrum of the national African American
population. Record numbers of poor and working-class members
were joined in the NOI by a large influx of black middle-class professionals who were fed up with the enforced lack of employment
opportunities and low salaries resulting from widespread racial discrimination found in American corporations, academic institutions, industry, and government. Malcolm believed these new,
better-educated converts could also educate and help find gainful
employment for the hundreds of former prisoners and high school
dropouts groping for a viable way out of the ravages of poverty.

Malcolm's appeal to a wide spectrum of African Americans and
the skyrocketing development of new temples and subsequent
growth in the economic power and political clout of the NOI
alarmed the FBI and other governmental law enforcement and
intelligence agencies in the State Department, CIA, and Justice
Department who jointly decided that Malcolm X, Elijah

Muhammad, and the NOI should be a top priority for national and international surveillance and containment. Thus on New Year's Eve, 1956, J. Edgar Hoover requested (and the following day received) official permission from the Justice Department for increased "technical surveillance" (wiretapping) of the NOI. Copies of the request were sent to the State Department and the CIA. Hoover falsely claimed that one of the reasons he needed approval for the wiretaps and other bugging devices was the NOI's "violent nature." The devious and fanatical Hoover, who absolutely despised black people (he later supervised a massive and vicious undercover campaign against Dr. Martin Luther King, Jr.), knew perfectly well that Elijah Muhammad strictly forbid any Muslim to carry, use, or advocate the public use of firearms or any other weapons and that every member was required to respect the laws of the United States.

Meanwhile, Malcolm's stature was growing exponentially among his peers and colleagues in the NOI. Some began to liken him to the great Christian evangelist and organizer St. Paul, who, like Malcolm, had emerged from prison and had been largely responsible for the rapid growth of his then renegade religion by proselytizing among the masses. One of Malcolm's associates also compared him favorably to the tall, ascetic Muslim evangelist Omar, who was chiefly responsible for the rapid spread of Islam six centuries after St. Paul popularized Christianity. A protector of the poor, a leader, and a fund-raiser for his nation's treasury, Omar was deeply respected, like Malcolm, for his great integrity among the people. The lives of the two religious and social activists paralleled in an eerie way as well: Like Malcolm, Omar was murdered by an assassin as he was about to address his followers. But Malcolm was not concerned with his status, personal ego, or reputation at this point in his life. He immediately and emphatically brushed aside any exaggerated claims, comparisons, or assertions about his "greatness" and focused entirely on the challenging tasks at hand.

Malcolm with Wilfred and Philbert, 1963.

(AP/Wide World)

The booming success of the NOI through 1956 meant that the economic fortunes of the sect were also rapidly improving. In five short years the number of temples had expanded nearly fourfold, and within the next three years national membership climbed to a hundred thousand from a base of just four hundred active members one decade earlier. This growth meant that millions of dollars in tithes, fees, donations, and revenue from a wide array of businesses, real estate holdings, and investments were flowing through the coffers of the organization. Malcolm and his lieutenants carefully monitored and administered this massive cash flow, and Malcolm was adamant that fellow ministers, financial and legal staff, and rank and file members alike not abuse or exploit this privilege.

Malcolm's exemplary behavior in these matters also greatly impressed Muhammad, and he gave Malcolm even more responsibility in the upper-echelon hierarchy that ruled the organization. As a result, jealousy and envy among some ministers and staff began to surface for the first time within the NOI. For the time being, this jealousy was contained and suppressed, but by the early 1960s it would begin to fester more and adversely affect the work and stability of the organization, which in some ways was beginning to expand too rapidly for its own good, as Muhammad had cautioned earlier. But in late 1956, Malcolm X was not affected by any of that. Much more personal matters began to take priority in his life for the first time in years.

The Two Bettys

Up to this point Malcolm had always been very careful to, in his words, "stay completely clear of any personal closeness with any of the Muslim sisters." Malcolm's rigid adherence to the dictates of Islam and the severe moral strictures of the NOI had made him feel that he "didn't have the time" to be with women. However, as the highly intelligent, charismatic, and handsome star of the NOI, he was being pursued by a great number of women both in and outside of the organization. But Malcolm had always used his characteristically stern discipline and aloof manner to firmly rule out even the possibility of becoming involved. On a number of occasions some of the women let out broad hints that Malcolm, the most eligible bachelor within the NOI, needed a wife. But Malcolm always made it clear that marriage held no interest for him whatsoever; he was much too busy. Then in 1956–57 Malcolm met and fell in love with two black women: Betty and Bettye.

Speaking of Islam's strict laws and teachings about women, Malcolm said:

> The true nature of a man is to be strong, and a woman's true nature is to be weak, and while a man must at all times respect his woman, at the same time she needs to understand that he must control her if he expects to get her respect.

These frankly sexist attitudes, albeit couched in the self-justifying excuse that a man was providing "protection" for weak women by being strong on their behalf, was obviously an impediment to Malcolm letting down his guard and revealing the core of vulnerability and even insecurity that lay at the center of his lingering distrust. Although he was no longer exploiting or abusing women, he was still harboring notions about the nature of women that were clearly reactionary and unworthy of the truly humane and caring man that Malcolm was becoming. Many of these patriarchal notions were being reinforced and supported by both Islam and the personal teachings and guidance of Elijah Muhammad. Malcolm waged an intense war within himself, as he had with so many issues in his extraordinary life, grappling with the obvious contradiction between fiercely insisting upon, and promoting "respect" for black womanhood from black men (as well as "protecting" them), and his respect for those women who expressed intelligence, independence, fortitude, and spiritual and emotional maturity.

Malcolm was reticent around women for other reasons as well. He openly testified that for personal reasons he considered it impossible for him to love any woman fully because he did not trust women. He claimed that his experience in the streets had taught him that they were "tricky, deceitful, and untrustworthy flesh." He insisted that he had seen too many men tied down or even ruined by women. Elijah Muhammad even encouraged him to stay single.

Beyond all the rhetorical bluster, religious dogma, evasive excuses, overt sexism, and male posturing lie a far more common and thus real and abiding reason for Malcolm to reject the love of a woman: a mortal fear of hurt and abandonment. Malcolm had been deeply scarred by the tragic and painful circumstances and experiences involving his own mother and the aimless, purely hedonistic relationships he had cynically chosen in the past. Malcolm had always been reluctant on some fundamental level to trust and confide in women enough to reveal just how vulnerable, insecure, and even fearful he often felt in their presence. The problem he had expressing genuine intimacy with anyone lay at the core of his dilemma. But Malcolm, who rarely talked about personal matters with anyone, did confide to Shorty his desire for a wife and children. Gradually, he began to prepare to do something concrete about his desires.

Malcolm stealthily and shyly pursued both Betty and Bettye as he tried to make up his mind about which one to propose to.

Bettye was the sister of one of his associates in the NOI. By all accounts she was a tall, stunningly beautiful woman with luminous, bewitching eyes who carried herself regally. Many men were attracted to her, but few felt confident enough to pursue her because they feared her equally impressive intellect. Unlike other men, Malcolm was not intimidated by her quiet dignity and serene self-confidence. After a brief courtship, Malcolm asked her to marry him in the fall of 1957. But he did not insist on an immediate answer to his proposal and gave her time to think it over.

During this same period, he met another woman named Betty Sanders. She was originally from Detroit and had joined the NOI in 1956 at Temple Number Seven in Harlem. Malcolm mentioned to his sister Ella that he had noticed her at various organizational functions the year before and was still intrigued by her though they still had not formally met. She was a tall, attractive woman with dark skin and brown eyes. She was also a college graduate of the Tuskegee Institute in Alabama, where she had majored in education, and was in New York pursuing a degree in nursing, one of the few professional areas then open to blacks. Betty, who by 1957 was known as Betty X, was also a regular lecturer on hygiene and the study of medical science in the NOI's girls' and women's classes.

Out of the blue one day, Malcolm asked Betty if she would like to go to the Museum of Natural History with him. (Malcolm often attended museums on his own when he was in any city.) Malcolm had often seen Betty X at the Thursday night Muslim Girls Training Class (M.C.T.) and General Civilization Class (G.C.C.), where the women and girls were taught various domestic skills and the philosophy of Islam. Malcolm periodically dropped in on these classes where Betty X was teaching. He would have brief, friendly small talk with her, but nothing more. So Betty was greatly surprised when Malcolm asked her out. For his part, Malcolm was still trying to convince himself that he was asking her out merely because he wanted to "help the women's classes" by showing her some museum displays on evolution that would help her in some of her lectures. At least, that's what he told her. Then on the day of the trip to the museum Malcolm telephoned and tried to cancel their date (he got cold feet but did not want to admit it). Betty's immediate response was, "Well, you sure waited long enough to tell me." Her polite but pointed response impressed Malcolm, and he suddenly found time to keep their date.

While at the museum, Malcolm began to ask Betty all kinds of questions. Impressed with her intelligence, he shyly and apologetically also began asking her personal questions. Betty, sensing that Malcolm was interested in her, repeatedly reassured him that she knew his interest was purely out of curiosity and brotherly concern. Later, Malcolm discovered from one of the other women in the temple that Betty X had a problem involving her foster parents, who were strict Catholics. After telling them that she was a Muslim, her parents gave her an ultimatum: either leave the Muslims or they would cut off her funds for nursing school. Betty X stuck with Islam, which further impressed Malcolm.

Malcolm, who had not yet heard from Bettye concerning his proposal, began to contemplate asking Betty X to marry him instead. Then Malcolm realized that it did not make any sense to be thinking such a thing because he still had not heard from Bettye. Besides, he barely knew Betty X. So he consciously started avoiding her. But in his mind he kept weighing the obvious advantages of marrying someone like her.

Malcolm knew deep down that neither Betty nor Bettye was anything like any woman he had encountered while he was a street hustler. Malcolm's ambivalence and indecisiveness about what to do stemmed from a fundamental human insecurity that many men (and women) face: the fear of rejection. Of course, he need not have worried. Both Bettye and Betty were very impressed with Malcolm's strength, intelligence, sincerity, and dignity. They also noticed, and were touched, by his natural shyness, which Malcolm vainly tried to hide from them. For Betty X's part, Malcolm made such an impression on her the first time she saw him walk onto the speaker's platform that she sat bolt upright on her chair. Her initial reaction, she explained, was "somewhat akin to respect, or maybe even fear." Although Malcolm insisted that he was going to pursue marriage his way, he was very smitten with Betty X and had decided to propose to her, despite the fact that he had not yet heard from Bettye.

First he consulted with Elijah Muhammad about his choice. Muhammad subsequently met Betty X when she was invited to Chicago to attend seminars for women teachers at the NOI national headquarters at Temple Number Two in Chicago. The Messenger was greatly impressed by her and told Malcolm she was a "fine sister" and that he had his blessings. Now Malcolm was determined to propose to Betty X. He never did get back in touch with Bettye.

Instead, on January 12, 1958, he got in his car and drove all the way from New York to Michigan, ostensibly to visit his brother Wilfred, now head Minister of Temple Number One in Detroit. The morning after his arrival, Malcolm called Betty X, and as soon as she answered the phone, he quickly interrupted and blurted out, "Look, do you want to get married?" Betty, initially taken by surprise, recovered sufficiently to respond affirmatively. He then told her to catch a plane to Michigan because "he didn't have a whole lot of time." Although he later boasted that he "knew she would say yes," he clearly had finally conquered his fear of rejection and was very happy that Betty X had accepted. With every other major commitment in his life, Malcolm acted swiftly and decisively once he made up his mind to do something. Matters of the heart were no exception.

After Betty X arrived in Detroit, Malcolm met her foster parents, who appeared to be very friendly and happily surprised, although Malcolm was not absolutely sure they were. They still did not approve of Betty leaving Catholicism to become a Muslim. The following morning, at his brother Wilfred's suggestion, Malcolm and Betty drove to Indiana, where Wilfred thought they could get married without delay. But when they arrived, they discovered that Indiana's law had been changed and now required a long waiting period. Malcolm and Betty then drove eighty miles to Lansing, Michigan where he introduced Betty to his brother Philbert's family. There Malcolm learned that he could get married that very day if he and Betty hurried. Within hours on January 14, 1958, Malcolm and Betty X obtained a marriage license and the necessary blood tests. They then rushed to a justice of the peace.

Because they had done everything in such a hurry, no family members attended the wedding.

Betty's nursing school schedule required her to fly back to New York, but she could wait four days to return. Malcolm had the assistant minister at Temple Number Seven take over for him until he and Betty returned. Elijah Muhammad made the bombshell announcement about the marriage at Temple Number Seven after his Sunday lecture. Some of the young brothers whom Malcolm had earlier counseled to remain single looked as if he had betrayed them, but everyone else, as Malcolm put it, was "grinning like Cheshire cats." The women in the temple were ecstatic and excited for Betty. One exclaimed, "You got him!" Later, Malcolm grudgingly admitted with a grin, "Maybe she did get me!" Not long after the wedding, Malcolm unexpectedly encountered one of Bettye's brothers, who told him that his sister had been waiting for Malcolm to get back in touch with her and that she had been looking forward to marrying him.

Although Malcolm barely knew Betty X when he married her, they gradually fell in love and had six daughters together. Their marriage was by far the best decision he ever made, Malcolm remarked. Finally, he had learned to trust and confide in a woman that he truly respected and loved for her finer human qualities. He also learned that when one person truly loves another, as Betty X did him, hiding and suppressing one's true emotions, strengths, or weaknesses is not necessary, because that someone will understand and accept the other person for what that person is. For Malcolm X, it was a great lesson to learn and embrace.

Malcolm and the Media

The activities of the NOI and Malcolm X had become increasingly high profile in the white media. On April 14, 1957 an incident in Harlem brought the Nation of Islam to the attention of the general American public for the first time. Two white policemen, breaking up a street scuffle between a drunken man and his wife, grabbed the drunken man, who then struck one of the policemen in the chest. The officer then hit the man with his nightstick as the man vainly tried to defend himself. The other officer then used his nightstick, too, and helped the first officer subdue the man. Like the Rodney King incident in Los Angeles thirty-five years later, the two officers then proceeded to pummel the man mercilessly until his head, face, and clothing were drenched in blood.

An angry crowd gathered and began to protest the police's excessive use of violence. Another bystander, a member of the NOI and Temple Number Seven named Johnson Hinton then protested, "You're not in Alabama!" and demanded that the policemen stop. This comment infuriated the white officers, and as Hinton was leaving the scene, a policeman collared him from behind, spun him around, and without saying a word clobbered Hinton with his nightstick. Despite the impact of the blow, which Hinton later testified in court was "terrific," he somehow managed to grab hold of the nightstick as it again began to descend upon him. As they struggled for possession of the nightstick, another policeman intervened and began clubbing Hinton. Soon many other officers joined the attack, and they collectively clubbed a hapless Hinton to the pavement.

Bleeding profusely and handcuffed, Hinton, who had never been arrested before, was taken to the Twenty-eighth Precinct house, where he was slammed into a chair. Stretched out on the floor in a pool of blood lay the drunk whom the police had beaten earlier. As Hinton sat in agony moaning and praying, another cop demanded that he "shut up" and then struck him in the mouth. When that failed to stop Hinton's anguished moaning, yet another white cop said, "I'll shut you up," and hit Hinton several times in the face with his fists. He then fetched a nightstick and began beating Hinton's knees. Then the officer kicked Hinton in the chest so hard that he and his chair were propelled against the wall. His head struck the wall, and he passed out.

News about the vicious brutalization of Hinton and the other man spread like wildfire throughout Harlem. Within minutes, more than two thousand Harlemites were in the streets angrily demanding retribution as they surged toward the station house. Panicking, the police started calling every influential and respected black citizen they could think of to try to restore calm. Less than a half hour after Temple Number Seven was notified that

Hinton had been beaten and jailed, a highly disciplined and trained contingent of Malcolm's FOI (Fruit of Islam) group appeared outside the 123rd Street police station. They stood there shoulder to shoulder in complete silence and impressive military formation. James Hicks, editor of *The Amsterdam News*, Harlem's and New York City's most prominent black newspaper, was summoned as a mediator, but the crowd demanded justice, not mediation.

As tempers flared, New York Police Inspector William McGowan and several other top police department officials implored Hicks to contact his good friend Malcolm X. They all agreed that Malcolm was the only man in Harlem who could manage the crowd and get it to disperse peacefully. Hicks found Malcolm and his new confidante, John Ali (NOI National Secretary years later), in the crowd (which was now quickly approaching 3,000) gathered at Seventh Avenue and 123rd Street. Malcolm made it very clear that there was nothing to negotiate; Brother Johnson had been unjustly brutalized, the police were responsible and were denying him crucial medical attention by holding him in the Twenty-eighth Precinct house. The police authorities then asked Hicks to arrange a meeting between them and Malcolm at Hicks' office.

When Malcolm arrived, Deputy Police Commissioner Walter Arm told him he wanted the demonstrators to move. He then said he was telling him, not begging him. Malcolm very calmly rose from his chair, donned his coat and hat, and without saying a word, began walking out. The police were in shock as Hicks followed Malcolm out and urged him to reconsider. Malcolm then returned to his seat, his bargaining position much improved with the suddenly humbled police department. In return for removing his men, Malcolm said he wanted access to Johnson Hinton to determine for himself whether he needed medical treatment. He was given assurances that, if Hinton did require treatment, he would be transported to a hospital.

Unaware of the severity and extent of Hinton's injuries, Inspector McGowan returned to the precinct. As soon as he saw Hinton, he knew that Hinton was in very bad condition and that the NYPD had a huge, unwinnable lawsuit on its hands. When Malcolm saw Hinton lying on the cold floor of a cell, practically unconscious, he had to hold back his shock and tremendous anger. McGowan then asked Malcolm if he would disperse the crowd if Hinton were taken immediately to Harlem Hospital for treatment. Through clenched teeth, Malcolm agreed.

The police had Hinton taken to the hospital in an ambulance. The now huge crowd followed on foot. People poured out of bars, restaurants, nightclubs, and other places, adding to the massive ranks. An immense crowd gathered outside the hospital. After treating him, the hospital authorities, fearing a riot, immediately released Hinton back to the police, but not before Malcolm sent a photographer to the hospital to take pictures of Hinton's injuries.

The disciplined army of Muslims and the angry spectators accompanying them resumed their vigil outside the station house. The police then asked Malcolm if he would use his great influence to avert violence and disperse the raucous crowd, which had grown to more than five thousand people. Malcolm agreed on the condition that Hinton would continue to receive medical care and the officers who beat him would be punished. After being told that these things would be done, Malcolm calmly strode to the door of the police station, stood silently, and made a subtle motion with his right arm and hand. The FOI members, who were experts at crowd control and security, quickly and quietly dispersed the crowd.

No one who was present at the police station had ever seen anything like it. The immediate obedience and respect accorded Malcolm by the crowd caused Inspector McGowan to fume that "no man should have that much power." What he really meant of course, as John Hicks later stressed, was that no black man should have that much power.

Malcolm was now a living legend and a black folk hero in the eyes of the African American population in Harlem. He was also becoming a marked man in the eyes of the NYPD and the FBI, who now put him and the Harlem temple on around-the-clock secret surveillance.

In an effort to avert any further violence, Malcolm decided that his own men in the NOI and FOI would not appear en masse at Hinton's arraignment. Malcolm appeared alone with an attorney and bail money. Hinton was released and staggered out of the courthouse. Malcolm's own doctor examined Hinton and had him admitted to Sydenham Hospital, where doctors discovered he had a blood clot on the brain as well as many other injuries to the head, face, neck, shoulders, chest, and knees. Hinton required over one hundred stitches to properly close the wounds in his head, and a steel plate had to be inserted in his skull because the wounds were so severe.

In the weeks that followed, enlargements of the photographs taken of Hinton at the hospital circulated throughout Harlem. Malcolm and the other members of the Harlem temple organized a number of street demonstrations and rallies on behalf of Brother Johnson Hinton. The same photographs were used later during the trial that ensued when Elijah Muhammad, on behalf of the NOI and Hinton, hired lawyers to file a million-dollar lawsuit against New York City and its police department. An all-white jury eventually awarded Hinton seventy-five thousand dollars. The award, later reduced to seventy thousand dollars, was the largest made for police brutality in the city's history at that time.

Demonstrating courage and disciplined restraint under great public stress and provocation from enemies was becoming a regular feature of Malcolm's leadership, and Harlem loved him for it. His achievements in publicly facing down American racism were now beginning to gain him, and thus the NOI, many non-Muslim followers and supporters. In Harlem, the country's most heavily populated black community, the *Amsterdam News* made the entire story headline news, and for the first time, as Malcolm stated, "the black man, woman, and child in the street were discussing 'those Muslims.'"

One of the many formerly non-Muslim individuals in the black community who was becoming increasingly impressed by the NOI was Malcolm's uncompromisingly independent sister, Ella. Within a year she joined the sect, and no one was more surprised and pleased than Malcolm who remarked that "We have a saying that those who are the hardest to convince make the best Muslims. And for Ella it had taken five years." Her primary reason for joining was that she recognized the great potential that her siblings Malcolm, Wilfred, Philbert, Hilda, and other young black men and women of vision, energy, and commitment were now bringing to the ranks of the organization. She was, however, far less sure of Elijah Muhammad and his alleged "divinity" and self-described status as a prophet and his racially-based version of Islam. As her son Rodnell Collins later said, "The only reason she joined was because she felt it was the best program for black people since the Marcus Garvey movement."

As the organization grew rapidly in the spring and summer of 1957, Malcolm hit the road again to spread Islam and the "glorious teachings of the Honorable Elijah Muhammad." He opened new temples in Pittsburgh, Buffalo, Richmond, and several more in California. Elijah Muhammad formally made Malcolm his national representative, which meant he was officially the number one minister among all the other NOI ministers in the United States. Malcolm had become Muhammad's most reliable and trusted man in the complex hierarchy of the organization. His first major assignment as the national representative was Los Angeles, California, where the NOI's presence was growing faster than anywhere in the country outside of New York.

The *Los Angeles Herald-Dispatch* was a black leftist newspaper that had forged an editorial and financial alliance with the Nation of Islam. In July, Sanford Alexander, the owner of the *Herald-Dispatch*, began publishing a weekly column by Malcolm entitled "God's Angry Men." The first installment ran on July 18, 1957. For the first time, Malcolm X was able to deliver Elijah Muhammad's message to thousands of people in their homes (the *Herald-Dispatch* was sold in every major American city). Malcolm learned as much as he could about journalism and the technical end of the newspaper business.

Elijah Muhammad himself had become a columnist a year earlier in the spring of 1956 when he started writing a weekly column called "Islamic World" for the extremely popular African American newspaper *The Pittsburgh Courier*, which was sold nationally. The *Courier* had been a major media force in the black community for more than forty years and had a legendary reputation both in the United States and abroad as one of the finest independent newspapers of its kind in America. In October 1957, the Messenger's column was renamed "Mr. Muhammad Speaks." With the strong economic support and sales assistance of the NOI, the *Courier* thrived. In June 1957, for example, NOI members sold nearly 100,000 copies. Thrilled by its skyrocketing sales, the newspaper then added Malcolm's column to its newspaper.

By 1957 Malcolm and the NOI were being represented by major news and information outlets on both coasts. Meanwhile, Malcolm was working with an excellent and highly respected black journalist by the name of Louis Lomax. Lomax, who later gained some notoriety of his own for two books about the civil rights and black nationalist movements of the 1950s and '60s and who eventually became a friend and confidante of Malcolm's, helped Malcolm develop a national newspaper for the NOI that Malcolm named *Muhammad Speaks*, after the title of the column that the Messenger wrote for the *Courier*.

Not surprisingly, Malcolm prepared himself for his newspaper work with diligence and intense discipline. Returning to his workaholic schedule of eighteen-hour days, Malcolm plunged into a study of editing, layout design, advertising, and news reporting. He also enlisted the aide of a brilliant black female editor and journalist who, like Lomax, tutored Malcolm endlessly on the techniques and dynamics of sound newspaper work. A perfectionist and taskmaster like his mother and Ella, she bossed Malcolm around, but he never complained. Malcolm was finally learning to take instruction from a woman in an environment of intellectual and social equality (and where a woman knew more about a subject that he was interested in than he did). This mature attitude stood him in good stead when he and Lomax struggled to develop the newspaper during its first year of operation. The first copies of the newspaper (whose first issue was called *Islamic News*) were typed, printed, and designed in the basement of Malcolm's home.

Two years earlier, in 1955, the Bandung Conference had been convened by many of the major political and cultural leaders of African and Asian nations who were leading and advocating revolutionary anticolonial struggles for national independence in the Third World. Not coincidentally, most of these emerging non-white nations were Islamic. For years, Elijah Muhammad had assiduously cultivated political and religious contacts in Africa and the Middle East, and his efforts at internationalizing the NOI began to pay off. Malcolm began to fill the crucial role of diplomat for the NOI in 1957 by meeting with many of these international political and religious leaders and other heads of state. He also began to serve as an official liaison for Muhammad at the United Nations.

At the same time, Malcolm was forging a political and personal friendship with Adam Clayton Powell, Jr., the legendary Harlem congressman and minister of one of the largest and most powerful churches in all of New York, the Abyssinian Baptist Church (with an all-black congregation of more than 5,000). Various Third World nationalists, such as Gamal Nasser of Egypt, Kwame Nkrumah of Ghana, and Indonesian President Achmed Sukarno (who had officially hosted the Bandung Conference), as well as Powell were instrumental in helping the NOI gain increased visibility and prestige on the global scene as a result of the efforts of Malcolm on behalf of the Messenger. By the end of 1957, Elijah Muhammad and the NOI had made contacts with a number of Islamic activists both inside and outside the United States.

In May 1957, a Pakistani journalist named Abdul Basit Naeem, who was living in Brooklyn, signed a contract with Muhammad to produce a glossy ninety-page booklet entitled *The Moslem World and the USA* to focus on international Islamic affairs and also to feature the Messenger's Savior's Day convention as its centerpiece. Savior's Day was celebrated by the NOI each year on February 26, which was allegedly the birth date of Wallace D. Fard, the mysterious figure whom the Messenger had met in Detroit in 1930 and who was regarded, in the elaborate and complex mythology of the NOI, as "God in person."

Throughout 1958, Malcolm continued to push for the Messenger's ambitious and increasingly successful economic and social program of building and maintaining farms, stores, restaurants, apartment complexes, office buildings, temples, banks, schools, health clinics, and cultural centers for members of the NOI throughout the United States. Malcolm and other ministers were busy recruiting scientists, engineers, accountants, entrepreneurs, teachers, journalists, scholars, economists, and farmers to its social and religious agenda, which now began to emphasize not only criticism of Christianity and Judaism as proper religions for African Americans, but also to resurrect the sometimes dormant idea that black people in America should have their own independent nation within the confines of the United States. Thus in many speeches during the late 1950s, Malcolm openly talked about the secular, political, and economic aspects of the NOI program as a means of attracting and harnessing the explosion of energy being generated by black youth and young adults as a result of the rising civil rights movement led by Dr. Martin Luther King, Jr., among many others.

In insisting on the establishment of an independent national "home" for African Americans in the South, Malcolm sought to find a pragmatic strategy for enlisting the militant and increasingly nationalist and social revolutionary perspectives of young black Americans in the service of the Messenger's global plan for forging ties of unity and mutual cooperation with the Nassers, Nkrumahs, Sukarnos, and others in the African and Asian anticolonial struggles. As confirmation of this plan, President Gamal Abdel Nasser of the newly formed United Arab Republic, a multinational coalition of Arab states fighting for an independent Palestine against Israel and for a Pan-Arab and Pan-African coalition throughout Africa, sent a cablegram to the Messenger thanking him for his support. Malcolm then sent the message to various black newspapers as part of a public relations campaign for the NOI.

The Messenger, Malcolm, and other ministers in the NOI became increasingly strident in their tone regarding Jews. The anti-Semitism expressed by the Messenger and endorsed at the time by Malcolm was seen as aiding and abetting the struggles of Muslims in Egypt, Syria, and Palestine who were united in their military and propaganda war against the Jewish state of Israel. It also reflected the notions promulgated by Fard and his major disciple, Muhammad, that Jews had historically aligned with whites against black people and that "Jesus could not have been a Jew because he was born in Palestine."

At the Savior's Day convention on February 26, 1958, Muhammad declared publicly that he was a prophet in the same line as Abraham and Moses and that he was performing the same historical role as Moses in telling Pharaoh to "let my people go." Though all other prophets had been persecuted and killed, the Messenger asserted, "No one can lay a hand on me because I am protected by Allah." He also said, "The other prophets had seen a revelation and were only revealing what they saw, but none besides me was taught directly by God."

Malcolm's sister Ella and many other black people saw this sort of outlandish and demagogic talk as foolish, dangerous, and delusional, yet they were as torn as Malcolm himself would eventually be between such rhetoric and the positive, dynamic, and productive programs, values, and activities of the NOI. To many of the Christians and even the agnostic visitors in the auditorium, much of what the Messenger said sounded like the blasphemous ranting of a man overcome with delusions of grandeur. Some began to leave after his speech while others (both within the NOI and outside it) held on in the belief that it was possible and necessary to make a critical differentiation about what they agreed with and supported in the NOI's program and organization and what they decidedly did not endorse, support, or go along with.

Muhammad's "Blueprint for the Blackman's Future" was also unveiled at the Savior's Day convention. With the support of African Americans and Muslims throughout the world, the Messenger said he hoped to build a three-million-dollar complex in Chicago that would include a "religious, educational, and business center" by 1961. He told the thousands attending the convention that newly acquired apartment buildings and the NOI temples, groceries, and markets were an infinitesimal indication of the economic power in the hands of African Americans.

A twenty-four-year-old named Louis X (later Louis Farrakhan), who had been recruited and mentored by Malcolm in 1955, sang "Pharaoh, Let Us Go" as FBI agents and local police surreptitiously conducted what they called a "fisur," an acronym for physical surveillance. Agents and police roamed the parking lots, noted the license plate numbers of every car, took photographs of anyone who might be a dignitary, and monitored eavesdropping equipment that recorded the speeches. Clearly, the conflict between the forces of the government, the media, and the NOI were coming to a head. Malcolm X knew and understood better than most people that something had to give.

Chapter 15

"Muhammad Speaks" and Malcolm X Is His Voice

By 1958, the scandalous discrimination against dark-skinned foreigners by white businesses in the United States had become the talk of the United Nations, which officially investigated this discrimination. Distinguished diplomats and other officials were often thrown out of restaurants (in some cases, bodily) by white bigots because of racist Jim Crow laws and because the foreign customers were regularly "mistaken" for African Americans. Another investigation by the United Nations revealed that diplomats were denied access to restrooms while traveling to and from New York and Washington, D.C. by automobile.

As egregious as these insults were, they paled beside what Muslims from other nations found to be the biggest disadvantage of all for them: the lack of Islamic houses of worship. Only seven cities in the entire country had orthodox Islamic mosques at the time. Most were quite small and in need of repair, such as the popular mosque built in 1934 in Dearborn, Michigan, an all-white suburb right outside Detroit. The largest was the Islamic Center in Washington, D.C., which had been erected in 1956.

In an attempt to build upon a growing brotherhood and out of a mutual criticism of America's political, cultural, and religious inadequacies, the Messenger repeatedly expressed his desire to be of service to Third World Muslims. To build on the work of the Bandung Conference in 1955, a second conference was held on

July 12, 1958, at the Park Palace in midtown Manhattan. This time, over 13,000 people participated in the weekend gala. Many prominent Third World Muslim leaders were present along with a number of local African American politicians.

One of the most important guests, a man whom both Muhammad and Malcolm X held in awe, was the legendary African American historian, columnist (for the *Pittsburgh Courier*) and scholar, J.A. Rogers. Rogers was widely considered an expert in ancient African and European history and had written a number of seminal texts on both, and the complex interactions between Africa, Europe, and the Americas. His books were, and still are held in very high esteem, by Black nationalists, Pan-Africanists, and students of African and African American history all over the globe. As the Messenger continued to speak before huge crowds across the country about the limitations, deceptions, and inadequacies of integration as a political and economic strategy on the part of blacks, Malcolm continued his new mission of promoting and strengthening the links between African Americans and Africa. With Muhammad's consent, Malcolm accepted an invitation to join the Welcoming Committee of the Twenty-eighth Precinct Community Council. The group's primary function was to welcome foreign dignitaries to New York. In that capacity, Malcolm and John Ali were at the airport on August 1 to welcome Prime Minister Kwame Nkrumah of Ghana to America. When John Ali handed Nkrumah several pamphlets about the Messenger, Nkrumah smiled and thanked him, saying he was "most interested in the plight of my people in America."

Then during the first week of December 1958, in one of the increasingly bizarre incidents that began to occur as the NOI's public profile rose, Captain Joseph (head of the Fruit of Islam security force) and John Ali brought a letter to the temple in New York that threatened to kill Malcolm X and the Messenger unless $50,000 in cash was left at a drop site in the black-owned Hotel Theresa in Harlem. The letter said, "Murder is not new to us. We could have killed Elijah Muhammad in Boston when he got off the plane. If Muhammad appears in Newark on December 14, it will be the last time." The letter frightened Elijah Muhammad. He told John Ali to notify the police and the FBI, which he did. The problem with the letter, the police told him, was that it bore no postal stamp to indicate its origins, nor did it mention any organizations or have any distinctive marks or detectable fingerprints.

The inability of the police to intervene or identify who might have sent the letter clearly rattled Muhammad. His blood pressure rose dramatically, and he called his wife, Clara, to have her return home from a trip immediately, which she did. After police assured him that the letter was probably nothing more than the rant of a harmless crank, Muhammad regained his composure and decided to speak in Newark, New Jersey, as planned. There the Messenger boasted before a crowd of thousands, "I have no fear. If I'm shot down, you stand up. What is there to be afraid of? We are greater than our enemies who enslave us." Muhammad received a standing ovation. Malcolm was unfazed. He was mildly fatalistic about these matters and had always maintained that he would probably die at the behest of his enemies anyway.

Malcolm holding "Muhammad Speaks," 1963.

(AP/Wide World)

On April 20, 1959, Muhammad and Malcolm co-sponsored a major gathering of radical Pan-Africanists in the New York area. Still hoping to acquire some funding from the newly independent Islamic nations in North Africa and the Middle East to build an Islamic Center on Chicago's South Side, Muhammad held the event to demonstrate that these newly independent African and Arab nations were immensely interested in alliances with African American Muslims. Dozens of highly regarded and prominent African Americans attended the event, including J.A. Rogers, Dr. John Henrik Clarke, and well-known jazz vocalist Dakota Staton, who provided entertainment at the gala affair. African diplomats also attended, among them Liberian ambassador Charles T. O. King, who emphasized the special kinship between his nation (populated and controlled by freed American slaves who had returned to Africa a century before) and those Africans who remained in America after slavery. CBS-TV covered the event, but focused on Malcolm and the NOI. In his speech, Malcolm X called for a "Bandung Conference" of Harlem leaders and urged civil rights groups to support an NOI-sponsored rally in Washington, D.C. in May.

> *The proposed Islamic Center would cost twenty million dollars and feature a new hospital, a traditional mosque (as opposed to the storefronts the NOI was forced to settle for in most cities), and an expanded University of Islam.*

The Messenger's courtship of Arabs paid off handsomely. In May 1959, Gamal Nasser invited him and his family to visit Egypt as official state guests. The invitation included a chance to make the *hajj*, which is the pilgrimage to Mecca. Excited by this great opportunity, Muhammad immediately started making plans for his first trip abroad. The Messenger planned to take his wife and sons Akbar, who spoke fluent Arabic and was going to serve as his father's interpreter, and Herbert (who later became business manager of boxing legend Muhammad Ali after he joined the NOI in 1964), who was coming along as official photographer.

> The hajj is the sacred rite of passage for Muslims worldwide. It is an arduous journey across hundreds of miles on a pilgrimage to Mecca, birthplace of the prophet Muhammad, to pay eternal homage to Allah and confirm one's spiritual commitment to Allah and the religion of Islam. Every Muslim is supposed to make this trip at least once in a lifetime, if possible.

When the FBI and CIA learned about the trip they mounted a COINTELPRO (counterintelligence program) to abort it. First, the CIA contacted the Egyptian ambassador in Washington to determine whether he knew what an "unsavory" character Muhammad was and that he preached an unorthodox and adulterated form of Islam. Similar violations of the Constitution had been used successfully in 1951 against Paul Robeson and black Communist leader William L. Patterson, who had lodged official charges of genocide against the United States with the United Nations. Muhammad now found it next to impossible to get his passport. The Chicago field office of the FBI wrote a memo to FBI headquarters that explicitly instructed the Washington D.C. field office to "put a stop" on Elijah Muhammad and his family "in the event they make application for a passport ..."

Muhammad's lawyers told him that the circumstances surrounding his passport trouble suggested high-level government involvement. Not to be undone by the illegal and unconstitutional machinations of the federal government, Muhammad decided that Malcolm should go on to Egypt while his lawyers battled the government. Malcolm was also instructed to inform Nasser that Muhammad's will to make the hajj would ultimately triumph over the will of the American government to prevent him from doing so.

The intrigue continued. On June 5, 1959, the FBI sent the CIA a memorandum regarding the Messenger's pending trip. The memo said the FBI had discovered that the main objective of the trip was to "impress his followers in the United States who contribute to his support by showing he is a well-known Moslem and has connections in the Moslem world." The CIA then contacted Ambassador

Mustafa Kamal of the United Arab Republic. After discussing the matter with the Americans, Ambassador Kamal was reported to have said, "It is religiously and politically unwise to give Muhammad any recognition when he visits Egypt." But Kamal refused to speak out publicly against Muhammad's trip, which was probably a wise move on his part. He had been an ambassador for little more than a year and had not been in the United States long enough to be well acquainted with the NOI. In addition, speaking out against the wishes of Nasser would have been political suicide. Unable to get other Muslims to publicly denounce Muhammad, American intelligence was forced to resort to other measures.

Meanwhile, the State Department's game of playing political football with Muhammad's passport came to an abrupt halt when William R. Ming Jr., a formidable attorney who also represented Dr. Martin Luther King Jr., lobbied to get Muhammad's passport approved. Ming told Muhammad that he had contacted the Chicago offices of Senators Everett M. Dirksen and Paul Douglas from Illinois. Ming complained that his client was an upstanding American citizen who was being unconstitutionally deprived of his right to travel. The office promised to look into the matter immediately. The mere mention of Dirksen, who had just been named Republican minority leader, quickly got the State Department's attention. When an aide called on June 19 to determine what the holdup was, an official in the passport division said that there "appeared to be no overriding political reasons which preclude issuance of a passport." Five days later, Muhammad received his passport. But the extended delaying tactics by government officials seemed to have worked on one level: By the time everything was in order for the trip, it was too late for Muhammad to properly prepare for the complete hajj. In the meantime, he had told Malcolm to go to the Middle East without him, because the invitation from Nasser was not an opportunity to be wasted.

Malcolm left the country on July 12, 1959, and the very next day Muhammad got the national exposure that he craved, although the slant of the coverage was not exactly what he or Malcolm had in mind. It did, however, mark a major turning point in the fortunes of the NOI, public knowledge of Islam in the

United States, and the internal dynamics of the American black nationalist movement that would have both positive and negative repercussions for years to come. And it happened on television. It made Malcolm a household name in middle America for the first time. It also made a star out of its host, who became a living legend in television broadcast news history.

On the evening of July 13, a former game show host and commercial pitchman named Mike Wallace, who anchored a new, provocative television show called *News Beat* on WNTA-TV in New York, ran the first segment of a five-part series on the Nation of Islam. The outstanding research for the program was primarily the work of Louis E. Lomax, the same well-respected black journalist who had helped Malcolm with the development of the NOI national newspaper *Muhammad Speaks*. Lomax, a highly ambitious news reporter and writer who also worked with Wallace, was trying to crack the almost impenetrable wall of racial discrimination and exclusion of black journalists that reigned supreme at all national televison networks. The packaging, tone, editing, and visual structure of the program was vintage Mike Wallace (who went on to work for more than twenty-five years as an anchorman on CBS-TV's immensely popular news program *60 Minutes*). The series, which ran for five consecutive evenings on Channel 13 in New York, had a national impact because news wire services and then newspapers and magazines spread information about it in deceptively shocking and frightening terms.

The program was given the highly provocative and sensationalist title of "The Hate That Hate Produced," which on a first, superficial glance appears to be a brilliant summation of aspects of the historical identity of the NOI and its teachings, but like all glib slogans, it misses the point of what it purports to be exposing. But the techniques of what some called ambush or "you are there" journalism that Wallace had mastered (and later in his career honed to a science) drove home the message that he wished to convey to a mass television audience: The Nation of Islam, its program, and its leadership were a dangerous menace to society and to all responsible Americans, black and white. In a famous introductory excerpt from the widely viewed and now classic televison documentary, Wallace stares dramatically into the camera and states:

> While city officials, state agencies, white liberals and sober-minded Negroes stand idly by, a group of Negro dissenters are taking to street-corner stepladders, church pulpits, sports arenas, and ballroom platforms across the nation to preach a gospel of hate that would set off a federal investigation if it were to be preached by Southern whites.

The brusque tone of outrage, moral indignation, self-righteous bluster, and rhetorical puffery, not to mention the intellectual hubris of Wallace's approach was matched only by the excited rush of intimidating images of "angry Negroes" that were flashed across the screen. As Malcolm pointed out in his autobiography:

> "The Hate That Hate Produced"—the title—was edited tightly into a kaleidoscope of "shocker" images ... Mr. Muhammad, me, and others speaking ... strong-looking, set-faced black men, our Fruit of Islam ... white-scarved, white-gowned Muslim sisters of all ages ... Muslims in our restaurants, and other businesses ... Muslims and other black people entering and leaving our mosques ... Every phrase was edited to increase the shock mood. As the producers intended, I think people sat just about limp when the program went off. In a way, the public reaction was like what happened back in the 1930s when Orson Welles frightened America with a radio program describing, as though it was actually happening, an invasion by "men from Mars" ... It's my personal opinion that the "Hate ... Hate ..." title was primarily responsible for the reaction. Hundreds of thousands of New Yorkers, black and white, were exclaiming, "Did you hear it? Did you see it? Preaching hate of white people! Here was one of the white man's most characteristic behavior patterns— where black men are concerned. He loves himself so much that he is startled if he discovers that his victims don't share his vainglorious self-opinion. In America, for centuries it had been just fine as long as the victimized,

> *brutalized, and exploited black people had been grinning,*
> *begging, saying, "Yessa Massa," and Uncle Tomming.*
> *But now, things were* different …

Predictably, white newspapers and news magazines joined in a collective, shrill chorus attacking the NOI and Malcolm X as "hatemongers," "a threat to good relations between the races," "black supremacists," "black segregationists," "violence-seekers," "Communist-inspired," and the like. The blatant hypocrisy and dishonesty of notoriously racist and all-white institutions such as the electronic and print media piously lecturing African Americans about civic responsibility in the realm of race relations struck not only Muslims, but most African Americans in general as patently absurd and deeply insulting given the daily onslaught of concentrated racism on every level of American life during the socially repressive 1950s. The civil rights movement of the period was encountering such ugly, intense, and sustained opposition to its fundamentally mild reforms such as voting rights and equality before the law that many historians and other commentators were saying that the reaction resembled the racist savagery of the post-Reconstruction era from 1880–1920 when thousands of African Americans were lynched, racist terror by the KKK and other groups were the norm, and Jim Crow segregation, oppression, exclusion, and exploitation had made it impossible for the ordinary black man or woman to make a decent living anywhere in the country.

During the late '50s when the "Hate …" documentary was produced, black people were still routinely being murdered, beaten, discriminated against, and denied the right to vote throughout the South, while the KKK and other white hate groups ran amuck by burning and bombing the homes, churches, and businesses of both black people in the movement and ordinary citizens outside it. Many African Americans found that white outrage, and aversion to honestly facing painful truths still all too often dictated their responses to blacks who didn't think that the United States was anywhere near as ideal, fair, just, or democratic as the official propaganda and mythology of the U.S. taught its citizens that it was.

The NOI's various temples throughout the country and Elijah Muhammad were subjected to a deluge of public attacks by the entire spectrum of American political and religious opinion. Even black Christian-oriented civil rights organizations weighed in on the issue, calling the NOI "irresponsible," "extremist," and "not reflective of the general sentiment of the Negro community." As far as the white media, the government, and the great majority of ordinary white American citizens were concerned, the general verdict was that something needed to be done to stop the NOI from spreading "lies" about "our great country" and "embarrassing us with their hate-filled philosophy in the eyes of the world." The fact that many were now denouncing the NOI as a cult struck Malcolm and the members of the NOI as particularly ludicrous given their current position as a respected segment of the Islamic faith that encompassed nearly one billion members throughout the globe.

Malcolm's phone and the phones of every temple in the country rang off the hook as the NOI was besieged by endless requests from press, radio, and television to "go on the record" in response to the numerous attacks against the NOI and especially Elijah Muhammad and Malcolm X. Malcolm now found himself consulting daily with the Messenger regarding what strategic and tactical methods should be used to combat this latest offensive against their efforts. Although some people in the NOI began to show signs of panic and even fear of the ferocity of the public attack on them, the Messenger stayed calm, patient, and focused. Muhammad, who as a child and adolescent, had personally witnessed lynchings and many other unspeakable atrocities and racist crimes against blacks, was not fazed by his latest challenge. He suggested that the impact of this bad publicity could even be transformed with the proper response.

Malcolm was personally amazed by his mentor's cool as he relayed some of the things that were being said about him and Islam. Malcolm admitted that he "could barely contain himself" because he was so livid about the charges. The Messenger counseled Malcolm, the other ministers, and the rank-and-file membership to calmly but forcefully stand up to the verbal assaults, death threats, and distortions and to "simply tell the truth" about what the black man is being forced to endure in such a racist country.

This advice was a balm for Malcolm and confirmed his own view of the situation. Now was the time to go on the offensive and not be pushed into a defensive position or public retreat with regard to the NOI's aims, values, and objectives. Malcolm was more than prepared to "fight fire with fire." Besides, Malcolm personally had had enough. Somehow his unlisted home telephone number got out, and his wife Betty was reduced to taking a continuous stream of phone messages or fending off abusive calls when Malcolm was out. No sooner would she put the phone down than it would immediately ring again. Life was becoming bedlam both in and outside the temple.

Because New York City was the major mass media headquarters of the United States and one of the most important news outlets in the world, and because Malcolm and his ministry were located in Harlem, most calls for the NOI were directed to him. Calls poured in from San Francisco to Maine and even from London, Paris, Stockholm, and Berlin. In all of the furor, however, Malcolm noticed some significant differences in the quality of the coverage in Europe as opposed to the United States. The Europeans never pressed the question of hate and were far more interested in a sober intellectual and political understanding of who Malcolm and Elijah Muhammad were and what the NOI stood for and why. In Malcolm's view "only the American white man was plagued and obsessed with being 'hated.' He was so guilty, it was clear to me, of hating Negroes." A red flag went up for Malcolm whenever he was asked whether or why the NOI taught "black supremacy." As part of his strategy to fight fire with fire Malcolm responded:

> *The white man is so guilty of white supremacy that he can't hide his guilt by trying to accuse the Honorable Elijah Muhammad of teaching black supremacy and hate! All Mr. Muhammad is doing is trying to uplift the black man's mentality and the black man's social and economic condition in this country. The guilty, two-faced white man can't decide what he wants. Our slave foreparents*

> would have been put to death for advocating so-called
> 'integration' with the white man. Now when Mr.
> Muhammad speaks of 'separation,' the white man calls us
> 'hate-teachers' and 'fascists!' The white man doesn't
> want the blacks! He doesn't want the blacks that in his
> mind are a parasite upon him. He doesn't want this black
> man whose presence and condition in this country expose
> the white man to the world for what he is! So why do you
> attack Mr. Muhammad? For the white man to ask the
> black man if he hates him is just like the rapist asking the
> raped, or the wolf asking the sheep, 'Do you hate me?'
> The white man is in no moral position to accuse anyone
> else of hate!"

Addressing the question of why members of the Fruit of Islam
were being trained in judo and karate, Malcolm pointed out that
the image of a black person learning anything suggesting self-
defense seemed to terrify the white man. He would deftly turn the
question around:

> Why does judo or karate suddenly become so ominous
> because black men study it? Across America, the Boy
> Scouts, the YMCA, even the YWCA, the CYP, PAL
> (Police Athlectic League)—they all teach judo! It's
> alright, it's fine—until black men teach it! Even little
> grammar school classes, little girls, are taught to defend
> themselves.

When Malcolm was questioned about how many members were
in the NOI in response to the criticism by some black Christian
leaders that the NOI had only a "handful of members" and were
not representative of the masses, Malcolm always had a scathing
response ready for both the media and what he viewed as his
"Uncle Tom" opposition from black Christians, "Whoever tells
you how many Muslims there are doesn't know, and whoever does
know will never tell you." Malcolm reserved some of his most vit-
riolic scorn and disdain for the "Bishop T. Chickenwings"
(Malcolm's caustic and satirical name for black Christian opposition leaders) who were so often quoted in the press regarding the

NOI's anti-Christianity. Malcolm would, he said, "fire right back on that":

> Christianity is the white man's religion. The Holy Bible in the white man's hands and his interpretations of it has been the greatest single ideological weapon for enslaving millions of nonwhite human beings. Every country the white man has conquered with his guns, he has always paved the way, and salved his conscience, by carrying the Bible and interpreting it to call the people 'heathens' and 'pagans;' then he sends his guns, then his missionaries behind the guns to mop up.

After pointing out that many of the greatest philosophers, prophets, religious figures, scientists, and political leaders in history were once considered dangerous heretics, demagogues, false prophets, and renegades, Malcolm would insist that Elijah Muhammad was in this line of the misunderstood and maligned leaders who ultimately made a great contribution to humanity. The jury was not yet out on that historical assertion, but Malcolm had once again performed brilliantly and shrewdly in the arena of public debate. He also made the social and intellectual positions of the NOI crystal clear on major questions. Certainly, Malcolm had come to embody what the true potential of the NOI and Islam in America was, and even what it could mean in time as both it and he continued to grow and evolve. Malcolm himself put the situation in far more subversive terms at the time:

> We, the followers of the Honorable Elijah Muhammad, are today in the ghettoes as once the sect of Christianity's followers were like termites in the catacombs and grottoes—and they were preparing the grave of the mighty Roman Empire!

As Malcolm's public profile grew, so did his masterful, creative, and scintillating use of language. A past master of the subtle and sometimes brutal art of signifying, Malcolm excelled at the droll practice of what the English call "one-up-manship." For example, Malcolm often used his extraordinary understanding and analysis of American history to confound his enemies and force doubters or skeptics to reconsider their sources. Whenever reporters, political pundits, or others raised questions about the country's support of African American civil rights, Malcolm would masterfully redirect and redefine the very terms of the discourse. Five years later, Malcolm reflected on these verbal battles:

> I can remember those hot telephone sessions with those
> reporters as if it were yesterday. The reporters were
> angry. I was angry. When I'd reach into history, they'd
> try to pull me back to the present. They would quit inter-
> viewing, quit their work, trying to defend themselves.
> They would unearth Lincoln and his freeing of the slaves.
> I'd tell them things Lincoln said in speeches, against the
> blacks. They would drag out the 1954 Supreme Court
> decision on school integration.
> 'That was one of the greatest magical feats ever performed
> in America,' I'd tell them. 'Do you mean to tell me that
> nine Supreme Court judges, who are past masters of legal
> phraseology, couldn't have worked their decision to make
> it stick as law? No! It was trickery and magic that told
> Negroes they were desegregated—Hooray! Hooray!—and
> at the same time it told whites 'Here are the loopholes.'
> But I don't care what points I made in the interviews, it
> practically never got printed the way I said it. I was learn-
> ing under fire how the press, when it wants to, can twist
> and slant. If I had said "Mary had a little lamb," what
> probably would have appeared was 'Malcolm X
> Lampoons Mary.'

Malcolm also asserted that his own bitterness was less against the white press (from whom he did not expect much anyway) than it was against those Negro leaders who kept attacking the NOI and Elijah Muhammad. Malcolm was told by Muhammad that he wanted his ministers to try their best not to publicly counterattack the leaders because one of the white man's tricks was to keep black people divided and fighting against each other. In the Messenger's view, this division had traditionally kept black people from achiev- ing the kind of political unity that was necessary for their collec- tive welfare.

However, public criticism showed no signs of abating, and other more conservative black leaders continued, in Malcolm's words, to "rip and tear into Mr. Muhammad and the Nation of Islam." When it appeared as though Malcolm and others within the NOI were afraid to speak out against these important Negroes, Muhammad's patience wore thin, and he gave Malcolm the green light to once again "return the fire." As usual, Malcolm was acerbic, satirical, and verbally merciless in his attack:

> *Today's Uncle Tom doesn't wear a handkerchief on his head. This modern, twentieth-century Uncle Thomas now often wears a top hat. He's usually well-dressed and well-educated. He's often the personification of culture and refinement. The twentieth-century Uncle Thomas sometimes speaks with a Yale or Harvard accent.*
> *Sometimes he is known as Professor, Doctor, Judge, and Reverend, even Right Reverend Doctor. This twentieth-century Uncle Thomas is a professional Negro ... and by that I mean his profession is to being a Negro for the white man.*

These acrimonious comments definitely had an effect. The outrage expressed by black leaders targeted by Malcolm often matched that expressed by their white counterparts. Malcolm was not surprised. He realized that most of them had never been "called out" and blasted publicly in such an acerbic manner before. Malcolm called these figures "black bodies with white heads" and viewed their disdain for the NOI and what it represented as indicative of their positions as puppets of white bosses who often served as president or board chairman of mainstream civil rights organizations. In this regard, Malcolm reserved his greatest scorn and contempt for such nationally known individuals and institutions as Roy Wilkins and the NAACP and Whitney Young and the Urban League.

Regardless of whether Malcolm's comments were considered by the general public to be unfair, Malcolm insisted that standing up for oneself and being completely honest in one's appraisal of what was necessary or of value in any public discussion of the serious issues and concerns facing African Americans was crucial. If that required one to sometimes transgress or even erase the boundaries of what was considered to be proper etiquette with regard to debate, then Malcolm was more than up to the task. To him, the NOI, and Elijah Muhammad, this discourse was war, and the stakes involving the liberation of people of African and Asian descent throughout the world from white American and European oppression were nothing less than human survival.

Famous national magazines such as *Life, Look, Newsweek,* and *Time* ran long, extensive stories on the NOI, replete with photographs, editorial commentary, and analysis.(One of the first major stories that the great black photojournalist, writer, and film director Gordon Parks ever did for *Life* after he became the first African American to ever work for the magazine in 1948, was on the "Black Muslims.") Many newspaper chains began to run not one story, but a series of three, four, or five "exposures" of the NOI. Even the staid and archconservative *Reader's Digest,* the most well-known and read mainstream magazine in America ran an article entitled "Mr. Muhammad Speaks" by none other than the co-writer of Malcolm's autobiography and the author of *Roots,* Alex Haley. Soon, other monthly magazines followed suit. The media spillover was so great and the attention so enormous that a popular Harlem radio show invited Malcolm to conduct a weekly talk show. During the next four years, three books about the "Black Muslims" were printed.

The net result of this publicity was that Malcolm X, Elijah Muhammad, and the NOI finally had the international forum that they had craved for many years. Mike Wallace's media hatchet job on the NOI had backfired. The notoriety, for all of its negative fallout, also had the unintended consequence of turning on thousands of African Americans who were otherwise unaware or only vaguely familiar with the NOI and its principles and values to an independent nationalist movement for fundamental social change. This movement was especially attractive to black youth and young adults who were not interested in (or saw as sorely limited) the civil rights movement led by the Southern Christian Leadership Conference (SCLC) and Dr. Martin Luther King Jr., the NAACP, the Urban League, CORE (Congress of Racial Equality), and others.

African American youth yearned for a more militant and dynamic expression of their alienation from and profound disillusionment with America and its endless empty promises of freedom, justice, equality, and democracy. African Americans of the period wanted much more than merely token integration or the condescending implication that if they "kept their nose clean, worked hard, and believed in America" everything would eventually be fine. What Malcolm X offered was an alternative to the other civil rights groups. As he, the NOI, and the Messenger made the exciting and dangerous transition into the 1960s, everyone (especially the FBI and CIA) recognized that Islam and the radical black nationalist movement was generally becoming a force to be reckoned with, and Malcolm stood at the epicenter of this historical development.

Chapter 16

The Nation of Islam and Third World Revolution

In 1960, Malcolm X turned thirty-five years old. He had been out of prison for nearly eight years and had spent nearly every waking hour since then working non-stop on behalf of the NOI, the national and international expansion of the religious and social philosophy of Islam, and spreading the teachings and values of the man called "the Messenger of Allah" and the "Honorable Elijah Muhammad." Malcolm now used his charisma, sharp intelligence, ambition, drive, and command of language not only to stimulate, but to educate his listeners, black and white alike, to learn and appreciate the far more profound and painful truths about society and history that American schools and most of its teachers were still far too bigoted, timid, or ignorant to know and articulate. His immense appeal to his many followers and the many other people who were simply intellectually or politically curious about his radical stance on the major issues of the day, lay in his ability to face the complex realities and stern challenges to his quest for freedom, justice and independence without fear or regret. He possessed the rare quality of genuine integrity and never allowed self-pity or bad faith to distract him from his ethical or social responsibility as a leader and teacher no matter what anyone else said. He had learned the invaluable lesson of being self-confident and assertive but without allowing his ego to guide or direct his decisions. The masses of black people in Harlem and throughout the nation sensed these things about him even when they disagreed with something he said or believed. In a word he had *respect*, something he personally valued and cherished more than anything.

It was these qualities that made him dangerous or even feared in the eyes of the government and his political as well as religious adversaries and opponents. They knew—like his supporters and colleagues did—that he was truly uncompromising when it came to principle; he might lose or be defeated in any given context, but *he would never back down in a fight*. This is what endeared him to the thousands of people who would routinely hear him speak or debate others in public. In 1960, Malcolm began making hundreds of appearances on television, radio, college campuses, as well as granting long interviews in newspapers and magazines. He now had a baby girl whom he named Attallah, "after the one who sacked Rome," Malcolm said. She had been born in 1958, but he rarely saw her because he was so busy and on the road. His marriage to Betty X even began to suffer because of his heavy schedule, but their ultimate devotion to each other and the cause of Islam kept them together, despite some rough times.

The year also marked a turning point in the direction of the NOI as it began to put greater public emphasis on the notion of a formal separation of the races and independent nationhood for African Americans. Muhammad felt certain that the political unity and religious authority growing out of the economic and cultural infrastructure that he, his ministers, and their followers were building would eventually win the NOI a grant of land and the power to administer it. Although nearly everyone outside the NOI (and privately even many members within it) saw this goal as little more than a utopian pipe dream or a purely symbolic gesture signifying alienation from the American mainstream, the Messenger maintained faith in the idea as a possible, if remote, alternative.

For Malcolm the situation was more complicated. His ambivalence was not so much with the idea of separate development and statehood, but with the focus on an isolated territory within the American empire that would lack any pragmatic and systemic linkages to the Third World nations struggling to free themselves from the ideological orbits or economic spheres of the United States and Soviet Union. To Malcolm, a truly radical and non-aligned Pan-Africanism forging institutional and social bonds linking the African (American) disapora, as well as the Caribbean, with Third World nations seemed a much more viable possibility in both the short and long term than a conventionally separatist movement within the United States.

The Messenger also favored an alliance with Third World countries that was more tied to the religious and social aspects of Islam than to one that explicitly addressed the political and economic dynamics of capitalism and imperialism. Economic development of the NOI and religious prophecy often took precedence over more overtly political and ideological concerns with Muhammad. He did not like communism because it was atheistic and was not convinced that socialism was a viable alternative to capitalism. In addition, Muhammad had always eschewed political protest that was not directly connected to the Nation of Islam and officially forbid his followers to join or participate in the civil rights movement, which he viewed as futile and misguided.

Malcolm addressing crowd in Harlem.

(AP/Wide World)

227

Although Malcolm X and the Messenger did not yet conflict on these and other issues and activities in the NOI, the rapidly growing national and international success of the newspaper *Muhammad Speaks,* which Malcolm had founded a mere three years before, began to reveal a barely discernible tension between Malcolm's public pronouncements (all officially sanctioned by Muhammad) and his private preoccupations. Malcolm's newspaper articles and public speeches revealed an intense interest in and support for the revolutionary nationalist and socialist movements in Cuba, Algeria, the Congo, Ghana, and many other places in Africa, Asia, and Latin America. As these national liberation movements intensified and previously obscure names such as Fidel Castro, Che Guevara, Patrice Lumumba, Frantz Fanon, and Abdul Babu began surfacing as internationally renowed leaders of social revolution in oppressive, colonized societies that were usually supported tacitly or openly by the United States government and corporations, nationalist, leftist, and even conventionally liberal organizations. In America these same agencies were being compelled to choose sides for or against capitalism, colonialism, and imperialism.

Malcolm found himself torn between his duty to the comparatively more conservative stance of the NOI (as defined by Muhammad's more politically quiescent strategy and program in the United States) and the intellectual, pragmatic, and visceral need that Malcolm and many of his friends, peers, colleagues, and acolytes felt to openly support the revolutionary positions being put forward by these movements and their leaders.

This difference in approach to these questions initially came to a head when Fidel Castro and his triumphant group of Cuban revolutionaries came to New York in September 1960 to have his new government formally recognized and inducted into the United Nations. The successful eight-year-long revolutionary struggle that culminated in the overthrow of the corrupt American-backed regime of dictator Fulgencio Batista on January 1, 1959, had electrified the Third World and made international heroes of Fidel Castro and Che Guevara, two of the most charismatic and dynamic political figures in the world.

What incensed the U.S. government and the CIA, however, was that in the months following the seizure of state power, Castro nationalized all Cuban industries, thereby confiscating and taking full economic and political control of foreign-owned companies (90 percent of which were previously owned by American corporations). He also took complete control of the island nation's many gambling casinos and other highly lucrative and illegal enterprises from the American Mafia. Castro and his new political apparatus also initiated massive changes and reforms in the country's infrastructure and created socialist models of development in the nation's schools, industries, medical and health facilities, legal system, and cultural institutions. By declaring in early 1960 that he was a Marxist and believed firmly in the ideology of communism, Castro, along with Guevara and their lieutenants and supporters both within Cuba and the United States became a major target of the CIA, the State Department, and the Mafia—who secretly collaborated with each other on plots to assassinate Castro and Guevara, among others, and to lead a right-wing counter-revolution to overthrow the new regime. The CIA was also authorized and determined to assist in the overthrow or assassination of other radical Third World leaders in Africa (the Congolese leader and freely-elected president Patrice Lumumba was a major target), Asia, and Latin America.

It was in this highly contentious and lethal atmosphere that Castro and his entourage arrived in New York. In August 1960, John Roselli, a leading Mafia figure with major gambling interests in Las Vegas and Cuba, met with top CIA operative Robert A. Maheu (who was also the chief business manager for the extremely eccentric billionaire Howard Hughes). Maheu asked Roselli if he would be interested in participating in a plot to recruit exiled, right-wing Cubans in Florida to assassinate Castro. However, on September 4 the Russian KGB based in Cuba intercepted a cable to the CIA base there exposing the plot, which was then widely disseminated to other governments in Latin America who were fighting for independence and were experiencing similar disruptions. Of course, when confronted with the evidence of a CIA-Mafia plot against Castro, the State Department, through its press spokesman denied any involvement and denounced the evidence as a forgery. Nevertheless, Roselli and Maheu met again on September 14, just days before Castro's trip to New York, to discuss an assassination of Castro before he arrived at induction ceremonies at the United Nations.

Other petty ploys meant to embarrass Castro were implemented. A plane carrying Major Juan Almeida, the Afro-Cuban whom Castro had appointed head of the Cuban army, was seized at the New York Airport at Idlewild on the grounds that it belonged to the Batista regime (Castro's government had not yet been recognized by the United States). Astonishingly, the plane was handed over to temporary receivership. When Castro arrived in New York, he was ordered to make a cash deposit of $10,000 to the Shelburne Hotel, where he planned to stay during his visit. The hotel owner made the ridiculous claim that the payment was a guaranty against damage, but delegates from other nations had not been required to make such deposits. Castro angrily refused to pay and threatened to sleep on the street if necessary.

Embarrassed by what he viewed as America's shoddy and intolerable treatment of the Cuban president, Love B. Woods, the African American owner of the Theresa Hotel in Harlem, offered rooms to Castro and his entourage for $21 a day for forty rooms. Castro immediately accepted the offer. Woods, who was a good friend of Malcolm's, was thrilled to have the Cuban revolutionary staying at his hotel, and so was most of Harlem, who saw the U.S. government's contemptuous treatment of Castro and the other Cubans as typical of white American incivility and arrogance. When the Cubans arrived they were greeted by a crowd of three hundred Harlemites. Most of these Harlemites were members of the recently formed Fair Play for Cuba Committee (FPCC); others were part of a coalition protesting America's refusal to grant a visa to Patrice Lumumba of the Congo.

Almeida and Cuban army captain Nunez Jimenez took a walk through Harlem on their first night at the Theresa Hotel and attracted a crowd of more than a thousand people. Almeida was already well known among Harlem's black and Latino residents. He had hosted an American delegation to Cuba in July 1960, which included Robert F. Williams, an NAACP official and, in the eyes of the staid organization, a renegade radical. Williams was also publisher of *The Crusader*, a small radical newspaper aimed at African American readers. On September 20, Castro extended an invitation to Williams and other NAACP officials for a private conference. Later that morning, Castro went to the United Nations, where Cuba and thirteen newly independent African nations were officially admitted to the world body of the United Nations.

African leaders had already come to the realization that despite their growing presence in the United Nations, their voices did not carry beyond the borders of New York City. For the most part, the American media ignored their activities, so they turned to African American leaders in Harlem for support. Four African American men, Manhattan Borough President Hulan Jack, James Lawson, the Reverend Adam Clayton Powell Jr., and Malcolm X, soon found themselves inundated with invitations to attend official embassy functions sponsored by the Africans.

One of the first manifestations of the new relationship was the April 16, 1960, anti-apartheid rally held in front of the Theresa Hotel. The keynote speaker at the rally was Kenneth Kaunda, president of the Zambian African National Congress of what was then Northern Rhodesia. Speakers representing Liberia, Kenya, and the United Arab Republic also addressed the gathering. Kaunda warned that "the Union of South Africa will ultimately fail" because of its vicious and abhorrent racial policies. "Freedom for Africa!" Kaunda shouted to the Harlemites at the end of his speech. The assembled African Americans responded with shouts of "Now, Now, Now!"

On September 26, 1960, the CIA's headquarters in Langley, Virginia, was notified that Malcolm X, in his capacity as a member of the Welcoming Committee of the Twenty-eighth Precinct Community Council, was to sponsor "a large reception for Castro" on October 2. A high-level government official, the CIA memo said, "had indicated a desire to discourage or prevent if at all possible such a reception from taking place as outlined above." However, the attempt to sabotage the meeting failed, and the

October 2 reception at the Theresa Hotel proceeded smoothly. Castro was so impressed by Malcolm X that he asked to meet with him on September 20. At half past midnight, to the chagrin of the State Department and the CIA, Malcolm and several other members of the NOI went to Castro's hotel room to discuss revolution with Almeida and the Cuban leader. The private meeting lasted for thirty minutes.

After Malcolm emerged from the meeting, bleary-eyed reporters asked him what memorable comments Castro had made. "Premier Castro told me," Malcolm said, smiling broadly, "that he felt at home for the first time since his arrival in this country last Sunday afternoon." A reporter then asked Malcolm X what he thought of Castro personally. Malcolm responded, "Any man who represents such a small country but who would stand up and challenge a country as large as the United States on behalf of his people must be sincere." Castro was well aware of the NOI's activities, Malcolm added, and had told him that Elijah Muhammad had quite a following in Central and South America. Another reporter asked if the meeting had been prearranged. "No," Malcolm replied. "The Nation of Islam is not in alliance with Mr. Castro or with any foreign powers on earth. The Nation of Islam is allied with Allah, in whom we believe. Hence, we cannot be affiliated with communism since it's atheistic."

On September 21, FBI agents visited Malcolm X at the Harlem temple to discuss what he and Castro had really talked about, but as usual, they learned nothing. Malcolm had long ago learned how to deal with the intrusive questions of J. Edgar Hoover's agents and, unlike many others, was never fearful of, or intimidated by them. On that same day, a CIA agent noted that "it is felt the information indicating a direct connection between the Moslem Cult of Islam and Castro is of particular interest."

The extemporaneous conference with Castro was a highlight in a year of many such triumphs in making alliances with African and Asian leaders:

- Malcolm and John Ali led a contingent of NOI members to New York's Idlewild Airport to greet Gamal Abdel Nasser, President of the United Arab Republic, on September 23.

- A week later on September 30, John Ali and Malcolm again met with ZANU (Zimbabwe African National Union) leader Kenneth Kaunda.

- John Ali and Malcolm also welcomed Sekou Toure of Guinea upon his arrival in New York.

In October, Ghanaian President Kwame Nkrumah returned to Harlem. After meeting with Nasser, Nehru of India, and Sukarno of Indonesia during the morning session of the U.N. Assembly on October 5, Nkrumah addressed a crowd of 1,000 gathered in front of the Theresa Hotel. At the rally, President Nkrumah, a leading force in Pan-Africanism worldwide, made a dramatic announcement that proved to have a profound impact upon Malcolm, who also addressed the rally. "The 20 million Americans of African ancestry," Nkrumah told the gathering, "constitute the strongest link between the people of North America and the people of Africa." "I am informed," he added to the delight of the African Americans in the crowd, "that black American leaders are beginning to grasp the tremendous advantage that is conferred on the United States by their presence in this country." The Ghanaian president was accompanied by his longtime friend (and future secretary-general of the United Nations) Alex Quaison-Sackey, whom he personally introduced to Malcolm. Like Nkrumah, Quaison-Sackey soon developed a close friendship with Malcolm.

Although both Malcolm X and Hulan Jack, the Manhattan borough president, denounced America's shamefully poor treatment of Africans living in the United States, no speech that day was more eloquent and forceful than of Harlem congressman Adam Clayton Powell Jr., who lambasted the State Department for pretending that Africans were not a force to be reckoned with in the U.N. General Assembly. "I attended four receptions given by African delegations last week," Powell said, "and the only representative of the American government there was myself." He warned that the United States would "be in trouble" if it continued this policy. "America without Africa is going to be a second-class power," he stated. Powell also complained bitterly about the blatant discrimination Africans were encountering, particularly in Washington, from hotels, restaurants, and real estate agents.

On the domestic front, the FBI discovered from their wiretap on Elijah Muhammad's phone that the Messenger was furious about Malcolm's meeting with Castro on September 20. Muhammad was afraid the U.S. government would try to link the NOI with communism and use this as an excuse to attack and decimate the sect as it had done in 1942 when Muhammad was arrested and put in prison for four years for counseling young men to evade the draft in World War II.

On October 31, 1960, the Internal Revenue Service's (IRS) intelligence division in Chicago notified the FBI that it might be possible to indict Muhammad for "alleged evasion of income taxes" for the years 1954–58. However, the counterintelligence proposal was abandoned after Chauncey Eskridge, a prominent black civil rights activist and Muhammad's attorney(who also served as legal counsel to Dr. Martin Luther King Jr.), produced records revealing that Muhammad had a net loss on businesses in his name for those years.

The FBI also leaked a scandalous story about the Nation of Islam that was riddled with lies and misinformation by using friendly sources at the New York *Journal American* (a paper owned by multimillionaire publisher William Randolph Hearst Jr., who was a close friend and confidant of FBI Director J. Edgar Hoover). The story, which ran on September 25, 1960, claimed that "Malcolm X and his Chicago headquarters" had been linked by the intelligence community to "international intrigue" with Nasser, Castro, and Premier Nikita Khrushchev of the Soviet Union in a "plot to win the minds of America's 20 million Negroes to use them in winning the allegiance of the newly independent dark-skinned nations in Africa." Three days later, Malcolm X resigned from the Welcoming Committee of the Twenty-eighth Precinct Community Council, to which he had been appointed for helping to disperse the crowds during the Johnson Hinton incident. In his letter to *Amsterdam News* publisher and editor, chairman of the council, Malcolm said he was resigning because the council, the police department, and the Hearst-owned newspaper had "failed to refute what you know are lies in the daily press."

On October 22, another government-planted report critical of Malcolm X's meeting with Castro, Nasser, and other prominent African Muslims surfaced in the *Amsterdam News*. According to the story, "two top representatives of the World Federation of Islamic Missions" criticized the Black Muslims for distorting Islam. The report identified the representatives as Maulana Muhammad and Yousse Shawarbi of Cairo, who served in New York as a member of the Supreme Council of Islamic Affairs. The story, to the deep embarrassment of the black newspaper, was based on deliberate misinformation. Shawarbi, who served as an advisor to the Yemen delegation to the United Nations, had appeared with Malcolm X on the NOI's national radio program, which was carried and aired in over eighty cities nationwide by the summer of 1960. Although the show was called *Mr. Muhammad Speaks*, the person usually doing the speaking was Malcolm X.

On November 5, Dr. Shawarbi accompanied Malcolm X to New York's Rockland Palace, where the Harlem temple was sponsoring an Afro-Asian bazaar. The bazaar drew 2,500 people, many of them African, Asian, and East Indian U.N. officials. "I have never denounced anyone," Dr. Shawarbi told the audience. "We are Muslims, and Muslims do not denounce each other. And I thank Allah that once a week the teaching of our faith can be heard on the air in this area."

As Malcolm X had predicted and foreseen, white American racism was resulting in the forging of political bonds between Africans and African Americans due to the atrocious treatment meted out to Africans living in the United States. Incidents such as the vandalization of Alex Quaison-Sackey's home in New Rochelle, New York was only strengthening the determination of the head of the Ghanaian delegation to the United Nations to join with African American leaders such as Malcolm and Powell in resisting and opposing such criminal behavior. That Quaison-Sackey had also received hate mail addressed to his home on April 4, 1960, confirmed his and many other Africans' conviction that the movement for civil and human rights was a key force in the development of unity between Africa and its diaspora. The letter that Quaison-Sackey received denounced his efforts to have U.N. sanctions imposed against South Africa for its apartheid policies. The racist who sent the letter identified himself as "a white American for a white South Africa" and added, "Negroes are not wanted in the United States."

These problems would persist throughout the sixties, and Malcolm would continue to be one of the most important forces in demanding that the United States do something concrete about it. But he knew that nothing substantial would be done until white America and its "criminal government," as Malcolm put it so many times, did something about the age-old problem of racial apartheid in this country. The struggle was intensifying and would only get much more intense and dangerous as the sixties wore on.

Despite a few setbacks, generated mostly by the media and government snooping, 1960 was productive both politically and personally for Malcolm. His newspaper, *Muhammad Speaks*, was doing very well after a rocky start in 1957. Syndicated black columnist Louis Lomax still helped Malcolm gather news and do layouts. C. Eric Lincoln, a young black scholar from the University of Pennsylvania who was writing his Ph.D. dissertation on the Nation of Islam, also did some work at the paper. Impressed by the high quality of the newspaper, Muhammad was receptive to Malcolm's suggestion that the Messenger offer Lomax and a young (and soon to be world-famous) author named James Baldwin (who was also a good friend of Malcolm's) high salaries as editors of *Muhammad Speaks*. However, both men declined.

C. Eric Lincoln *went on to publish the first major mainstream book on the NOI called* The Black Muslims in America *in 1961. Louis Lomax's book on the NOI,* When the Word Is Given, *was published in 1963. James Baldwin spent hours interviewing the Messenger in his home in Chicago and included a long section on Elijah Muhammad and the NOI in his best-selling book* The Fire Next Time, *which was published to critical and commercial acclaim in 1963.*

The FBI had learned through its extensive network of telephone wiretaps and from their own informants in the NOI that dissension was beginning to brew within the hierarchy of the NOI, especially after Elijah Muhammad's twenty-seven-year-old first son and heir-apparent Wallace had been indicted by a federal grand jury for draft evasion back in August 1957. The FBI had been trying to "neutralize" Wallace because it believed that he would inherit and lead the NOI upon the death of his father Elijah. Members of the organization had been told that Wallace (named in honor of Wallace D. Fard, the sect's actual founder) would be "the one."

The handsome, bright, talented, and articulate Boston minister known as Louis X (later Farrakhan) was recruited by Malcolm to join the NOI in 1955 and was widely considered to be his most outstanding disciple. (Malcolm even had some complimentary things to say about Louis in his autobiography, which was, of course, written before Malcolm was aware of the role that his disciple would eventually play in his demise.) A highly accomplished concert violinist and college graduate, Louis X was once denied an opportunity to play with a symphony orchestra in the United States because of the color of his skin. Louis was also known as an excellent singer and songwriter; he even played the ukulele. In 1960, he wrote the words and music for a song that he independently produced for the Nation of Islam. Entitled "The White Man's Heaven Is the Black Man's Hell," it was an immediate underground hit in black communities throughout the country. Sold at NOI events and carried by a number of black record stores across the United States, the record's irresistible beat and Louis's melodious voice might have easily made it a Top 100 hit had it not been for its scathing lyrics denouncing the racism of the white man and praising the eventual end of white domination on earth. Within six months, the NOI had sold over 10,000 copies of the song.

The record confirmed what many others had been telling Louis X for years: If he abandoned the NOI, he could become as big a star as Sam Cooke or Nat King Cole. But Louis was dedicated to the NOI. While still enjoying the success of his first record, he wrote and produced a play with a Muslim theme. Entitled Orgena ("a Negro" spelled backwards), Louis X's play, which dealt with God's final judgment of white people and usually featured its author in the starring role, drew large crowds of African Americans.

Speculation was rife about who would inherit the NOI because Elijah Muhammad, who had experienced severe asthma attacks off and on since childhood, was seriously ill by 1958. His recurrent bronchial disorder had become so severe that he spent hours a day hooked up to an oxygen tank. This fact, and Wallace's incarceration, precipitated a major crisis in the organization just as it was taking off as a leading force in the African American movement of the time.

The FBI's Philadelphia office began to detect hints of trouble concerning Muhammad's possible successor as early as 1958, after it learned of comments made by none other than the twenty-five-year-old Boston minister Louis X (who became Louis Farrakhan in August of that year). At the offices of the *Pittsburgh Courier*, an African American newspaper giving extensive coverage to Muslim events, one of the editors asked, "When is Malcolm X taking over for the old man?" The question apparently caught Louis X off guard, and he launched into a tirade against the newspaper's coverage. The paper, Louis said, reported on Malcolm's speeches and public appearances, but never gave "the Honorable Elijah Muhammad top billing." If Malcolm X were "weak," Louis told the editor, he might "try to take control" of the NOI, but he said he doubted if the idea had entered Malcolm's mind.

The truth was, that no other member of the Nation of Islam had enjoyed the meteoric rise in the NOI that Malcolm had, and as Louis X's touchy answer to the *Pittsburgh Courier* editor's question suggested, many ministers were becoming jealous of Malcolm's growing influence and popularity. Some even accused him of nepotism and cronyism, and as some of Malcolm's appointments indicated, there appeared to be some truth to this charge. Malcolm had awarded ministerial positions to Leroy and Osborne Thaxton, two men he had converted in prison, and he even offered Shorty, also a Malcolm convert, an opportunity to join the NOI, which was nixed by Elijah Muhammad because of a personality conflict between the Messenger and Shorty. Malcolm also appointed his brothers Philbert, Wilfred, and Reginald (who had been reinstated) to ministerships.

Despite the backstage bickering, backbiting, and envy, however, Malcolm steadfastly maintained to everyone in the NOI that he was not interested in "taking over" for the Messenger. In an effort to dispel the rumors about his eventual ascendancy, Malcolm told a crowd of thousands at the Savior's Day Convention on February 26, 1959, "If anything should happen to the Messenger, the program would be stopped because Allah appointed the Honorable Elijah Muhammad only to do the job he is doing."

But as 1960 ended, a number of complex new challenges were surfacing within the NOI that, in addition to the ongoing realities outside, would sorely test its will and ability to survive in spite of all of its apparent success. As the new year emerged, however, Malcolm remained cautious but optimistic about the future. And on the home front, Betty gave birth on December 25, 1960 to her and Malcolm's second child, a girl named Qubilah.

Chapter 17

Civil Rights vs. Human Rights

In 1961, Malcolm X was quickly becoming one of the country's most sought-after speakers, and his message was now overtly challenging the mainstream civil rights philosophy of Dr. King and others. Malcolm began to emphasize the necessity of the movement to address the liberation of African Americans in terms of *human rights*, instead of always focusing or relying on the constitutional legalities and protections of conventional political discourse. In making this subtle but significant shift in the focus of his public statements, Malcolm hoped to link this concern with the Messenger's emphasis on building and sustaining independent social, religious, and economic institutions that were owned and controlled by African Americans. This two-pronged strategy sought to drive an ideological, social, and cultural wedge between those bourgeois African Americans who upheld the notion of integration and assimilation as a method of acquiring freedom, justice, and equality in the United States in the areas of employment, wages, housing, health care, and education and an emerging, more militant generation of workers, students, and social activists who insisted on a more autonomous course for pursuing these goals. Malcolm and Muhammad, as well as the rest of the NOI, also wanted to make a critical analysis and repudiation of the ways in which Christianity in the black community (especially in the

South, which was the regional base of the civil rights struggle) worked to advance and support the bourgeois vision over and against the nationalist and Islamic position of separation and independence.

One of the most effective ways that the NOI was making a major impact on the views of many African Americans, especially in large urban areas, was in its many social and educational rehabilitation programs to morally reform and to physically and psychologically treat ex-convicts and drug addicts. Malcolm had also called for an expansion of the organization's numerous literacy programs. By 1961, the success rate of the NOI in these areas was so impressive that even *The New York Times* began praising its efforts. The newspaper even carried a story about how some mainstream social agencies had asked representatives of the Muslim programs for clinical suggestions and assistance. Elijah Muhammad finally began to allow curious whites to attend the previously all-black public rallies that the NOI had become famous for. The Messenger reasoned that if the general population could hear the truth about what black people needed and wanted, it would be hopefully less inclined to support and finance the civil rights movement, which only helped blacks to remain dependent on the white man and his largesse.

Malcolm's popularity as a speaker surged. He began debating a very wide range of white and black intellectuals, scholars, activists, leaders, theologians, and pundits on television and radio. He was also much more frequently interviewed in mainstream American magazines and newspapers. In addition, Malcolm's popularity as a speaker grew rapidly among college students. By 1963, he would be identified by *The New York Times* as the second most requested speaker on the national college circuit in the country after Arizona Senator Barry Goldwater, the Republican candidate for President in 1964.

On May 24, 1961, Malcolm was invited to speak at a program hosted by the Harvard Law School Forum entitled "The American Negro: Problems and Solutions." Before an audience of nearly

2,000 people, Malcolm insisted that the NOI was not a political organization but a religious one, and after talking about the status of Elijah Muhammad as a prophet of Allah, once again pressed for the separation of the races and an independent nation with land provided to African Americans as reparations for slavery and subsequent exploitation. He also stated that the United States government should assist this new country for a period of fifty years until it could become self-sufficient. This was the only way, Malcolm insisted, that the ongoing racial crisis in America could be solved.

Elijah Muhammad introducing Malcolm, 1961.

(AP/Wide World)

Malcolm also pushed the Messenger's claim that Allah planned to destroy all opposition to Muhammad through a War of Armageddon if whites persisted in their evil ways against black people. It was a curiously conservative, passive, and intellectually tepid performance by Malcolm, but the Messenger had upbraided him on a number of recent occasions for being too outspoken in a secular manner. Although Malcolm humbly submitted to the will of Muhammad and the two men displayed a public front of unanimity, a noticeable tension was developing between Malcolm and the Messenger on what goals, strategies, and tactics should be used to advance the NOI and the cause of Islam.

The Civil Rights Movement Goes On the Offensive

As Muhammad retreated to a more conspicuously religious and racial conservatism and Malcolm found himself trapped between his desire to be more publicly active and outspoken in political matters and his loyalty to following the more insular dictates of his older mentor and sponsor, the civil rights movement began pursuing its aims and objectives more forcefully. Mass demonstrations, boycotts, sit-ins, marches, and what civil rights activists called "direct action campaigns" began sweeping the country. As these efforts rapidly accelerated, the NOI and Malcolm suddenly found themselves in the unenviable position of trailing behind the masses. Though Malcolm never openly questioned the Messenger's position on these matters, he did begin to wonder when he would be allowed to broaden his scope.

Malcolm was paying very close attention to the impact of Ella Baker and an organization called "Snick" (or SNCC, Student Nonviolent Coordinating Committee), a dynamic group whose members included such luminaries of both the civil rights and black power movements as Bob Moses, Julian Bond, John Lewis, James Forman, Ruby Doris Robinson, Diane Nash, Ivanhoe Donaldson, Joyce Ladner, Stokely Carmichael, H. "Rap" Brown, Fannie Lou Hamer, and many others. But under Ella Baker's leadership and guidance, SNCC broke away from the SCLC (Southern Christian Leadership Conference). SNCC organized the first black college student-led sit-ins in the South on February 1, 1960, which spread like a prairie fire throughout the country and were quickly becoming a major recruiting force and influence on a group that Malcolm X and the NOI especially coveted: young black college and high school students.

As a woman in the SCLC, Baker was contending with an organization of all black male ministers, the great majority of whom shared the predominant sexist view of virtually all American churches, black and white, that God meant women to be subordinate (a belief that was also shared by the Nation of Islam). Additionally, she was disappointed that Dr. King and the leaders of the SCLC did not share her belief that the southern civil rights movement could be made a "mass force" emerging as a counterbalance (and rival) to the NAACP.

However, with the students of SNCC, Baker had finally found a group that valued her wisdom and experience. As the young people banded together to form SNCC, Baker urged them not to limit their sights. She told them they must look beyond lunch counter sit-ins, focus on "more than a coke and a hamburger," and work to change the social structure of the entire country. At the founding Raleigh, North Carolina Conference in April 1960 and in the years following, "She kept daring us to go further," said now Congressman John Lewis, who would later become SNCC chairman. Lewis said he considered Baker "our personal Gandhi, the spiritual mother, I guess I would call her, of SNCC." Baker's ideas on participatory democracy and her unshakeable belief that people must fight for their own freedom and not rely on leaders to do it for them were adopted by SNCC as their own. As the highly idealistic and creative organization, which welcomed both black and white women and men to its ranks as both leaders and participants, began to develop an office, staff, and political identity, Baker continued to serve as its guiding force. Her ideological and organizational model of mass action and leadership was a real and important challenge to the entire movement.

As these events were happening around Malcolm in 1961, he began to feel increasingly restless about the public role he felt the NOI should have been playing in the startling developments taking place within the civil rights movement. On May 4, 1961, an integrated group of seven black men, three white men, and three white women known collectively as "the Freedom Riders" boarded two Greyhound and Trailways buses and left Washington D.C. at the start of what was supposed to be a two-week trip to test their right to mix black and white people in bus stations throughout the South. They encountered few major problems until they reached Alabama. In the town of Anniston, a mob of racist whites wielding clubs, tire irons, baseball bats, chains, and bricks surrounded one of the buses when it pulled into the terminal. They beat savagely at the windows with pipes and clubs and slashed the tires as the bus pulled away. A few miles outside town, the tires went completely flat. The pursuing mob caught up with the bus and set it on fire, setting off a massive wave of smoke inside the bus. As the choking Freedom Riders stumbled off the bus just before the fuel tank exploded, they were greeted with hundreds of blows from bats, clubs, bricks, fists, and chains.

Meanwhile, the second bus managed to escape and head for Birmingham, a tough iron and steel center notorious for its bigotry and harrowing racial violence. CBS Correspondent Howard K. Smith was at the terminal when the bus arrived. Some thirty to forty men were milling around outside the station. They were members of the KKK, a local reporter told Smith. The men dragged the Freedom Riders off the bus, pushed them into a nearby alley, and clubbed them into a bloody pulp with lead pipes, brass knuckles, keyrings, fists, and feet. One of the passengers (a white male) was paralyzed for life by the beating. Another black man fell at Smith's feet, his face a bloody, unrecognizable mess. "They ... just about slaughtered those kids," Smith said later. After a while, one of the thugs glanced at his watch, and the mob dispersed. Only then did Eugene "Bull" Connor's racist police officers, whose station house was just three blocks away, arrive at the terminal (most of the local police, including Connor, belonged to the Klan). Later Smith saw some members of the gang standing in front of Connor's office laughing and talking. Badly shaken, Smith, who had covered Nazi Germany before World War II, felt he had witnessed another *Kristallnacht* (a term for the two-day period in November 1938 when angry mobs attacked Jews in Germany and Austria and destroyed their homes and businesses). He told CBS radio listeners that the mob reminded him of the worst Gestapo thugs.

As a result of this and many other bloody mob scenes that followed (hundreds of other Freedom Riders immediately took up the struggle where others left off), national and international attention became focused on the South's brutal racial injustice and threw the newly elected Kennedy administration into confusion. As many of the nation's citizens looked on in horror (or delight), Malcolm cooly surveyed and monitored what was taking place as the year ended. Inside, however, he was seething. Despite the numerous successes of the NOI and his higher profile as a national representative of the Messenger, Malcolm was deeply dissatisfied. He knew and understood that the NOI could not sit back and not take a proactive stance on the civil rights movement while many African Americans, as well as some whites, were putting their lives on the line for the struggle.

There was grumbling both within the NOI and in the general African American population that "the Muslims talk a good game but rarely do anything unless it affects Muslims." Although Malcolm thought it was patently absurd to act as the Freedom Riders did by allowing themselves to be violently attacked without acting in self-defense, he recognized what incidents like these indicated. If the cause of Islam was to grow and prosper in the United States, Malcolm privately confided to some friends and associates, it would have to become more directly involved in the mass protests, demonstrations, public resistance activities, and grassroots organizing that the civil rights movement was exhibiting throughout the South, and increasingly in the North as well. Of course, its methods and response would have to be markedly different from "turning the other cheek" or tolerating the brutality of their enemies, but ultimately it would not be enough to merely call on Allah and the "Honorable Elijah Muhammad" to confront and attack problems that only mortal men could resolve.

Changes in the NOI

Malcolm's analysis of the new challenges to himself, Muhammad, and the NOI was slowly but surely leading him to a confrontation with the small, fragile man who, despite ever-worsening health problems, still maintained control of the fortunes of his organization and nearly all the members within it. However, even within the NOI, other changes were beginning to take place regardless of whether the Messenger wanted them. And Malcolm would either be participating in or endorsing those changes.

By the end of 1961, the NOI was flourishing, with national membership at an all-time high. Hundreds of millions of dollars were flowing into the coffers of the various temples, which were now located in nearly every state of the country. Elijah Muhammad had finally been allowed to travel throughout the Muslim world in Africa, Asia, and South America and upon his return directed that the temples formally change their names to mosques in accordance with Islamic law and custom. There was also a sharp climb in the number of Muslim-owned and operated small businesses. The various stores, restaurants, retail clothing outlets, supermarkets, farms, and other businesses were all designed to demonstrate to African Americans what they could do and accomplish for themselves if they would unify and trade with each other, hire each other for employment, and keep capital flowing in black communities, just as other national minorities did. Recordings of Mr. Muhammad's speeches were now regularly being broadcast across America over small radio stations. In Detroit and Chicago, school-age Muslim children attended the NOI's two Universities of Islam through high school in Chicago and through junior high in Detroit. Starting from kindergarten, they learned black history, and from the third grade on they studied Arabic.

Malcolm was instrumental in most of these changes and was happy and honored to have also played a role in Muhammad's eight children all becoming deeply involved in key positions within the NOI. Because Malcolm felt that the Messenger's six sons and two daughters should not have to continue working for white employers, he initiated a special fund-raising drive within the mosques to enable those of Muhammad's children working outside the NOI to be employed instead by the organization. Muhammad agreed, the fund drive proved successful, and his children all gradually did begin working for the NOI. Herbert

Muhammad became publisher of Malcolm's newspaper *Muhammad Speaks,* and the others worked in various business enterprises within the NOI, except for Wallace and Akbar Muhammad. Wallace, who had completed his prison sentence for refusing the draft, was initially made minister of the Philadelphia mosque until he was finally suspended from the NOI and subsequently broke ranks with his father in 1963. Akbar Muhammad, who was a student at the University of Cairo in Egypt, also broke with his father and adopted orthodox Islam over his father's ersatz and idiosyncratic version.

Despite the general good fortune that the NOI had experienced over the past decade since Malcolm's involvement, there were increasing signs during 1962 and 1963 that the organization, and particularly Elijah Muhammad, was headed for major trouble as a result of a rapid series of both external and internal problems that began to seriously undermine and sabotage the organization's efforts. Malcolm himself began to notice that conflicts associated with the jealousy and envy of other ministers toward Malcolm were taking their toll. These self-inflicted wounds, as well as problems imposed from the outside world, were gleefully noted and recorded by the FBI and CIA, who accelerated their undercover surveillance and sabotage of the NOI's programs in the United States and abroad. This stepped-up campaign of harassment, infiltration, and "dirty tricks" against the NOI, Malcolm, and Muhammad was especially aimed at driving wedges between the Messenger, his family, his top lieutenants and advisors in Chicago, other jealous ministers throughout the country, and Malcolm X, and also making it extremely difficult for targeted mosques in major cities to function effectively. Toward these twin objectives, local police in these cities began to collaborate with the FBI to use violence against the leadership and membership of these mosques.

While all this was taking place, government agencies and bickering factions within the NOI began to take advantage of Muhammad's increasingly failing health, which was now serious enough to warrant around-the-clock medical attention. After a series of long speeches given at a number of huge rallies that NOI ministers had organized across the country, the Messenger badly aggravated his long-time bronchial asthmatic condition. At sixty-two, the once spry and energetic Muhammad was now so ill at times that he was bedridden for extended periods. Even during simple personal conversation he would suddenly start coughing so often and violently that it racked his small body. He soon had to cancel several appearances at big city rallies, and Malcolm increasingly assumed more of these obligations. People in Muhammad's family, the hierarchy of the NOI, its membership, and Malcolm all began agonizing over the Messenger's weakening condition.

Doctors were so concerned that they recommended Muhammad move permanently to a much drier climate. The NOI purchased a home for him in Phoenix, Arizona. In Phoenix, Malcolm began to notice the ever-increasing number of intelligence and security agents who were regularly monitoring and tracking the Messenger's and his every move. After a number of months, it was reported that the Arizona climate did vastly improve the Messenger's health and relieve much of the suffering. From 1962 on, Muhammad spent most of every year in Arizona.

Muhammad finally decided, at his doctor's recommendation, that he could no longer take on the massive administrative or decision-making duties that he had carried before, even with all his aides. Because he could no longer allocate as much time or energy to helping Malcolm decide which of the many public speaking, radio, press, and television requests Malcolm should accept nor could he help Malcolm with organizational matters that Malcolm routinely brought to his attention for advice and consultation, the Messenger decreed that Malcolm should assume these duties and make the final decisions in his absence. Malcolm felt touched and deeply moved at the level of trust the Messenger displayed in Malcolm's judgment as a leader. Muhammad told Malcolm that he should do whatever he thought was wise or in the best interests of the NOI. "Brother Malcolm, I want you to become well-known," Muhammad told him one day. "Because if you are well-known, it will make *me* better known. But, Brother Malcolm," he added, "there is something you need to know. You will grow to be hated when you become well-known. Because usually people get jealous of public figures." As Malcolm later grimly noted,

"Nothing that Mr. Muhammad ever said to me was more prophetic."

The Ronald Stokes Episode

On April 27, 1962, an event transpired in Los Angeles that marked a very ominous and disturbing trend in relations between the NOI and the police and served as a menacing foreshadowing of the government's role in, and encouragement of racist police violence against black organizations, citizens, and activists through the rest of the decade. On that day, Ronald X Stokes, who was the twenty-eight-year-old secretary of Mosque Number Twenty-seven (which was the major NOI mosque in Los Angeles), and his wife and another Muslim went to a dry cleaners a block away from the mosque. Stokes, who worked at the cleaners, was able to get clothes cleaned at a discount and often took the suits and dresses of fellow Muslims there. As they were leaving the cleaners with their clothing, two LAPD officers approached them. One of the two white officers asked Stokes whether he had a license to sell clothing. Stokes told the officer that he was not selling the clothes nor were they stolen, but the belligerent officer refused to believe him and made several racial slurs. "We didn't do anything," Stokes said angrily. "You're only doing this to us because we're Muslims." Fearing violence, Stokes told his wife to return to the mosque, which she did. "Stop talking with your hands," one officer demanded. He then grabbed Stokes and twisted his right arm behind his back.

When Muslims inside the mosque heard gunshots, they rushed out to assist Stokes and the other man. At about the same time, an armed special police officer stationed at a nearby dance hall happened by and began firing at the Black Muslims. Although Stokes was dying from a shot in the head, police handcuffed him and hit him in the head with their nightsticks. Within ten minutes seventy-five LAPD officers arrived at the mosque. At least six more unarmed Muslims were shot, and a dozen more received less serious injuries. While they were lying on the ground, LAPD officers kicked them. One of the Muslims was kicked so hard in the mouth that his lower dental bridge was broken in half. The Black

Muslims were unarmed, but one police officer was shot in the arm by an errant shot from a police revolver, and six more were wounded. Moments later, the police entered the mosque. Once inside, they ordered Black Muslim males to line up against a wall.

Instead of just searching the men, the police deliberately ripped their suit jackets up to the neckline. The police then ripped each man's trousers from the bottom of the inner seam to the belt loop, then snatched them off. Then they openly mocked and ridiculed the men. "We shot your brother outside," one white police officer taunted while searching them. "Aren't you going to do something about it?" After the last black male was disrobed, they were ordered to march single file to waiting police cruisers outside. "Run, nigger, so I can kill you," another white officer said. Still more attempts were made to provoke the men. "I broke my stick on the head of one of them niggers," a Muslim later told reporters he heard one officer say. In response, other white officers said, "You should have had the new kind [with a metal rod centerpiece], it wouldn't have broken." As the Muslims were unloaded from one police cruiser, a white officer was overheard telling another one that he had been "looking for ten years to kill the Black Muslims." Stokes, meanwhile, was lying in his blood on the sidewalk. The other injured Muslims were not given medical attention for two days. Each of the arrested Muslims had been placed under a $10,000 bail.

This viciously racist and lawless attack was praised and supported by none other than the modern architect of the LAPD, Police Chief William H. Parker, who on May 1, 1962, told a grand jury that unless something was done about the Black Muslims, there were "bound to be more frequent" clashes between police and members of the NOI. Four days later, as 2,000 people attended Stokes's funeral, Los Angeles Mayor Sam Yorty, who had been accused many times in the past of ignoring complaints of African Americans and Mexican Americans about extensive police brutality, echoed Parker's assessment of the Nation of Islam. "I would like to have the Muslims dealt with," Mayor Yorty told reporters, "through the many fine leaders in our Negro community."

Yorty was alluding to planted and false reports that indicated national civil rights leaders had condemned the Nation of Islam instead of the LAPD for the incident. Nothing could be further from the truth. The murder of Stokes, which received international attention and condemnation, had so repulsed moderate black civil rights leaders that each had called Elijah Muhammad's home to express their outrage over obvious violations of the law and the rights of his followers, and when the media failed to retract the false reports, civil rights activists called their own press conferences to rebut them. Roy Wilkins, Executive Secretary of the NAACP, issued a news release accusing the media of deliberately misinforming the public. In a letter reprinted in *Muhammad Speaks*, Wilkins refuted the "incredible report" circulating in Los Angeles that

> ... *some sections of the Los Angeles Negro community here are remaining silent because Stokes was a leader in the Muslim movement. We urge our Los Angeles branch to press in all possible ways to bring the guilty police to account and to rally other groups to do likewise. The national office supports fully the protests which the Los Angeles branch has lodged in the brutal police killing of Ronald Stokes.*

The outpouring of support came from across the entire spectrum of the African American civil rights community. Veteran black labor leader A. Philip Randolph visited the Messenger's home in Chicago to offer his support, and letters of condolence were sent by Dr. King, James Farmer of CORE (Congress of Racial Equality), who had initiated the idea of the Freedom Riders, and many others. In a speech in Washington D.C. Farmer said, "CORE stands shoulder to shoulder with the NAACP and other human rights organizations in condemnation of such police brutality."

The enraged response of Malcolm X, among other officials and rank-and-file members of the NOI, was scathing and denounced the LAPD, the Mayor's Office, and the general atmosphere of racist terror that was sweeping the nation in 1962. In the past month alone, in retaliation for black pastors engaged in voter registration drives, five of their churches had been bombed in Alabama and Louisiana, and the home of Dr. Cuthbert O. Simpkins, a prominent black dentist who was a leading member

Dr. King's SCLC in Shreveport, Louisiana, was also bombed in an assassination attempt. It was the second time in three months that an attempt had been made on Simpkins' life.

On Muhammad's orders, Malcolm flew to Los Angeles to conduct his own investigation and deliver the eulogy for Stokes. He was so outraged about the murder and the subsequent police cover-up that many in the NOI who agreed with him thought and hoped that there would be some physical retaliation against the police. Malcolm accused the police of using "Gestapo-like tactics and false propaganda" regarding events surrounding the lethal raid. "Stokes was murdered in cold blood," Malcolm told the *Los Angeles Herald-Dispatch*.

Nine days later the LAPD and the D.A.'s office poured still more gasoline on the fire they had set when a coroner's jury ruled that Stokes's murder was a "justifiable homicide." The next day, the same jury began an investigation to determine whether the state should begin a probe of the "cult" (the NOI). By this time, many members of the NOI in Los Angeles and throughout the country were seriously considering attacking the police. After such a heinous miscarriage of justice, a number of veterans of the NOI and other supporters began to feel that if they did not defend themselves against people invading their own mosques (it was considered sacrilege for people with arms to enter a house of worship), then what good was all their militant rhetoric about self-determination and self-defense? It was time to act, many black people insisted. But they wondered what position the Messenger would take on this issue.

When Malcolm was sent to Los Angeles he was given strict orders from Muhammad to prevent any further violence. Not only did Muhammad want to prevent any unnecessary deaths of his own followers, but he was also deathly afraid that any violent response by the NOI would only give the "white devils" in authority another excuse to slaughter and create mayhem for his people. He instructed Malcolm to verbally attack the police, the Mayor, and other forces responsible in the harshest terms possible and to investigate any legal grounds for suing the city and the LAPD for their actions.

Of course, Malcolm did not need any motivation from the Messenger to do as he requested. He was as angry as he had ever been in his life, and openly wept when told that Stokes, whom he knew personally, had left a widow and two children. He privately told some members of the NOI that he would have gladly led an army of Muslims into battle against the police, but when he broached the idea to Muhammad, the Messenger was aghast. "There's already been one bloodbath. Why do we need another? I told you we would lose some good soldiers in the war with the devils," Muhammad added, "and we will lose some more. Allah is the Best Knower. He will settle the score." Malcolm's anger began to subside a bit, and after calming down, he abided by Muhammad's decision.

Malcolm X, Elijah Muhammad, and his followers led a raging international broadside of verbal attacks on the authorities that lasted for weeks. Many foreign leaders, including Nkrumah and Nasser, also joined in on the attack and issued public statements condemning the murder of Stokes and the unforgivable act of invading and desecrating a sacred house of worship. On May 12, 1962, writing in his column for the *New Crusader*, Muhammad made his harshest public criticism yet by declaring,

> *There is no justice for us black people. There is no future for us nor our children in 'civilized' America. This country's police force, using the tactics of brute savages, have behind them the government to kill us—judging from the government's silence. I have hundreds of followers now in jails, state and federal penitentiaries, for no other reason than they are Muslims. Therefore it is useless to appeal for justice to the state prosecutors of the U.S.A. since no justice will be given us from them!*

Chapter 18

Disillusionment and Renewal

As he had done in the Johnson Hinton case, Malcolm obtained photographs showing the injuries to Stokes and had them converted to large posters. The photos were also published in August in a special edition of *Muhammad Speaks*. For weeks, anyone who ventured in or near a Black Muslim mosque saw gruesome autopsy pictures. At a rally in Boston, Malcolm stood behind the enlarged photos and declared that police would really have seen some action had they harmed women during the attack. "Stokes died protecting his wife," Malcolm said. "One of the easiest and quickest ways to die," he told the audience, was to "put your hand on a Muslim woman ... This applies to all so-called Negro women. If she is black, keep your hands off her."

Malcolm also issued bitter denunciations of the behavior of the police. "The brothers' pants were cut off them by the police," Malcolm X told a crowd of 8,000 at a rally held at Detroit's Olympia Stadium. "They were jabbed in the rectums to try to get them to fight so the police would have an excuse to shoot them."

For weeks after Stokes's murder, Elijah Muhammad continued his relentless attack on the federal government, particularly the FBI and the Justice Department, to pressure them in to launching an investigation to determine whether police had violated the civil rights of his followers. On May 26, 1962, he surprised civil rights leaders by calling upon them to form a coalition with the Nation of Islam. "There could be no better step taken," the Messenger wrote in the newspaper, "to bring about an end to the free killing of our people than the uniting of the NAACP and the Muslims and all national groups that are for justice for our people. I am sure," he said, "Allah will avenge the attack and killing of my followers by the lawless, brutal police force. The murder of one of my followers will always cost the U.S.A. plenty," the Messenger declared.

On June 4, a Boeing 707 airplane carrying 130 passengers crashed on takeoff from Orly Airport in Paris to New York. Within minutes of the crash (the worst involving a single aircraft in aviation history), Atlanta's mayor was notified that 124 of the plane's passengers were members of the Atlanta Art Association. Elijah Muhammad portrayed the crash as Allah's chastisement of America for the Stokes murder. "More of this will come," the Messenger ominously intoned. Malcolm's remarks were even more caustic and bitter, saying among other things that he and the NOI had been "praying" that Allah would

> in some way let us know that he has the power to execute
> justice upon the heads of those who are responsible for the
> lynching of Ronald Stokes on April 27. And I got a wire
> from God today … somebody came and told me that he
> had really answered our prayers over in France. He
> dropped an airplane out of the sky with over 120 white
> people on it …

These incendiary remarks were subsequently published on June 6 in the *Los Angeles Herald Tribune*. The FBI later gave a tape recording of this speech to Mayor Yorty of Los Angeles. Upon receiving the tape, Mayor Yorty gave copies to the local media in Los Angeles.

A firestorm of criticism of Malcolm's remarks came from both outraged white politicians and African American civil rights leaders. On June 8, the former black General Secretary of the United Nations and Nobel Peace Prize Winner of 1950, Ralph Bunche, castigated Malcolm for his comments. In an address to delegates at an SCLC convention in Atlanta, Ralph Bunche said that Malcolm's comments "saddened and sickened me." "Ralph Bunche," Malcolm said in rebuttal, "is an international Uncle Tom. I feel sorry for him." Dr. King reiterated his sympathy and support for the Black Muslims who had been unjustly murdered and wounded. He told the convention that he, too, felt repulsed by Malcolm's comments on the crash. "I do not feel that hatred expressed toward whites by Malcolm X is shared by the vast majority of Negroes," King said. "While there is a great deal of legitimate discontent and righteous indignation, it had never developed into a large-scale hatred for whites."

Malcolm giving a speech, 1963.

(Corbis)

In the meantime, the Stokes case was costing the NOI a fortune. The law firm of Miller, Malone, and Brody charged Elijah Muhammad $60,000 to handle the lawsuit against the city of Los Angeles and its police department. Just three weeks earlier on May 17, Malcolm had joined several black leaders in Los Angeles for a rally that drew 3,000 people at the Second Baptist Church. The highlight of the rally was an announcement from the NAACP that it would support the NOI's call for an investigation into the illegal raid on a house of worship. Malcolm controlled his anger during the press conference, but later told his top aides in New York that the lack of direct action in response to the murder of Stokes was one of the several indicators why the Muslims were seen as "all talk and no action." Malcolm's speech at the rally, which received thunderous and loud applause from the crowd, evoked comments by Mayor Sam Yorty, who portrayed the speech as an incitement to violence. When a second rally was scheduled, Elijah Muhammad privately expressed fears about what Malcolm might say next. "I don't know who's to control Malcolm," he said to a member of the Los Angeles mosque. "Just tell Malcolm to cool his heels."

But despite the typical fire-and-brimstone speeches and rhetoric of Malcolm and Elijah Muhammad, the increasingly militant black movement in the United States was beginning to show signs of a growing impatience with the NOI, especially as it related to Muhammad's imposed withdrawal of the organization regarding secular political activity in America. Furthermore, the suspicious silence on the issue of self-defense by Muhammad (and his insistence that Malcolm "tone down" any references to violent retribution for racist acts) had some concerned that Muhammad and the NOI were starting to sound like the black Christian preachers whose "turn the other cheek" philosophy he and Malcolm had routinely attacked and held up to public ridicule in the past.

Muhammad's and Malcolm's bitter contentions about the tragic loss of innocent lives in the airplane catastrophe did little to assuage the agony and intense anger of the Muslims in Los Angeles as the white police officer who murdered Stokes falsely testified that the fatal wound was struck only after the unarmed Stokes moved his hands "menacingly." A jury agreed and held that his murder was a case of "justifiable homicide." This latest racial injustice was only the beginning of a concerted national assault on the NOI programs, leaders, followers, and philosophy in a disturbing number of attacks over the next two years that mirrored the spiraling rash of murders and unjust imprisonment of black and white civil rights workers throughout the country. In this atmosphere of racist harassment, assault, infiltration, and sabotage, the United States pressed its various investigations of the NOI, Malcolm X, and Muhammad via such aggressive and openly hostile governmental agencies as the House Un-American Activities Committee (HUAC), the FBI, and the Justice Department.

Another case of white policemen invading and raiding NOI mosques and killing or wounding Muslims emerged in Monroe, Louisiana. Brandishing weapons, police attempted to enter the NOI mosque. When the head minister and other unarmed members attempted to stop them, a fight ensued. Seven Black Muslims were arrested and later charged with aggravated assault. They were convicted and sentenced to six years in prison on March 5, 1961. The Louisiana Supreme Court upheld these convictions, and the U.S. Supreme Court refused to hear an appeal on the case.

The incessant legal and political battles, the FBI soon learned, were taking a tremendous toll on Muhammad's health. After the government approved HUAC's probe of the NOI, Muhammad ordered Malcolm to cancel all college campus appearances, because these public talks and debates (which Malcolm had been engaging in since late 1960) gained the NOI "no new converts," the Messenger said, despite all evidence to the contrary. Because Malcolm was committed to debates and speeches at almost forty colleges in October alone, he cited "throat problems" as the cause for his sudden cancellations. The real reason for the cancellations and other tactical retreats was not only Muhammad's ongoing health problems, but also his fear of the government's campaign to sap the strength of the organization by keeping it entangled in legal and economic problems. For the time being at least, Muhammad who was now based permanently in Phoenix, Arizona, needed to take a long rest and reevaluate what directions he wanted the NOI to take. In addition, because of the increasing jealousy and envy of Malcolm's status by other ministers in the organization and Muhammad's gradually evolving concern that Malcolm was becoming too important and too high-profile, the Messenger decided to "clip Malcolm's wings" until he could decide what public role he wanted his number one minister to play.

But while the Messenger worried about his health and internal administrative matters, another far more dangerous domestic problem was brewing in the NOI that directly involved Muhammad. A fire was burning in the NOI, the FBI had learned, much to its delight. All it had to do, the Chicago field office told J. Edgar Hoover, was fan the flames.

The Messenger vs. His Secretaries

While Malcolm was fighting the LAPD in the Stokes case, Muhammad's secretaries' long-standing private grievance against Elijah Muhammad threatened to spill over and become public. On May 10, 1962, several of them discovered the curious and coincidental nature of their relationship with the Messenger: He had had secret adulterous affairs and children with six of them. This startling bombshell was not known to anyone in the NOI, let alone the public, except for two people in the upper circle of the NOI and two of his eldest sons, and they had been sworn to secrecy. Malcolm was one of those who did not know.

The secretaries themselves were unaware that Muhammad had given each one of them the same absurd spiel that his sperm was "divine seed." Of course he had been lying to all of them about his affections and marital intentions. None of the women seemed to take the revelation harder than the Messenger's personal secretary at the Chicago headquarters, Tynetta X Nelson. On May 17, 1962, she called the Messenger at his new home in Phoenix, Arizona. As FBI agents recorded and monitored the conversation (the FBI had known about the Messenger's extramarital affairs and the personal identities of all six women through their surveillance since October, 1961), she argued with him about his promiscuity and asked him about rumors that he was involved with the other secretaries. As Muhammad proceeded to deny everything, Nelson called him a liar and told him that she "wasn't going to have it" and that she was going to leave him for someone else. The Messenger replied, "Oh, you don't have anyone else. Come on, don't talk to me like that." Ending the conversation, Nelson snapped, "But if you try a trick like that again! …" and abruptly hung up.

While this intrigue was going on, Malcolm remained a stalwart fighter for the NOI and continued to invoke the Messenger's name in glowing terms. Unaware of his beloved mentor's many violations of the sacred Islamic law against adultery and sins of the flesh, Malcolm ended 1962 the way he began it: speaking out forcefully and eloquently against all forms of racial, social, religious, and political oppression and exploitation throughout the United States and the rest of the world. As always, his speeches were credited to the "guidance, wisdom, truth, and divine leadership of Allah's Messenger and Holy Apostle, the Honorable Elijah Muhammad."

Malcolm was so busy with the daily business of running the NOI that he was not aware of the severity of the discord in Chicago. Aside from the paternity charges and rancor between Elijah Muhammad and his six mistresses, his wife Clara and son Wallace were bitterly unhappy with the Messenger. When Malcolm came to Chicago for Savior's Day in February 1963, Wallace informed Malcolm of the lurid charges that had been made by one of the six women, Ola X Hughes.

The 1963 Savior's Day convention was the shortest in NOI history, lasting only one day instead of a long weekend because NOI officials in Chicago were trying to keep the rumors about Muhammad from spreading. They reasoned that if the visitors stayed longer, they would certainly hear about the scandals, which thus far had been quarantined in Chicago. Elijah Muhammad missed the convention completely. The more than 3,000 people attending the convention were told that he was too ill to appear. Malcolm was assigned to run and coordinate the event, which only triggered more jealousy and hostility on the part of Muhammad's children (except for Wallace).

Malcolm was thankful that few Muslims outside Chicago had heard the allegations about the Messenger's extensive indiscretions. He remained in Chicago for several weeks after the convention while Muhammad recuperated from stress related to "family matters." During his stay, Malcolm discovered to his shock and severe disappointment that almost all of the allegations were true.

All the women who had worked for the messenger as personal secretaries and who had become pregnant were young, unmarried, and mesmerized by Muhammad's authority over the NOI and his supposed "divine powers." Some of these young women had joined the NOI in the vain hope of marrying Malcolm. Two of them, Evelyn and Lucille, had even dated Malcolm in the 1940s, and he and Evelyn had even once seriously considered marriage. Ironically, Malcolm had personally recommended most of the young women involved for the highly coveted secretarial jobs, and Muhammad had even offered to give Malcolm's wife, Betty, a secretarial position just days before she and Malcolm eloped.

As a former hustler in his ex-Detroit Red days, Malcolm had once taken great and perverse pride in being a procurer and manipulator of women. Now as a mature, moral, and responsible man, all he felt was intense shame and guilt for having unintentionally placed so many eager young girls and women in a situation where their innocence and ambition had been exploited. In sincerely trying to help them and by putting so much faith and trust in Elijah Muhammad, Malcolm had failed to heed a primary rule that all street hustlers learn: Never trust anyone completely. Although he had once said he never trusted anyone completely, even as a Muslim, he had to admit to himself that he had made an exception of his mentor and "surrogate father" Elijah Muhammad. "All the wind was taken out of his sails when he realized what the Messenger had done," his brother Wilfred recalled.

Malcolm quietly contacted three of the former secretaries to verify what was being said. After hearing their accounts, he wrote Muhammad a long letter about the matter and asked for an appointment to discuss it. In April 1963, Malcolm went to Phoenix to confront the Messenger. He spoke candidly with him, and Muhammad was equally blunt. Yes, Muhammad openly confessed, he had done all the things of which he stood accused.

Shaken and afraid of the consequences for the NOI if this shocking news were released to the national membership and trying desperately to find a workable compromise to maintain his relationship with Muhammad, Malcolm suggested that the scandal be broken to the faithful gradually and in biblical terms. He and Wallace, Malcolm said, had been searching the Bible and the Qur'an for authority to support the view that a leader's private failings do not diminish his public achievements. The Messenger seemed pleased with that: "You always have had such a good understanding of prophecy and of spiritual things," he said to Malcolm in a soft, slow way. "You recognized that's what all of this is—prophecy. You have the kind of understanding that only an old man has … I'm David in the Bible," the Messenger went on. "When you read about how David took another man's wife, I'm that David. You read about Noah, who got drunk—that's me. You read about Lot, who went and laid up with his own daughters. I have to fulfill all these things." The sixty-five-year-old Elijah Muhammad was clearly willing to risk everything for which he and his many followers had worked for more than three decades to continue his sexual dalliances.

Dismayed and appalled by Muhammad's matter-of-fact admission of guilt, obvious megalomania, and fatalistic indifference to critics of his brazen abuse of power, Malcolm went to Wallace to see whether they could come up with some plan to rescue the NOI from what appeared to be its almost certain demise. Already some people in Chicago were leaving the organization because of the rumors. Malcolm, however, was determined not to allow the old man's hypocrisy to destroy what he and so many others had helped build with the NOI in the past ten years. He asked Wallace what he thought could be done to "help" his father and stop his selfish and self-destructive course.

Wallace, the once heir-apparent who had been banished by his father for questioning his morality, was pessimistic about a solution. He had already tried to discuss the matter with his father, he told Malcolm, but "my father doesn't want to be helped. He doesn't want to mend his ways." Wallace also told Malcolm that

Muhammad was so angered by his son's questions that he suspended him as minister of the Philadelphia mosque. When Malcolm asked Wallace why he supposed that his father felt that way, Wallace's answer was chilling in both its simplicity and its implications: Muhammad had been worshipped as the final prophet for so long that he had convinced himself it was true.

The deadly combination of dishonesty, hypocrisy, jealousy, envy, fear, hubris, paranoia, and hatred—traits that Malcolm had always associated with "white devils" and their lethal doctrine of racism—was about to poison and infect the NOI in a particularly virulent way. The one organization Malcolm and so many other African Americans had grown to love, protect, honor, support, and nurture for more than thirty years was on the verge of unraveling before the eyes of the world. Once again, Malcolm's indomitable faith and sense of what was good, necessary, and right was about to be shaken to its core. But not before white America's racist madness, and a rapid series of traumatic, world-shattering events was to plunge the entire country into a major crisis of despair, depression, and disbelief.

The Battle of Birmingham

Since Alex Haley's articles on the NOI, Muhammad, and Malcolm X had appeared in *Reader's Digest*, dozens of mosques had opened. By January 1963, there were at least 120 mosques across the country, most of them so new that only one-third had been assigned numbers. Between Malcolm's proselytizing and media attention, Muhammad said, there was no telling how large or how fast the NOI would grow.

On February 16, 1963, Malcolm sent a telegram to Attorney General Robert Kennedy concerning a recent police raid on a mosque in Rochester, New York, which was very similar to the armed invasions of white police officers in Monroe, Louisiana, and Los Angeles, California. Once again Muslims were shot and arrested on trumped-up charges. The NOI had to spend still more money to pay lawyers for the defense of Muslims on frivolous charges. Clearly the government-backed policy of local police harassment was succeeding.

Malcolm understood very well that, even though the NOI was still growing at a rapid rate, he and the NOI would soon be consigned to political irrelevance and eventual oblivion if they did not come up with an independent, creative, and inventive way of asserting the NOI's ideas, principles, and values within the framework of militant African American political and social discourse and activity. Black people needed much more than just religious promises of divine intervention, admonitions to pray, iconic leaders, or institutions that merely focused on and ultimately included only those folks who made a personal commitment to the programs and doctrines of the Nation of Islam or any one social and spiritual entity.

As Malcolm privately battled to keep internal struggles from tearing the NOI apart, he also made increasingly profound (if subtly hamstrung) public contributions to the intellectual discourse and social analysis of African American politics and culture. As Malcolm fought valiantly to maintain a tenuous balance between the delicateness of addressing private concerns and the aggressive demands of public organizing, he began to find his own niche in the wide array of ideological, social, and spiritual challenges to both African American nationalism and "mainstream" politics-as-usual.

Elijah Muhammad had been upset about Malcolm's efforts in 1961 and 1962 to induce the NOI to abandon its policy of political noninvolvement; at the time, Muhammad not only forbade Muslims to participate in the civil rights movement in any capacity, but he also did not permit them to vote because the system was corrupt. However, the civil rights campaign in Birmingham, Alabama during the spring and summer of 1963 convinced Malcolm of the supreme urgency of direct action against racism. What occurred in Birmingham represented the ferocious battles and severe tests African Americans were going to have to undergo to gain freedom, justice, respect, and human rights in the United States. Without successfully combating racist forces directly, Malcolm insisted, neither he nor the NOI would be able to fulfill its secular or religious mission.

On April 3, 1963, Dr. King's SCLC organization and SNCC launched a concerted political campaign for voting rights, equal access to all public facilities, desegregation of schools, housing, and health care, and equal opportunity in employment that centered on the industrial city of Birmingham. Birmingham had a notorious and much-deserved reputation as one of the most racist, segregated, and violent cities in the entire country, and outside of Mississippi, the state of Alabama had one of the worst records in the South for enforcing and protecting the rights of its African American citizens. Racist violence of all kinds against blacks was so widespread and the bombing of black churches, schools, and private homes was so frequent that African Americans sarcastically and fearfully referred to the city as "Bombingham." If the joint forces of the SCLC and SNCC were to make any headway at all, they were going to have to face the organized wrath of some of the most reactionary and ruthless white politicians and police forces in the entire nation.

While the internal problems of the NOI raged on and Malcolm struggled to find some solution to them that wouldn't completely destroy the NOI, the civil rights movement in Birmingham was besieged by a paroxysm of racist violence as the KKK, armed white citizens, the police, the Mayor's office, and the cocky, bantamweight Governor of Alabama (and sworn, committed segregationist), George C. Wallace, unleashed a torrent of organized and spontaneous mob action against the nonviolent demonstrators. Led by Dr. King's SCLC, as well as the younger activists and leaders in SNCC, thousands of African Americans had taken to the streets in peaceful protest only to be viciously assaulted by clubs, sticks, rocks, police dogs, fists, and gunshots. The notorious Eugene "Bull" Connor, "Chief of Public Safety" for Birmingham and one of the most feared and despised racists in the entire South (which was saying a great deal), trained his police force to immediately attack black men, women, and children if they had the nerve to demonstrate in "his town." "No niggras *sic* are going to tell me what to do!" Bull roared, as thousands of African American demonstrators were beaten, arrested, and jailed, including many children, Dr. King, and his top aides and associates.

Meanwhile, Malcolm continued his verbal attacks on Dr. King's movement in numerous speeches throughout April and early May. His most bitter denunciations came after many small children were injured in a protest in Birmingham on May 3. The black children were injured after the adults tried to physically defend themselves against a massive assault by a white mob and the local police. "Real men don't put their children on the firing line," he said. "The lesson of Birmingham is that the Negroes have lost their fear of the white man's reprisals and will react today with violence if provoked." Malcolm also criticized the blatant hypocrisy of white liberals who advocated integration but did not practice what they preached. "The northern liberals," he said, "publicly advocate desegregation but flee to the suburbs when the Negroes approach. Washington was desegregated. What happened? The whites fled to the suburbs."

On May 13, Malcolm attended an antisegregation rally outside the Theresa Hotel. Civil rights leaders had "closed their eyes to what's going on here in New York and California," Malcolm said, referring to the Stokes case. "I don't condone what's going on in Birmingham, but we also have segregation here."

During the same rally, Alfred D. King, Dr. King's younger brother, was the last speaker to address the crowd, and he was booed loudly by the assembled throng of over 3,000 when he insisted, "Nonviolence is the most effective way to achieve our goals." The Harlem audience was in no mood after the ongoing racial atrocities committed against African Americans in Birmingham and the rest of the country to hear or accept anything that did not address the absolute necessity of self-defense (soon after King's brother arrived in Harlem his home in Atlanta, Georgia and a black hotel where Dr. Martin Luther King was visiting were bombed by white racists). "We want Malcolm! We want Malcolm! We want Malcolm!" the crowd roared.

The following day, Malcolm returned to Washington, D.C. where he continued his attacks on the FBI and the Kennedy administration. Before an audience of 400 in the studio at WUST-AM radio, he rebuked the president for failing to take action to protect civil rights activists who were being brutalized in

Birmingham. The only difference between President Kennedy and Alabama Governor George C. Wallace, Malcolm said, was that one was a wolf and the other was a fox. "Neither one loves you," Malcolm told the audience. "The only difference is that the fox will eat you with a smile instead of a scowl." The weekend bombing in Birmingham, he added, was proof that King's turn-the-other-cheek philosophy was unworkable, and that African Americans should therefore "stay away from the white man. But if he turns his dogs on your babies, your women, and your children, then you ought to kill the dogs, whether they've got four legs or two!"

The very same day, President John F. Kennedy told reporters that he was deeply concerned about what he called the "growing extremism" of African Americans, citing the Nation of Islam and Malcolm X's comments as examples. During a meeting with Alabama newspaper editors on May 13, both the president and his brother, Attorney General Robert Kennedy, agreed that the Black Muslims might pose a threat to national security if the nonviolent attempts to end desegregation remained "stifled" by white violence.

Malcolm's response to the Kennedy brothers was swift and direct. During a speech on May 16, 1963, in Washington, Malcolm sharply dismissed the "extremist" label that the President and the Attorney General had pinned on him and the NOI as a vain effort to avoid their own responsibility in failing to provide protection for American citizens in Birmingham. Malcolm then accused President Kennedy of trying to blame advocates of black racial separatism for the failures of integrationists.

"President Kennedy did not send troops to Alabama when police dogs were biting black babies," Malcolm said sternly. "He waited three weeks until the situation exploded," he added, alluding both to the violent reaction of those blacks attacked by whites and the bombing of (local black leader) Reverend Shuttlesworth's home. In his talk with Alabama editors, Malcolm said, "Kennedy did not urge that Negroes be treated right because it is the right thing to do. Instead, he said that if the Negroes aren't well treated, the Muslims would become a threat. Instead of attacking the Ku Klux Klan and the White Citizens Committees," Malcolm X concluded, "Kennedy attacked Islam. We don't want to mix with whites, and he therefore attacked us as extremists." Once again, Malcolm's implacable and brilliant logic cut through the haze of evasions, lies, and hypocrisy of those in authority who claimed that they were "concerned" with the human and civil rights of African American citizens.

Chapter 19

The Chickens Come
Home to Roost

The last six months of 1963 were some of the most tumultuous, event-filled, and tragic periods in American history. It was not surprising given the complexity of his life's astonishing journey that the thirty-eight-year-old Malcolm X would once again be at the epicenter of the societal storm.

After a period of five weeks during which thousands of African Americans had been exposed to some of the worst, sustained racial violence in the country since WWII, the blacks finally had had enough and fought their tormentors in the streets, setting off what the white newspapers called a "riot." One week after the police attack on the children and one day before Dr. King's hotel room was bombed, the city's black community erupted. During this retaliation, several whites were attacked by blacks. It was only then that the federal government became alarmed enough to respond in an official way to the racist terror in Birmingham. Just five months earlier at a meeting in early January with Dr. King, Kennedy had told King that the administration had no plans to propose any civil rights legislation. A deeply disappointed and frustrated King had vowed to colleagues that the movement's pressure on the government would not end until the government finally found the courage to act. By June 1963 President Kennedy had watched the television footage of dogs, beatings, arrests, and firehoses nightly on the news like the rest of the country and was finally determined to act.

After dragging his feet on the issue of civil rights for nearly two years, the president appeared on television to address the nation on the evening of June 11, 1963, exactly one month to the day of the Birmingham Truce Accord (the city had promised to take steps toward desegregation and fair hiring practices). Announcing his intention to send to Congress the most sweeping civil rights bill in history, the president was, in an opportunist act of both political self-interest and personal conscience, suddenly sounding like Malcolm X and Martin Luther King, Jr. combined, speaking the exact same words these two giants had been speaking and writing since the mid-1950s:

> Now the time has come for this nation to fulfill its prom-
> ise. The events in Birmingham and elsewhere have so
> increased the cries for equality that no city or state legisla-
> tive body can prudently ignore them. The fires of frustra-
> tion and discord are burning in every city, North and
> South … We face, therefore, a moral crisis as a country
> and a people. It cannot be met by repressive police action.
> It cannot be left to increased demonstrations in the streets.
> It cannot be quieted by token moves or talks. It is time to
> act in the Congress, in your state and local legislative bod-
> ies, in all of our daily lives … A great change is at hand,
> and our task, our obligation, is to make that revolution,
> that change, peaceful and constructive for all.

Earlier that same day, in one of those weird synchronicities of history that seemed to characterize the sixties era, Governor George Wallace of Alabama made his infamous stand in the schoolhouse door by making a big public show of trying to prevent a young black man and woman (James Hood and Vivian Malone) from entering the University of Alabama's major auditorium to register for that semester's classes and thus ending segregation at that university. As the civil rights historian Taylor Branch points out in his 1988 Pulitzer Prize winning book "Parting of the Waters:

America in the King Years, 1954–1963, Wallace's so-called "stand" was carefully scripted, orchestrated, and arranged in cooperation with federal authorities who let Wallace make his racist speech as a face-saving device before he stepped aside and allowed Hood and Malone to enter the school.

Just a little past midnight that same evening, Medgar Evers, the civil rights leader and NAACP president in Jackson, Mississippi, was shot in the back and killed right in front of his front door as his wife and children watched in horror. He had just returned from an NAACP meeting and had just emerged from his car to walk to his front door with his house keys in his hand when he was shot. The authorities in that assassination took thirty-four years to arrest and convict his murderer, a leading KKK member named Byron de la Beckwith. He was finally brought to justice in 1997.

Malcolm addressing reporters, 1963.

275

On that same day Dr. Martin Luther King Jr. announced that a massive march was going to be held later that summer in Washington, D.C. Little did anyone imagine at the time that this march would become the largest demonstration and march of its kind in American history and would go down in history as a major watershed in the civil rights movement. This march and its aftermath also accelerated Malcolm's commitment to a much more secularized political radicalism and marked the beginning of the end of his personal and spiritual dependence on Elijah Muhammad and the NOI.

Malcolm's new stance would be a recognition of the necessity for an internationalist perspective on the African American movement and that ultimately only a revolutionary transformation of political, economic, and social relations on a global scale would ever truly address and move beyond the ideological systems of both racism and the limitations of a strictly racial nationalism. Furthermore, Malcolm's quest for a viable religious identity and rigorous moral stance would evolve well beyond the illusions of idolatry and a too rigid dependence on racially-based dogmatic principles. He would come to understand and advocate a position that did away with the delusional "necessity" of so-called "divine men" and ego-based prophecies. Now Malcolm would make the transition to a truly advanced position that would join the battle against the evils of racism with the battles against capitalism and imperialism as well. Finally, he would also begin to see the backwardness of reactionary gender-based attitudes and values.

How Malcolm would come to these insights and begin to put them into action in the last twenty months of his life constitutes one of the most astounding achievements of the twentieth century, and is the basis of his true legacy to his admirers and detractors alike. These transformations would begin in the later summer of 1963 and rapidly accelerate in late fall and early winter of 1963–64.

The March on Washington

The March on Washington for Jobs and Freedom was originally the brainchild of the seventy-four-year-old legendary African

American labor leader A. Philip Randolph (1889–1979), who first conceived the idea in 1941. When it finally materialized on August 28, 1963, as the March on Washington, it was coordinated and organized by Randolph's protégé and longtime collaborator Bayard Rustin. The march drew a multiracial crowd of 250,000 people on the nation's capitol to demonstrate for civil rights and equal opportunity for all Americans.

> A. Philip Randolph was the founder of the Brotherhood of Sleeping Car Porters, one of the first major black labor unions in the twentieth century as well as a major force in the Congress of Industrial Organizations (CIO) in the 1930s. He became the first black official in the AFL-CIO when the two unions merged in 1955. Both Randolph and Bayard Rustin were committed socialists until they reached middle age.

Randolph, along with leaders of the civil rights movement such as Whitney Young of the Urban League, Dr. King of SCLC, John Lewis of SNCC, James Farmer of CORE, and Roy Wilkins of the NAACP, worked together despite some internal conflicts to pull off the march. During the march on Washington, Dr. King gave his famous "I Have a Dream" speech and younger, more radical black voices, such as those of SNCC, had the opportunity to address a large international audience for the first time. By all mainstream accounts, the march was a rousing success.

But not everyone was pleased. One of the major voices of dissent was Malcolm X, who attended the march only as a critical observer. (Muhammad had strictly forbidden all NOI members to participate in the march.) Malcolm dubbed the event "The Farce on Washington" and reserved some of his most scathing and brilliant insights for the leaders of the march, whom he derisively called the "Big Six," and the march itself. In one of his most famous speeches, "Message to the Grassroots," which was delivered in Detroit on November 10, 1963, Malcolm said that the march enabled the federal government to pretend that it was supportive of the civil rights agenda while undermining and sabotaging any militant and substantive political organizing of blacks in Washington, D.C.

The spontaneous energy of previously unorganized "ordinary" black men and women of the working classes and the poor were on the brink of engaging in a leaderless mass action in the nation's capitol. People were advocating lying down in the streets and roads, on airport runways, and on government lawns in a mass action to keep the politicians in Congress, the Senate, and the Presidency from conducting their normal business. Malcolm emphasized that many of the African Americans who were openly suggesting this sort of activity were the younger generation of blacks, who were more defiant of the authorities and less fearful of the consequences of their actions. They were fed up with the slow and passively gradual pace at which the civil rights movement was progressing. Like Malcolm, many were seriously considering far more radical actions that would demonstrate just how urgent the desire for freedom from the tyranny of racism was.

According to Malcolm, the march essentially domesticated this impending mass force, taming it enough so that a "reputable" and "dependable" leadership could co-opt the direction and focus of it. Instead of militant, subversive action with a concrete focus on truly radical transformations of political economy and racial ideology, the shift was to a nebulous, "we all believe in love, tolerance, and integration" view that failed utterly to address real-life issues and concerns such as education, housing, health care, employment, institutional racism, economic development, and political power. By avoiding substantive ideas or intellectual and practical solutions to these pressing questions, the Big Six and the government (especially the Kennedy administration) could ignore or minimize the role of the black masses in the drafting and execution of public policy.

Why would the Big Six be a party to such betrayal? Malcolm observed that wealthy and powerful white liberals from the corporate world made substantial contributions to the coffers of the Big Six's organization, called the Council for United Civil Rights Leadership. He identified white millionaire philanthropist Steven Currier as the liaison between the Kennedy's and the civil rights leaders, who all agreed to meet at the Carlyle Hotel (owned by the Kennedy family) in New York. In Malcolm's analysis, Currier promised the Big Six more than a million and a half dollars to be split between their organizations in exchange for their political loyalty to the Kennedy's. The way to demonstrate their loyalty was to ensure that the march was controlled and led by them and their more moderate views. In this way, Malcolm said, the form and content of what could and could not be addressed at the march would be dictated by the Big Six leadership coalition and the Kennedy administration. In summing up his assessment of the march and its political meaning (or lack thereof) Malcolm stated:

> As soon as they got the setup organized, the white man made available to them top public relations experts and put the news media across the country at their disposal, which then began to project these 'Big Six' as the leaders of the march. Originally, they weren't even in the march. You were talking that march talk on Hastings Street, you were talking march talk on Lenox Avenue, and on Fillmore Street, and on Central Avenue, and Thirty-second Street, and Sixty-third Street. That's where the march talk was being talked. But the white man put the Big Six at the head of it; made them the march. They became the march. They took it over ... This is what they did with the march on Washington. They joined it. They didn't integrate it; they infiltrated it. They joined it, became a part of it, took it over. And as they took it over, it lost its militancy. It ceased to be angry, it ceased to be hot, it ceased to be uncompromising. Why, it even ceased to be a march. It became a picnic, a circus. Nothing but a circus, with clowns and all ... with clowns leading it, white clowns and black clowns. I know you don't like what I'm saying, but I'm going to tell you anyway. Because I can prove what I'm saying. If you think I'm telling you wrong, you bring me Martin Luther King and A. Philip Randolph and James Farmer and the other three, and see if they'll deny it over a microphone. No, it was a sellout. It was a takeover. When James Baldwin came in from Paris, they wouldn't let him talk, because they couldn't make him go by the script .... They

> *controlled it so tight that they told those Negroes what*
> *time to hit town, how to come, where to stop, what signs*
> *to carry, what songs to sing, what speech they could*
> *make, and what speech they couldn't make; and then they*
> *told them to get out of town by sundown. Now I know*
> *you don't like me saying this. But I can back it up. It was*
> *a circus, a performance that beat anything Hollywood*
> *could ever do, the performance of the year ....*

Despite Malcolm's brutally honest assessment of the political and ideological limitations of the march and its leadership, Malcolm confided privately to friends and select associates in the NOI that although he disagreed with King's methods, he admired him for at least taking a public stand. Malcolm realized that despite the cautious attitudes of the conventional civil rights leadership, in the end they were demanding far more than merely civil rights, which were already supposed to be protected by the Constitution anyway. In taking a public position against racial tyranny and oppression, they were standing up for the humanity of black people. Therein lay the revolutionary potential of the struggle. "If only the energy demonstrated by its many participants could be guided in a more radical and internationalist direction," Malcolm thought. Malcolm's qualified and reluctant admiration for King was one more indication that Muhammad's influence on his spokesman was waning.

Muhammad's isolationist policy had clearly outlived its practicality in a period when African Americans were risking and losing their lives for the right to be treated as human beings. Merely talking tough was not going to be enough for the NOI to sustain its credibility with the general African American population. Black folks were demanding results, even from Muslims. More and more it appeared that the primary benefits of membership in the NOI were increasingly limited to the Messenger, his family, and his favored lieutenants, aides, and ministers. The poorer rank-and-file members, many of whom had remained loyal to the organization for nearly twenty years, were becoming even poorer as a result of the excessive tithing and other financial demands on them. And they were doing the lion's share of the work for the NOI. Moreover, the emergence of radical young militants like Stokely Carmichael, James Forman, and many others from groups such as SNCC made the civil rights movement seem more progressive and realistic than the NOI, which was bogged down by its "white devil" rhetoric, religious dogma, dependence on the deification and idolatry of Elijah Muhammad, and the Messenger's refusal to commit the considerable resources of the NOI to expanding and advancing the black movement beyond the confines of the NOI itself.

Meanwhile the impending revelation to the world of Muhammad's multiple extramarital affairs was putting tremendous pressure on Malcolm to stem the tide of what was rapidly threatening to tear apart the NOI. Malcolm was preparing to persuade several trusted ministers within the NOI to help him carry out a strategy to save what they all most valued in their lives. Elsewhere, however, an even larger problem loomed for the movement, and once again that problem was located in Birmingham, Alabama.

The Sixteenth Street Baptist Church Bombing

Just two weeks after the lofty rhetoric and enormous public display of human brotherhood and racial harmony in Washington, D.C., the entire country was brought back down to earth and forced once again to face the horrific reality of racism in America. A bomb went off during Sunday school services at the Sixteenth Street Baptist Church in Birmingham on the morning of September 15, 1963. Four young black girls, ages 11 to 14, were killed instantly, and hundreds were injured when the church, a major center of community and civil rights activity, was completely destroyed in the blast. The physical impact of the bombing was so great that parts of the charred limbs of the victims were found embedded in the brick and mortar of the rubble. Although the civil rights movement had suffered many deaths and murders over the past decade, no event in modern civil rights history had appalled the world more than this brazen, savage act.

Gary Thomas Rowe, Jr., a high-level FBI informant paid to infiltrate the local chapter of the Ku Klux Klan, had called FBI headquarters at least an hour before the blast to advise the Bureau what was about to occur (Rowe, who had a long criminal record, had on one occasion admitted killing a black man in cold blood. He had also participated in beating civil rights workers while Birmingham police stood by laughing.)

The children's deaths in the bombing caused the greatest crisis yet in the short six-year history of Dr. King's leadership of the SCLC. The national outcry from African Americans was huge, fierce, and immediate. The Brooklyn, New York branch of the Congress of Racial Equality (CORE) sent King an urgent telegram in the wake of the bombing urging him to abandon the philosophy of nonviolence. It was time, the CORE message stated, to "unshackle the hands of Negroes in Birmingham" and allow them to "defend themselves and their children." At a meeting at Town Hall in New York just days after the bombing, black writers John O. Killens and James Baldwin made a similar plea to King, advising him that Mahatma Gandhi's philosophy was unworkable when "white Americans acted like Nazis." "I can no longer be asked to love those who killed and persecuted Negroes," Killens said during the rally protesting the murders. The United States was also roundly denounced and condemned by many African and Asian leaders throughout the world including Ben Bella of Algeria, Achmad Sukarno of Indonesia, and Ho Chi Minh of Vietnam.

Nine days after the bombing and speaking before 600 SCLC delegates in Richmond, Virginia, Martin Luther King publicly defended his philosophy of nonviolence by saying that the nonviolent struggle had received a "serious blow" due to the bombings. "It is more difficult now", he added, "to get over to the Negro community the need for nonviolence." But, King said, "Those who call for retaliatory measures do not represent the Negro masses and their leaders." But neither Malcolm nor many other emerging radical black leaders and activists, not to mention many members of the "Negro masses" saw it quite that way.

Many Third World leaders refocused on the NOI and especially Malcolm X as the salvation of African Americans. The American intelligence community began paying particularly close attention to Malcolm's extensive activities at the United Nations (he even had a small office there) as well as to his endless meetings and strategy sessions with other African American radicals and nationalists in Harlem. Both the FBI and the CIA were afraid that if Malcolm X assumed control of the NOI in the wake of either illness or scandal involving Elijah Muhammad, the sect would become more politically active and thereby pose a threat to national security.

Malcolm was still urgently searching for a viable compromise that would allow him to move the NOI in a more dynamic and secularized political direction, but at the same time maintain and consolidate the NOI's religious identity and committment to Islam. The last thing Malcolm wanted was a head-to-head confrontation with Muhammad that would cause a major split or rupture in the NOI. Malcolm realized that this extremely delicate balancing act required both the organization and Muhammad to recognize that the way of the future lay in becoming more flexible and open to non-Muslims in the African American community and in modifying or even rejecting certain aspects of NOI's current religious and theological doctrine. Malcolm X was conflicted about his own political and moral stance. He desired much more contact and collaboration with his many non-Muslim friends, colleagues, and associates in the United States who shared many of his views, but he was also quite pleased with, and even dependent on, his extensive international Muslim ties. However, he was beginning to see that these two groups and their goals need not be mutually exclusive, but he did not know how to convince the Messenger and many other ministers in the NOI of that.

He was certain that the rank-and-file membership was more open to a more secularized political direction than the leadership was, but he knew that unless a synthesis of ideological and religious positions could be worked out soon, he and very possibly the NOI itself were doomed. He hated to think about these issues in such melodramatic terms, but the events and circumstances of the past year had left him no choice. Malcolm realized that Muhammad would blame him if the NOI went into rapid decline or collapsed because of public revelations about Muhammad's adultery, and Malcolm knew that if these problems couldn't be resolved in-house, he would be threatened with death by Muhammad, as well as many others in the NOI who remained loyal to Muhammad.

Sustaining him during this crisis, as always, was his faith: in Allah, in Betty, in his children, in the African American community, in his siblings, and in Islam. Despite the many secret agendas of others, the petty jealousies of some colleagues, the unscrupulous intrigues of governmental agencies such as the FBI and CIA, and the widespread opposition and hostility of white racists throughout the country, Malcolm felt strong and clear-minded. In spite of everything, he felt, in the words of the traditional black idiomatic expression, "no ways tired." He was determined, as he always was, to go all the way wherever the path led him—even to his own demise. He intended to do all he could to avoid it if possible, but if he could not, he was prepared to do what his sense of right, and what justice told him was best. In this respect he was a great deal like his longtime ideological counterpart and nemesis, Dr. Martin Luther King Jr. But as he reflected on what direction to go next, another major event intruded upon his life that also had far-reaching effects and consequences on the world.

The Assassination of President John F. Kennedy

When President Kennedy was assassinated in Dallas, Texas on November 22, 1963, the nation mourned and grieved the loss of a man who had been, at age 43, the youngest man ever elected president of the United States. However, not everyone shared in the outpouring of grief and sorrow that was expressed throughout the country. One of those who did not mourn was Malcolm X. Like many people in the NOI, he had been deeply angered and outraged by President Kennedy's agonizingly slow and sometimes indifferent response to the mild demands from the civil rights movement. Despite this suspect record, the president was well regarded by many African Americans who saw him as someone who had the potential to grow beyond an often opportunist tendency to forsake principle for political expediency. President Kennedy's speech in June 1963 about the need for his administration and the country to seriously address and combat racial injustice had gone a long way toward repairing faltering relations with many African Americans.

Yet the NOI remained unimpressed with Kennedy. When an official asked Elijah Muhammad about closing the University of Islam the day after Kennedy's assassination to demonstrate that Muslims shared in the country's loss, he remarked privately that, "This isn't a day of mourning for the Muslims," and "That devil's death doesn't concern us; it's time for the Christians to mourn, not the Muslims." However, the Messenger was not so naive or short-sighted enough to think that he could possibly say anything like this in public and not suffer the wrath of the entire country, especially because so many blacks were also mourning the president's death. So Muhammad put on an entirely different face in public. While many other Muslims in the NOI were quietly celebrating the president's death as more evidence that the white man's rule would end by 1970 (another of Muhammad's many "prophecies"), the Messenger himself remained curiously mute on the subject. He now wanted to make absolutely sure that none of his ministers, especially Malcolm X, said anything that could be construed as negative or disrespectful about the tragedy. The last thing Muhammad wanted was something that could provoke a white backlash against the NOI and Muslims generally, so he issued an edict calling for complete silence on the subject of the president's death.

To further ensure that the general public received the impression that he and the NOI shared in the country's grief over the loss of "their president," Muhammad, who generally approved each page of *Muhammad Speaks* before it was printed, called the editors and ordered a new front page for the December 6, 1963, issue. He wanted his column on the front page, he said, with a large photograph of the slain commander-in-chief. "After all," he said, "he wasn't bad for a devil." The FBI agents monitoring his phone calls noted that he laughed upon making the statement. Then the

Messenger called his son into the room and told him to call Malcolm X. Muhammad then dictated the exact words he wanted his national spokesman to say in the likely event that he would be asked to comment on the president's assassination. "My father said that we should say that we are sorry about the death of our president," Malcolm X was told as he listened in disbelief.

Malcolm was stunned, angry, and disillusioned by the Messenger's command. For Malcolm to have to make a public statement that neither he nor Muhammad believed was true was, for Malcolm, another sign of the Messenger's fall from grace. It was the biggest lie Malcolm had ever been asked to tell "in the name of the Messenger," and he could not do it. He was deeply hurt and saddened by the turn of events. "How can I say that after what I've been saying about Kennedy and the fall of America?" he asked one of his associates rhetorically. But his fellow NOI members said that ministers have no choice in the matter; the statement was an order, not a wish or plea. "Well," Malcolm said sadly, "you don't understand."

Nine days later, the Messenger was scheduled to speak in New York at Manhattan Center, but he fell ill a few days after the assassination and was unable to attend. Of course, Malcolm was the designated replacement. There was nothing out of ordinary about his speech. What was unusual, officials from the Harlem mosque recalled, was that Malcolm used extensive notecards that evening. He wanted to make sure that he did not stray from what the Messenger wanted him to impart. His associate, Sharon X, felt that he seemed particularly apprehensive about making the speech. Sharon and the others had never seen Malcolm use a prepared text before. He usually spoke extemporaneously or referred to his notes sparingly. This time he read what he had written beforehand word for word.

The assembled crowd of 700 people included some white reporters who were especially interested in what Malcolm had to say about the assassination. But Malcolm stuck to his prepared talk for the duration. The theme of the talk itself was standard fare. He had reiterated the substance of it (which was mostly Muhammad's official position) on many occasions, as if on automatic pilot: God was wreaking, and would continue to wreak, his vengeance on white America until it allowed its black population to be independent of it.

During the latter part of the speech, Malcolm noted how crucial the black vote had been to President Kennedy in what was at the time the closest presidential election in American history in terms of the popular vote. He then condemned Kennedy's decision to wait until African Americans finally began to fight back against the white racist terrorism in Birmingham before ordering troops to the city. He denounced the late president for undermining the original intent of the March on Washington by essentially paying off the civil rights organizations that had staged it, and for claiming a central role in its success to curry favor with African American voters in the upcoming election of 1964. He also castigated the late president for "twiddling his thumbs" while Patrice Lumumba of the Congo, the Diem brothers of South Vietnam, and four innocent little black girls in Birmingham were all murdered on his watch.

Then having grabbed the attention of his audience, which contained a substantial number of black non-Muslims who hoped that Malcolm would finally break free of the political constraints that Elijah Muhammad had imposed on him, Malcolm surprised the gathering by abruptly ending his talk with his customary genuflection to the Honorable Elijah Muhammad's teachings and guidance and opened the floor to questions. A reporter in the audience asked him the inevitable question about Kennedy's assassination and his personal feeling about it. For a few minutes Malcolm stuck to the official party line and the instructions that the Messenger had given him. But then Malcolm's sense of personal integrity and great need to be true to himself and his beliefs overcame his previous inclination to blindly obey Muhammad's order that he hold his tongue or lie about his feelings.

Malcolm had been the only national figure to speak out against America's central role, via the CIA, in the gruesome assassination of Prime Minister Patrice Lumumba in the Congo. No black leader before Malcolm X had addressed the American public regarding American war crimes against the people of Vietnam. No black leader had openly criticized the Kennedy administration for bullying Castro and attempting (through the CIA and the Mafia) to have him assassinated. Suddenly, Malcolm believed the moment had come to truly speak for those who could not or would not speak for themselves. He also knew that this moment was a final turning point in his relationship with the NOI. From now on he was determined that he would speak only for himself, in his own name, for what he genuinely felt and believed.

He looked up at the reporter and uttered what became one of the most infamous quotes of modern American history: "This [the assassination of Kennedy] is simply a case of chickens coming home to roost. Being an old farm boy myself, chickens coming home to roost never did make me sad; they've always made me glad." Then a huge smile erupted on Malcolm's face as if he were immensely relieved to have finally gotten it off his chest. Many in the crowd, which was mostly made up of Muslims, laughed loudly and applauded. But John Ali, now National Secretary of the NOI, did not laugh. Nor did the other high-ranking NOI officials who were on the stage with Malcolm. For they knew that while denouncing one authority figure, Malcolm had simultaneously defied another.

Of course Malcolm's statement about chickens roosting was not merely a clever metaphor. He was acknowledging the painful truth that the racist violence white America routinely visited on people of color throughout the world, and particularly in the United States, was coming back to haunt it and even take someone it considered important. The old adage of "what goes around, comes around" was very much on Malcolm's mind and that of many others who had grown weary of begging those in authority for humane treatment and the resolution of severe problems that threatened not merely the citizenship of African Americans, but their very lives. More than one hundred activists and ordinary citizens, black and white, had been killed by racists in just the past five years of the civil rights movement.

Back in Chicago, Muhammad had just finished recording a message of condolence to the Kennedy family, a blatantly insincere piece about how saddened members of the NOI were over the assassination. A Los Angeles radio station reporter had called for the Messenger's comments, and he had repeated that the NOI, like their fellow Americans, were "deeply shocked by the assassination of the president, and shared the nation's grief." When the reporter asked what he thought about Malcolm's comments, the Messenger was aghast and would not reply because he still could not believe that Malcolm had spoken out on the president's death in direct opposition to his order. When John Ali confirmed that what the reporter claimed Malcolm said was true, Muhammad knew that he could no longer depend on Malcolm to do his bidding. As he had with his wife, mistresses, children, and many others who had once believed so fervently in him, but had now been thoroughly disillusioned or banished, the Messenger now moved to isolate his surrogate son.

The next day Muhammad summoned Malcolm to confer with him in Chicago. Muhammad took his time before coming to the point. Finally he asked, "Did you see the papers this morning?" Of course Malcolm had. Muhammad told Malcolm that his comments about Kennedy had seriously damaged the NOI's image. Malcolm was therefore forbidden to make any further public statements. This action was necessary, Muhammad said, to distance the NOI from his intemperate remarks. Muhammad understood that denying Malcolm, who was so popular with most of the NOI membership, the right to speak on behalf of the NOI was far safer than banning him outright from the organization. Even more importantly, this action would prevent him from publicizing the sordid details of the Messenger's illicit affairs.

When Malcolm returned to New York on December 3, 1963, he discovered that Mosque Number Seven members had already been told that he had been silenced. So had the media. The following day, John Ali called a press conference in Chicago to officially announce that Muhammad had suspended Malcolm from the NOI for ninety days for his remarks about the late president. The statement read:

> Minister Malcolm Shabazz, *addressing a public meeting at*
> Manhattan Center *in New York City on Sunday,*
> December 1, *did not speak for the Muslims when he made*

*comments about the death of the president, John F.
Kennedy. He was speaking for himself and not the
Muslims in general, and Minister Malcolm has been
suspended from public speaking for the time being. The
Nation (NOI) still mourns the loss of our president.*

During a brief telephone conversation later the same day, the
Messenger had told Malcolm that he intended to suspend him for
ninety days for appearance's sake, that the punishment would be
moderately enforced, and that things would go on as usual. So
Malcolm was stunned when he heard talk about his "indefinite suspension" over the airwaves. He immediately called the Messenger
for confirmation. As FBI agents listened in on Muhammad's
tapped phone, Muhammad said, "Yes, they have it from here, that
you have been suspended for the time being ... that you will not
be making any public speeches for the time being. There is no definite time set .... This is for the best." The suspension from public
speaking would not affect Malcolm's administrative and ministerial duties at the mosque, Muhammad said. The punishment was
limited to all public speaking, including lecturing at the mosque.

Humiliated and trying hard to conceal his anger, Malcolm
called back again later that evening, still in a state of disbelief
about his suspension. Muhammad again gave vent to his displeasure about Malcolm's statement:

*You should have known better than to talk about the presi-
dent like you did ... I told you to lay off because it was
too hot. There is a time and place for everything ... I
don't like to do a thing like that [suspension], but I had no
alternative. You made me look like a fool. People are
looking to me if I would back you up. Such talk as that
could get us into trouble when the man [Kennedy] is not
even cold in his grave.*

Malcolm decided to swallow his rage about the suspension for
the time being, at least in public, and when asked by reporters
about it, he acted and sounded contrite and assured the media that
the Messenger was correct to chastise and suspend him. But those
who knew Malcolm well, such as Alex Haley, could feel his hidden

rage. Even the FBI was astonished that Malcolm had been able to fool so many others about his real feelings about the suspension. Hoover had even instructed his agents to offer Malcolm money to inform on his NOI foes and Elijah Muhammad. Malcolm, who would never cooperate with the government in such a way under any circumstances, categorically refused their bribe. When questioned about the suspension by *The New York Times*, CBS, and *Newsweek*, Malcolm insisted that he "should have just kept my big mouth shut" and that "anything that Mr. Muhammad does is all right with me. I believe absolutely in his wisdom and authority." He told another journalist that "Mr. Muhammad suspended me from making public appearances for the time being, which I fully understand. I say the same thing to you that I have told others— I'm in complete submission."

Malcolm's talent for clothing rebellion in submissive garb helped him to remain in the news and to continue as a public figure despite having been told to be silent. The press was full of speculation about whether he would stay in the NOI or venture out on his own. Meanwhile Malcolm discreetly leaked information to the *Amsterdam News* about what his future plans "might be." When asked privately by his old friend and journalist, Louis Lomax, about how long the suspension would last, Malcolm replied, "It better not last too long. I'm thinking about making a move on my own." He told another person, "It's hard to make a rooster stop crowing once the sun has risen."

On December 6, in response to constant media speculation (and a phony FBI news leak), Muhammad still insisted to the media that he and Malcolm were "still brothers. I hope such rumors do not get out of hand ... Malcolm and I have not split by any means. We are still brothers and I still think Malcolm is a wonderful worker of mine. But what I say is, we have rules; we must obey them." The following day Malcolm and Muhammad had a very amiable conversation, and Muhammad told Malcolm he looked forward to seeing him soon. This conversation initially confused the FBI who thought that a reconciliation was on the horizon, especially after Muhammad said to Malcolm, "We

Muslims don't act like Christians seeking revenge and so forth when something goes wrong ... Islam makes us true brothers and we have true unity."

Then, in late November the FBI uncovered evidence that the Messenger's wife of over thirty years, Clara Muhammad, had essentially left her husband because of his serial adulteries. She was now living in Washington and was spending a fortune on a large apartment that her guilt-ridden husband was reluctantly paying for. At the same time, informants and other surveillance devices planted in Philadelphia told them that Wallace was extremely unhappy with his father and had been contacting Malcolm regularly since his suspension. According to intelligence reports Wallace was now providing Malcolm with salacious details about his father's extramarital affairs. Whether Wallace was primarily motivated by a desire to cause a permanent split between his father and Malcolm, as the FBI suggested, or whether he was merely crying on Malcolm's shoulder, as Malcolm believed, was not clear.

Whatever Wallace's motives, the FBI was determined to exploit each man's weaknesses. The FBI began issuing bogus news stories about a deepening leadership crisis in the NOI. Most of the planted news reports focused on allegations that Malcolm was trying to take over the NOI by spreading rumors about Muhammad's private life. For the Messenger, who thought that the issue of his extramarital affairs had been hushed, the rumors about his son Wallace were heartbreaking. Upon receiving proof from other officials in the Philadelphia mosque, he knew he had to suspend him. He was angrier with Wallace than he was with Malcolm. In Harlem, members were told that Malcolm was no longer in charge and that they should avoid associating with him. Although Muhammad had said that Malcolm's suspension was only for ninety days, what members of the Harlem mosque were told about Malcolm's status after his suspension ended made it clear that the Messenger did not want Malcolm to return to the NOI.

Then on January 2, 1964, nearly five weeks after Malcolm's "chickens come home to roost" speech, Elijah Muhammad once again called Malcolm on the carpet for his refusal to remain silent and read him the riot act. Muhammad informed Malcolm that he was no longer his national representative or the Harlem mosque's minister. The NOI, which was trying to paper over the rift between Malcolm and the Messenger, did not inform the press about this latest development, nor did Malcolm inform the media about his new diminished status. Muhammad was livid about Malcolm's discussion with other East Coast ministers about Muhammad's extramarital activities. "I've been hearing about Malcolm this and Malcolm that, and even Malcolm being the leader," the Messenger fumed as Malcolm listened on his home phone in New York. "Now this one [minister] and that one is getting jealous. You are my property, and I am your property." "Yes sir", Malcolm replied. "You made an error," Muhammad continued. In response Malcolm said, "I asked your permission in a letter before I said anything, and I understood that it was all right."

At this Muhammad shouted,

> *I certainly didn't say any such thing! I can't understand why you took this poison and poured it out and told them [the other ministers] … You can't use fire to fight fire. One must carry a basket of water and not fire … I thought you were referring to something else. I thought you had a sly scheme or shrewd plan to undermine me, but it won't work, sir, not this time!*

Dumbfounded, Malcolm said nothing. He and the Messenger both knew that he had very clearly admitted to his moral transgressions when Malcolm confronted him with the evidence nearly a year earlier in Phoenix, Arizona. He had implied then and in a subsequent letter that it was okay for Malcolm to prepare the NOI for news about the scandal. Now the Messenger was refuting everything. Muhammad paused to catch his breath and then continued his harangue. "If anyone had told me that you were going to use things like that, I wouldn't have believed it. If you love Allah, then you must love me as the Messenger of Allah." After pausing again to catch his breath, he went on with his tongue-lashing. "Why are you checking into my personal affairs?" Malcolm X replied that he had not inquired into the illicit relationships. "I heard about it in Chicago [during Savior's Day, 1963]. I talked to Wallace about it, and he already knew about it." As it turned out, it was Louis X

(Farrakhan), along with two other ministers, who went to Muhammad with his version of what Malcolm had said about the secretaries. Malcolm was not aware of this fact at the time.

As the FBI continued to plant fake news items in mainstream newspapers in a vain effort to facilitate and exacerbate a final split between Malcolm and Muhammad, the Messenger became suspicious because the FBI made the incredibly stupid error of referring to Malcolm X in their news reports as "Malcolm Little." Because everyone in the NOI and outside it never referred to Malcolm using his "slave" surname, Muhammad knew that the reports were false and the result of an attempt by whites to destroy the NOI. Muhammad put an end to these attempts by releasing a statement in the pages of *Muhammad Speaks* that there was no discord in the NOI and that Muhammad did not view Malcolm X as the enemy, nor was the NOI an enemy of his. Muhammad wanted the editor of the newspaper to make sure that the article also stated the following:

> *We believe Malcolm is a believer as he has always*
> *preached that he was. It is not true that Malcolm is trying*
> *to ruin or run Muhammad's family, and we don't believe*
> *Malcolm is against us or that we are against Malcolm.*

Of course, most of what the Messenger had stated was also false, but it was one sure-fire way to relieve some of the media and surveillance pressure on him and the NOI.

As Muhammad spent the next two weeks preparing for the annual Savior's Day convention, he reflected on the fact that for the first time in twelve years, Malcolm would not be there to introduce him. When Muslims looked toward the stage for the man "most likely to succeed the Messenger" they would not be reassured by the presence of either Malcolm X or Wallace Muhammad, both of whom were now banished. So, for the first time, the Messenger faced the most joyful occasion of the NOI's year with trepidation and dismay. Despite all of his many followers, his wealth, and his ministers, lieutenants, aides, mistresses, and flunkies, Elijah Muhammad now felt very much alone.

Chapter 20

A New Beginning Leads to the End

A s Malcolm prepared to take his first-ever family vacation in Florida after seven years of marriage, certain anti-Malcolm elements in the NOI began to think about ways of finally eliminating him. A few days before he and his family left their home in Queens for Miami, Captain Joseph of the Harlem FOI called a fellow FOI member Anas M. Luqman, a war veteran and an explosives expert, and told him to attach a bomb to Malcolm's car that would detonate when the key turned in the ignition. Luqman immediately quit the NOI, told Malcolm, and then gave the details of the hare-brained scheme to the New York *Amsterdam News*. The failed scheme quickly convinced officials at Chicago NOI headquarters that Captain Joseph was too inept to orchestrate the assassination.

In Chicago, the Messenger had chosen none other than Louis Farrakhan, minister from the Boston mosque, to replace Malcolm as speaker at the Savior's Day convention. It was not a surprise. Aside from being one of the men who betrayed Malcolm to Elijah Muhammad, the handsome musician, singer, and orator had mastered the sound of his mentor, Malcolm X, in his oratory ("I styled my delivery and whatnot after Malcolm X," he said). But Farrakhan lacked Malcolm's brilliance, grace, and fury.

Malcolm went to Miami with his wife Betty Shabazz and their three daughters: Attallah, Qubilah, and Ilyasah. Malcolm was in Miami against Muhammad's wishes, but at the invitation of a twenty-two-year-old boxer named Cassius Clay. Clay had been a supporter of the NOI since he was seventeen and a (secret) member for three years, and he idolized Malcolm X. This attachment deeply worried Elijah Muhammad who to this time had kept his distance from the young boxer because he opposed professional boxing. But the Messenger's major concern was that he did not want the NOI's name associated with failure after Clay's upcoming February 25, 1964, title fight with Sonny Liston, which he felt certain Clay would lose.

> *Cassius Clay, who later changed his name to Muhammad Ali, had only fought twenty professional bouts at the time he met Malcolm X. In the eyes of many boxing "experts" and most of the public, Clay was destined to lose his first heavyweight championship fight to the widely feared and seemingly invincible champion, Sonny Liston.*

However, both Clay and Malcolm had far more faith in Clay's ability to win than Muhammad did. Malcolm was the person most responsible for Clay becoming a member of the NOI. Cassius's brother Rudy was a member before Cassius, and they would go to mosques together in whatever city they happened to be in. Sometimes Malcolm happened to be teaching at the mosques they attended, and like so many others, Clay was so attracted to Malcolm's teaching that Clay would always sit up front. When Malcolm visited Clay's training camp in January 1964, he was six weeks into his suspension. He served as the boxer's spiritual advisor at Clay's request, despite the silence imposed upon Malcolm by the NOI.

Malcolm was also there the night in February when Clay "shook up the world" and beat Liston to win the heavyweight title and (at the time) become the youngest man ever to become heavyweight champion. Alex Haley remembered that "Cassius wasn't going to have it without Malcolm being there, and Malcolm was there.

Malcolm called me before the fight and said it was sure to be one of the greatest upsets in modern times ..." Clay wanted Malcolm to be with him so desperately that he paid for the family's round-trip plane tickets, hotel accommodations, and other amenities. It was, Clay said, an anniversary gift for Malcolm and Betty. At Malcolm's request, Clay also got the ticket for seat number seven in the arena. Malcolm considered seven his lucky number, and he earnestly believed that being in that seat would enhance his friend's chances for an upset. Clay enjoyed going along because everything Malcolm had suggested up to then had worked to his advantage. He and Malcolm had become very close friends, and Clay viewed him as a mentor.

Malcolm with Muhammad Ali, March 1964.

After the fight, Elijah Muhammad called Clay and offered him the new name of Muhammad Ali as a reward for his victory. The following day, which happened to be Savior's Day, the Messenger proudly told the members of the NOI that he had personally renamed the champ and that the rumors about the former Clay being a member of the organization were true. The newly named Ali, sincerely humbled by the Messenger's gesture, felt more than a little guilty because there had been other members of the NOI who had been waiting for more than thirty years for the removal of their Xs and the bestowal of their holy names by the Messenger but who had not yet received them. Ali humbly pledged to do everything in his power to live up to the faith that the NOI and the Messenger had shown in him. In pledging his devotion to the old man, Ali found himself in the middle of a major conflict and crisis involving Malcolm and the Messenger.

Once again Elijah Muhammad had taken advantage of his position to undercut Malcolm's influence with a member of the NOI. The fact that the Messenger would suddenly embrace Ali after avoiding him and predicting that he would lose was characteristic of the Messenger's opportunism and blatantly manipulative attitude. Nevertheless, the trusting and open Ali spent several days after Savior's Day in New York with Malcolm. Ali was very optimistic that Malcolm soon would be reinstated by the NOI because Malcolm told Ali so when he asked.

On March 2, 1964, the new heavyweight champion told reporters that his "outrageous statements" (about how the Messenger was divine and so forth) were nothing compared to those they would hear from Malcolm in a few days, when his ninety-day suspension was to end. Elijah Muhammad was furious when he heard about Ali's comments on the suspension. On March 6, he called Ali and told him that he should not be spending time with Malcolm, because he was suspended indefinitely. If Ali ever wanted to become a minister himself, Muhammad said, he would be wise to avoid Malcolm. Ali promised to sever their relationship immediately. Malcolm was deeply saddened by Ali's decision, but he understood and refused to hold a grudge against him.

Malcolm had assumed that if he were not reinstated, Ali would side with him.

The following day, Elijah Muhammad went through the motions of celebrating his forty-fifth wedding anniversary, even as his wife Clara made plans for a separation. That same evening, Malcolm met with several confidants whose opinions he trusted to discuss plans for the immediate future. The next morning on March 8, 1964, Malcolm announced on the *Today Show* that he had broken with the NOI because its leader was morally bankrupt. He held a press conference later the same day and announced that he was forming two new organizations, one secular and political and the other religious. The political organization was named the Organization of Afro-American Unity (OAAU), which was named after the Organization of African Unity (OAU) in Africa. The religious organization was to be called Muslim Mosque, Inc., an independent religious group that would practice and advocate only orthodox Islam (in this case, the Sunni branch), as opposed to the ersatz, idiosyncratic, and racially-based version created by Muhammad and his mentor Wallace D. Fard. Malcolm X stated that the Black Muslim movement had "gone as far as it can" because it was too narrowly sectarian, dogmatic, and inhibited. He also stated that he was now prepared to cooperate in local civil rights activities in the South and the rest of the country because he understood that every campaign for specific objectives could only

> *heighten the political consciousness of the Negroes and intensify their identification against white society ... There is no use deceiving ourselves. Good education, housing, and jobs are imperatives for the Negroes, and I shall support them in their fight to win these objectives, but I shall tell the Negroes that while these are necessary, they cannot solve the main Negro problem.*

Four days later on March 12, 1964, in a formal press conference at the Park Sheraton Hotel in New York, Malcolm further clarified the relationship between his secular political body and his religious one. He said that all black non-Muslims were welcome into the OAAU as long they were politically committed to its program and objectives and that the identity and function of the OAAU and

Muslim Mosque, Inc. would remain separate and independent of each other. Politics and religion would not mix in Malcolm's new entities. He had learned his lesson from the NOI that an irresponsible, dogmatic, and narrow synthesis of religious doctrine and political ideology was ultimately a self-destructive course.

A number of Malcolm's positions in the spring of 1964 changed over the next few months as he and his colleagues fine-tuned his new organizational program. For example, as a member of the NOI, Malcolm had maintained that "separation", meaning a separate nation-state or a return to Africa was the only solution for black people in the United States. In the March 12 statement, he amended this position, stating that the solution was a "long-range program." Just two months later in May 1964, Malcolm discontinued altogether any advocacy of a separate nation and asserted that African Americans should fight in the United States as a whole to independently determine their political destiny.

In the March 8 and 12 press conferences, still hoping to avert any major conflict with the NOI and particularly Elijah Muhammad, Malcolm continued to praise the Messenger for his mentorship, analysis, and program, and declined to discuss publicly the "internal differences" that had "forced" him out of the NOI. Soon after Muhammad began to assail Malcolm in public for his "hypocrisy" and "hereticism," among other absurd charges, Malcolm decided to take off the gloves and eloquently defend himself and his new intellectual, political, and religious independence from the Messenger and the NOI. In speaking of this development Malcolm asserted, "I made an error, I know now, in not speaking out the full truth when I was first suspended."

Having now completely conquered any personal fears, misgivings, or regrets regarding his transcendence of the NOI and its limitations, Malcolm moved forward quickly and aggressively to make up for lost time in the national and international arena of the African American struggle. In his March 8, 1964, statement, Malcolm made his new thrust very clear:

> *Because 1964 threatens to be a very explosive year on the*
> *racial front, and because I myself intend to be very active*
> *in every phase of the American Negro struggle for human*

rights, I have called this press conference this morning in order to clarify my own position in the struggle— especially in regard to politics and nonviolence ... Internal differences within the Nation of Islam forced me out of it ... But now that it has happened, I intend to make the most of it. Now that I have more independence of action, I intend to use a more flexible approach toward working with others to get a solution to this problem. I do not pretend to be a divine man, but I do believe in divine guidance, divine power, and in the fulfillment of divine prophecy ... I'm not out to fight other Negro leaders or organizations. We must find a common approach, a common solution, to a common problem. As of this minute, I've forgotten everything bad that the other leaders have said about me, and I pray they can also forget the many bad things I've said about them. The problem facing our people here in America is bigger than all other personal or organizational differences. Therefore, as leaders, we must stop worrying about the threat that we seem to think we pose to each other's personal prestige and concentrate our united efforts toward solving the unending hurt that is being done daily to our people here in America ... Our political philosophy will be black nationalism. Our economic and social philosophy will be black nationalism. Our cultural emphasis will be black nationalism ... We must control the politics and the politicians of our community. They must no longer take orders from outside forces. We will organize and sweep out of office all Negro politicians who are puppets for the outside forces. Our accent will be on youth: we need new ideas, new methods, new approaches. We will call upon young students of political science throughout the nation to help us. We will encourage these young students to launch their own independent study, and then give us their analysis and their suggestions. We are completely disenchanted with the old, adult, established politicians. We want to see some new faces— more militant faces ... Concerning the 1964 elections:

*We will keep our plans on this a secret until a later date—
but we don't intend for our people to be the victims of a
political sellout again in 1964 ... Whites can help us, but
they can't join us. There can be no black-white unity until
there is first some black unity. There can be no worker's
solidarity until there is first some racial solidarity. We cannot think of uniting with others, until after we have first
united among ourselves. We cannot think of being acceptable to others until we have first proven acceptable to ourselves ... Concerning nonviolence: It is criminal to teach
a man not to defend himself when he is the constant victim of brutal attacks. It is legal and lawful to own a shotgun or a rifle. We believe in obeying the law ... we should
be peaceful, law-abiding—but the time has come for the
American Negro to fight back in self-defense whenever
and wherever he is being unjustly and unlawfully
attacked. If the government thinks I am wrong for saying
this, then let the government start doing its job.[1]*

After this powerful start, Malcolm hit the ground running. In
April 1964, he made the first in a series of highly significant
speeches at public rallies in Harlem organized by Muslim Mosque,
Inc. The purpose of these talks and lectures was outlining and for-
mulating the ideology and philosophy of a new movement. Many
observers agreed that these speeches were the best he ever gave.
Malcolm also began accepting many speaking engagements outside
New York in cities such as Boston, Cleveland, and Detroit.

One of Malcolm's most important, prescient, and intellectually
profound political speeches was given in Cleveland, Ohio on April
3, 1964, and was called "The Ballot or the Bullet." This speech
contained an astonishing number of eerily accurate and prophetic
observations and analyses of the future of African American politics. In addition, the speech is notable for its highly sophisticated
analysis of the mainstream American political and economic system. Malcolm was one of the first black political activists to point
out that elements of a radical black nationalism were present and

1. *Printed with permission, Pathfinder Press.*

growing in such conventional organizations as the NAACP and CORE, as well as SNCC, and that these forces were about to erupt.

El-Hajj Malik El-Shabazz

From April 13 to May 21, 1964, Malcolm went on a whirlwind tour of the African continent, meeting with a wide array of radical political leaders, intellectuals, scientists, students, diplomats, workers, peasants, religious officials, and expatriate African Americans promoting a Pan-African and internationalist vision of political, economic, cultural, and religious solidarity and mutual support networks between his organizations in the United States and independent African nation-states. On April 20, 1964, Malcolm X made the hajj to Mecca.

The long trip around Africa and to Saudi Arabia was expensive. Once again, Malcolm's sister Ella helped out. She was now well off financially as a result of her financial and business acumen and had several real estate holdings, which included lucrative properties in both Boston and New York. She had left the NOI after only a couple of years because of her fierce disdain for, and distrust of, both Elijah Muhammad and Louis Farrakhan. She was also studying orthodox Islam on her own and had been saving money to take the hajj herself, but she told Malcolm that it was more important that he go. She was deeply proud of how her brother had grown into such a mature, dignified, and widely respected leader of international renown. As Malcolm made the trip to North Africa he thought about how supportive Ella had always been of him, and he was genuinely humbled by her generous gesture.

While on the hajj, Malcolm experienced an epiphany that further transformed and expanded his already rapidly evolving consciousness. During the pilgrimage he shared food, clothing, lodging, and spiritual communication with hundreds of thousands of Muslims from all over the world. He met, talked, broke bread, and prayed with white Muslims from Europe as well as those from Africa, Asia, and Latin America. He was touched by the honesty and sincerity of this massive global commune of true brotherhood and moral unity. He wrote numerous letters and postcards to friends, family, and professional colleagues and associates (including some friendly white acquaintances in the media and academia) about the warmth, generosity, harmony, and compassion he felt and experienced on this spiritual and religious retreat.

As he meditated and read the Holy Qur'an daily (Malcolm was by all accounts a major scholar of biblical texts), he reflected deeply on the meaning of his life and the extraordinary events and circumstances that had formed and shaped it. At a mere thirty-nine years of age he had seen, shaped, and participated in many of the most pivotal and world-transforming events of his time. Alone in thought among a huge group of fellow believers, Malcolm fully grasped and understood the purpose and meaning of his life. He had finally found both the theoretical and practical ideas and methods of making his role in the global quest for freedom and justice a living reality. He wrote to people in America about the possibility that World Islam would eventually be the solution to the problem of racism in the United States. But he was neither naive nor Pollyanna in his assessment. Although he duly praised the love and many friendships he saw and shared in during the hajj, Malcolm understood that it would be a long struggle for Americans to acquire this kind of lofty consciousness.

As he stated upon his return to the United States, brotherhood was always a two-way street, and like Muslims throughout the world, he was not about to settle passively for a mere promise of respect and unity from his fellow citizens. The path to justice, freedom, and equality on the basis of human rights and a fundamentally different political and economic system, Malcolm said, was going to require immense sacrifices, as well as a far different conception and expression of social relations and morality. But Malcolm felt that he was on the verge of a new beginning when he arrived in the holy city of Mecca a week later.

Malcolm was treated like royalty in Africa. He was the honored state guest of many presidents, prime ministers, and revolutionary leaders while there. He journeyed to Egypt, Nigeria, Ghana, the Sudan, Morocco, Senegal, Liberia, and of course Saudi Arabia, where he gave numerous speeches, lectures, and talks at universities and cultural centers and on radio and television programs. He celebrated his thirty-ninth birthday in Algeria as an official guest of the revolutionary Algerian government. He was officially and formally recognized by the heads of state in Ghana and Saudi Arabia (the highest honor any foreign dignitary can receive in Africa).

Malcolm also appeared at the Summit of the Organization of African Unity (OAU), the U.N.-like body of Africa, where he introduced a petition charging the United States with violating the human rights of African Americans. Muslims and other African leaders were very impressed with his highly detailed and thorough presentation and were quite receptive to his idea of their supporting his petition in the United Nations. Those listening to him for the first time were also deeply impressed with Malcolm's encyclopedic knowledge of international law.

Many Africans also saw him as an American spokesman for their grievances with the U.S. government as well. Subsequently, several African and Arab diplomats, notably U.N. General Assembly President Alex Quaison-Sackey of Ghana, arranged for Malcolm to open an office off the same corridor where other "provisional governments" (such as the PLO and South Africa's ANC) had space. Still a private citizen, Malcolm X now had the status of a world statesman and was treated as such in the Third World. The CIA closely monitored all of Malcolm's travels and was deeply distressed by the considerable political progress he was making in his relations with nations that the U.S. government was trying desperately to control during the Cold War.

Upon returning to New York on May 21, 1964, Malcolm held a press conference and announced that several African and Asian nations stood ready to support his U.N. petition. Within days of his return, five members of the NOI's Newark Mosque Number Twenty-five were recruited to kill him. Wilbert X Bradley, Robert X Ben Thomas, Wilbur X McKinney, Talmadge X Hayer, and Leon X Davis met with someone who to this date remains unidentified, but who allegedly trained them in the art of assassination and paid them for their time.

During the summer of 1964, Malcolm began receiving terrorist threats via numerous crank calls, some of which came from FBI agents trying to scare him and some of which came from angry pro-Muhammad Muslims. Captain Joseph, the Harlem FOI chief, authorized the NOI's harassment campaign against Malcolm. "Every five minutes," a former member of the Harlem mosque recalls, "a different soldier would go to the telephone and call Malcolm's house. Sometimes we would say something threatening; sometimes we would just hold the phone and hang up. The idea was to unnerve Malcolm and Betty and maybe push them to the breaking point."

On June 5, Malcolm was informed that a colleague in Phoenix had obtained signed statements from two of the Messenger's former (and now banished) NOI secretaries who testified that the Messenger was the father of all their children. The two women, afraid for their lives, were now living in seclusion in Los Angeles. Malcolm's colleague, James 67X Warden, intended to press for a paternity suit against Muhammad. Still criminally involved in try-ing to intensify and exploit the hatred developing between the two factions in the NOI, the FBI sent a summary of the entire conver-sation to all domestic and military intelligence agencies, including the Secret Service.

On June 10, the Messenger made a special tape to be distributed to male NOI members only. The topic of his speech was "Hypocrites," which unmistakably referred to Malcolm X. "The white man has offered rewards for people to lie on the Messenger of Allah," Muhammad intoned. "This hypocrite is going to get blasted clear off the face of the Earth." Those who doubted that the hypocrite [Malcolm X] would be killed, Muhammad said, should keep their eyes on the events of June 24. "I'm going to show the world," he concluded. Later that evening, Muhammad's son-in-law and Muhammad's son Elijah Muhammad, Jr. summoned the best karate experts in the Chicago mosque to go to Detroit and await orders for a "special assignment." Other NOI enforcers, as Malcolm soon discovered, had received similar orders.

As the overwhelming pressure on him grew, Malcolm refused to back down. On June 13, he spoke by telephone with the host of a Boston radio program and went into great detail about Muhammad's extramarital escapades. As the summer of 1964 wore on there were a couple of incidents in which NOI-sponsored "hitmen" stalked and harassed Malcolm, as well as his sister Ella and her son Rodnell. But each time something would occur to scare the men off. On one occasion Malcolm was even approached at knifepoint by a group of men who issued verbal threats about his impending death. Malcolm and his wife Betty contacted the police on these occasions, but he knew it was a futile gesture. Malcolm was absolutely certain, although he could not prove it, that local police and the FBI were part of larger government program of harassment, and he did not trust the police or the FBI to act on his complaints—of course, he was right.

The Messenger commanded his lawyers to take back Malcolm's house in Queens, his automobile, and "all papers, files, and other material pertaining to the NOI." The deed and bill of sale for the small house and car were officially in the NOI's name, although Muhammad had always assured Malcolm that these and other possessions were "gifts" to Malcolm for his outstanding service to both him and the NOI. Malcolm had always remained strictly honest and trustworthy with regard to finances and had never taken any of the hundreds of millions of dollars that the NOI raised, unlike a number of the other high officials and the Messenger himself. Malcolm had subsisted on a relatively small salary and expense account from the NOI. He owned virtually nothing, and he and Betty and their three children depended entirely on the monies generated by Malcolm's lecture fees, articles, media appearances, and the like. So he legally fought the Messenger's incredibly petty and miserly attempt to seize the few assets he had in the world.

While all this intrigue continued in the U.S. and abroad, Malcolm miraculously continued to work very hard on a wide-ranging number of projects and activities in America, Africa, and Europe. On June 28, 1964, he announced the official formation of the OAAU (which he had promised to create in his March 8 press conference), and which was to be committed to "doing whatever is necessary to bring the level of civil rights to the level of human rights." On July 4 and 5, 1964, he gave another major series of brilliant speeches and lectures entitled "Harlem and the Political Machines" and "The Second Rally of the OAAU." Then he went to Africa for another tour. On July 17, 1964, while attending the United Nations as a representative of the OAAU, Malcolm reiterated his appeal for support before the delegates from thirty-four African nations at the OAU Summit Conference.

On September 21, 1964, nine days after an excerpt from Malcolm's upcoming autobiography had appeared in the *Saturday Evening Post* magazine, a civil court judge in New York ruled against Malcolm in the legal dispute with Muhammad over his home and ordered that Malcolm and his family vacate their residence in East Elmhurst, Queens by January 31, 1965. Malcolm and Betty were devastated, but Malcolm pressed on.

From early September to November 24, Malcolm toured Africa for a third time, going to eleven African nations and meeting with heads of state in each country. By this time, Malcolm had become acquainted and had long meetings with every prominent African and Arab leader, and with them, Malcolm was organizing a genuine coalition to politically challenge the United States and the European nations of Britain, France, and Portugal who had colonial governments in Africa. The CIA was even more alarmed, and a number of memorandums went out to section chiefs throughout the African continent and Europe that "Malcolm X must be stopped at all costs."

Malcolm was showered with offers to remain in Africa as an official in various governments there, not simply because the leaders admired his expertise, but also because they were fearful that Malcolm would be assassinated if he returned to the United States. Kwame Nkrumah of Ghana offered Malcolm an important cabinet post, which Malcolm humbly declined. Ben Bella of Algeria and Egypt's Nasser also made offers to Malcolm asking him to serve in their governments. Malcolm X thanked them both and told them that he had to continue working and organizing in the United States because that was where his people and destiny were.

Saudi Arabia gave Malcolm twenty-five scholarships for American Muslims interested in studying Islam and eventually becoming teachers, or imams. It also assigned Ahmed Hassoun, a highly regarded Islamic scholar, to return to the United States with

Malcolm to instruct members of Muslim Mosque, Inc. on practicing and propagating true Islam. Malcolm was also promised a multimillion-dollar mosque to be built anywhere in the United States. When Malcolm later announced that it would be built in Los Angeles, he also announced that Akbar, Muhammad's youngest child and a gifted student at the University of Cairo in Egypt, would be a teacher there.

On November 5, while Malcolm was still out of the country, a follower of his named Kenneth Morton was ambushed and beaten by NOI thugs sent by the Harlem mosque leadership. Returning to New York on November 24 and pushing on with his hectic schedule despite the continuing harassment and threats, Malcolm left for London only a week later to participate in a well-attended debate at Oxford Union. He also spoke at the London School of Economics and returned to the United States to speak at Harvard University during this time.

On the first anniversary of Malcolm's suspension from the NOI, in the most ominous sign yet that the Messenger intended to have Malcolm killed, an editorial appeared on the front page of the December 4, 1964, issue of *Muhammad Speaks*. Entitled "Boston Minister Tells of Malcolm—Muhammad's Biggest Hypocrite," the article was written by none other than Louis Farrakhan (formerly Louis X), Malcolm's former protégé who had been recruited by Malcolm nearly ten years earlier. Farrakhan wrote:

> *If any Muslim backs a fool like Malcolm in building a*
> *mosque, he would be a fool himself …. Only those who*
> *wish to be led to hell, or to their doom, will follow*
> *Malcolm. The die is set, and Malcolm shall not*
> *escape … Such a man as Malcolm is worthy of death ….*

These chilling words were placed in the newspaper right next to a photo of the Messenger sitting between Muhammad Ali and his brother Rahman holding and pointing to a passage in the Holy Qur'an. The symbolism was unmistakable: the Messenger was sending Malcolm a clear death notice.

Now given the full Islamic name of El-Hajj Malik El-Shabazz, as a result of his successful hajj, Malcolm was weary and nervous, but undaunted. Summoning unbelievable reserves of courage and sheer intellectual and moral stamina, Malcolm refused to run or hide from his enemies. The FBI and CIA, smelling blood, also moved in for the kill with various agents gloating to their superiors that Malcolm's days were numbered. By the end of 1964, Malcolm's file in the FBI alone was well over four thousand pages.

In the New Year's 1965 edition of *Muhammad Speaks*, Malcolm's former paper, the Messenger disowned his son Akbar for his support of Malcolm and his embrace of orthodox Islam over his father's brand just as he had banished his eldest son Wallace for helping Malcolm reveal his violations of moral principle. Throughout the Messenger's column he labeled his son a hypocrite, the worst epithet in Islam, just as he had labeled Malcolm.

The Final Hour

On Christmas Day, 1964, Malcolm received another sign that his tormentors were getting closer. Another good friend who had chosen Malcolm over the NOI and left the sect to join him was targeted for death. Leon 4X Ameer, the karate expert who had heard the Messenger's hysterical eight-hour monologue in September on the necessity of killing Malcolm, was beaten senseless by members of the Boston mosque in his hotel as terrified guests looked on. The first assault was stopped by a police officer who just happened to stop by the hotel. As Ameer was preparing to check out of the hotel later that evening, a second group of Muslims burst into his room and beat him so badly that they assumed he was dead. They dumped his bloody body in a bathtub and left. Once again, a policeman just happened to drop by after the damage was done. The officer went into the hotel room and followed the trail of blood to the bathroom. Ameer was rushed to the hospital, but he remained in a coma for several days. He later testified that the leader of the attack was Clarence 2X Gill and went on to identify others, but none of them was convicted of anything more than minor assault charges.

Malcolm knew that the Messenger was trying to draw him into a fight, but he refused to take the bait. However, the Muslims in the NOI were relentless. A physical confrontation between

Malcolm's bodyguards and another group of Muslim "strongarm" men took place in Philadelphia where Malcolm was appearing on a radio program on December 29, 1964. But this time a detective suddenly appeared and interceded. Malcolm called his wife Betty and told her to have his rifle and shotguns near the door when he got home and to not let anyone in until he got there. FBI agents also taped this conversation and noted that both the Army and Secret Service had, for some strange reason, been advised of the attack.

Malcolm continued to concentrate on building a broad-based political coalition with prominent civil rights leaders and activists, particularly Dr. King, with whom Malcolm had become friends since their brief meeting at the Capitol building in Washington, D.C. They had since spoken by telephone several times, which also upset the FBI. A black attorney and fellow activist named Clarence Jones, who was close to both men, tried to arrange a physical meeting between them. But scheduling conflicts and urgent politicking by members of King's staff who felt that a public meeting with Malcolm would damage King's reputation with liberals kept the two apart.

Malcolm decided to retaliate against Muhammad for the attempts on his life by publicly revealing as many of the NOI's false teachings as he could. When he appeared on the popular television talk program the *Irv Kupcinet Show* on January 30, 1965, he described the Messenger as a liar and a coward. Malcolm dismissed the notion that the white media was using him to discredit Muhammad; as he saw it the Messenger had done a great job of discrediting himself:

> *What Elijah Muhammad is teaching is diametrically opposed to the principles of Islam and the Muslim world itself. The religious officials at Mecca ... and those authorities at the top of Islam theology totally reject what Elijah Muhammad teaches as being ... Islam. On the other hand, what he is teaching can easily be defined as a religion, but it cannot be labeled Islam.*

Malcolm X then added that because there were so few Islamic scholars and mosques in America, it was easy for "any phony or faker to come along with a concocted, distorted product of his own making and say that this is Islam." When asked, "Are you by inference saying that Elijah Muhammad is a faker and a phony?" Malcolm X explained that he had once believed in the Messenger more than the Messenger believed in himself, but that belief changed when the Messenger

> *was confronted with a crisis in his own personal life and*
> *he did not stand up as a man. Anybody could make a*
> *moral mistake, but when you have to lie about it and be*
> *willing to see that murder is committed to cover up their*
> *mistakes, not only are they not divine—they are not even*
> *a man.*

In a final series of talks, interviews, lectures, and speeches given in New York, Paris, and London before black and white audiences, Malcolm spoke at length about the need for the African American struggle to establish political and ideological links with revolutionary movements throughout the world, particularly in Africa, Asia, and Latin America. He consistently made historical and contemporary connections between racism and capitalism and critiqued the latter as fundamentally responsible for upholding, defending, and supporting racial discrimination, exploitation, and oppression and said that "all thinking people today who have been oppressed are revolutionary" and that "this is the era of revolution." He also did extended analyses and critiques of the political and economic situations in Africa, Asia, the Caribbean, and the United States and made connections between those and the struggles in the Congo, Vietnam, China, and South Africa.

On February 9, 1965, Malcolm flew to Paris from London but was mysteriously refused entry by the French government. Speculation was rife that French intelligence had reliable information that Malcolm was going to be assassinated, and the government quickly intervened to save itself the embarrassment of a prominent American being killed on French soil. Malcolm was forced to return to London.

On February 13 Malcolm returned to New York. The next day, during the early morning hours, Malcolm's family home in Queens was firebombed. Earlier that day Malcolm's phone rang so often with terrorist death threats that his wife Betty, now four months pregnant with twin daughters, said she felt as if she were having a nervous breakdown. The children, Attallah, age six, and Qubilah, age four, were awakened by the sound of shattering glass and the smell of smoke in their bedroom. Qubilah woke her sister and the two dashed to their parents' bedroom. By the time Malcolm and Betty realized what was going on, the fire, set by Molotov cocktails, was raging completely out of control. Malcolm rushed his wife and four daughters to safety on the front lawn, and did not realize until later that he was standing in subzero weather in his underclothes. The next day Malcolm moved what little remained of the family belongings out of the house. Juanita Poitier (actor Sidney Poitier's wife), Ruby Dee, Sammy Davis, Jr., and many others collected and raised money for the uninsured family.

Thomas X Wallace, Ruby Dee's brother, who was also viciously beaten after he quit the Harlem mosque to follow Malcolm, invited his hero's family to live with him until things settled down. Malcolm reluctantly accepted the offer. Ordinarily, he would not have accepted the offer for fear of endangering others, but the constant, relentless harassment and attacks had worn him down. "I'm just about at the end of my rope," he told a colleague. He was dog-tired. Tired of staying up all night to protect his family from attack, tired of arguing with his distraught wife over the constant dangers she and the children were facing, and tired of being hounded by the FBI and the CIA.

By now, he knew he could not escape. His only prayer was that his children and his wife would. So he prepared himself for the inevitable. As he said to famed black photojournalist Gordon Parks on February 19, "It's time for martyrs now. And if I am to be one, it will be in the cause of brotherhood. That's the only thing that can save this country. I've learned it the hard way—but I've learned it." The following day in a phone conversation with collaborator Alex Haley, Malcolm openly acknowledged the probable role of other sinister forces, besides the NOI, in his demise:

> The more I keep thinking about this thing, the things that
> have been happening lately, I'm not at all sure it's the
> Muslims. I know what they can do, and what they can't,

313

*and they can't do some of the stuff that has been recently
going on … The more I keep thinking about what happened to me in France, I think I'm going to quit saying it's
the Muslims.*

After a final OAAU meeting that same evening, Malcolm
refused his friend Earl Grant's invitation to spend the night at his
apartment. You have a family," said Malcolm. "I don't want anyone
hurt on my account. I always knew it would end like this."

The final day of Malcolm's life was a Sunday. He was scheduled
to give an afternoon speech for his followers of the OAAU at the
Audubon Ballroom in Harlem. Nothing went as planned. The
three other speakers who were scheduled to speak all cancelled.
Understandably, Malcolm was nervous and strangely ill-tempered
and curt with his aides. This behavior was unusual because he was
always calm and very courteous to his staff. He apologized to them
for his short temper. Important business regarding the organization's charter was to be shared with his followers, but the staff had
not had enough time to finish and asked Malcolm if it could be
handed out next Sunday instead. Malcolm was not pleased, but he
quietly complied. He finally turned to one lieutenant standing
next to him and said with a tinge of sadness and irritation, "The
way I feel today, I shouldn't even be here."

A few brief minutes passed as Benjamin X Goodman (Karriem),
a longtime friend and colleague from the old NOI days, introduced
Malcolm with a flourish. Malcolm, who hated long, flowery intro-
ductions of speakers, especially himself, had always told Brother
Benjamin to "make it plain," which meant brief, with no elabora-
tion, and to the point. Now he fidgeted a little as Benjamin said,
"I present to you … a man who would give his life for you …" A
deluge of applause drowned out his name as the audience of several
hundred applauded loudly and vigorously. The rising applause continued as Malcolm strode toward the microphone and became
a standing ovation before it finally subsided. Malcolm greeted his
listeners as he always did with "As-Salaam-Alaikum."
Enthusiastically the crowd responded, "Wa-alaikum-Salaam."

Suddenly a loud disturbance erupted down front near the stage.
Two men started to argue. One of them said loudly, "Hey, get your

hand out of my pocket!" As Malcolm held up his arms, he said gently, "Brothers, please ... cool it ... It's alright ..." The bodyguards instinctively moved toward the commotion, leaving Malcolm temporarily unprotected. As they did, a smoke bomb was detonated. Once again the audience's attention was diverted.

At that moment a man stood up near the front rows with a sawed-off shotgun hidden inside his coat jacket and shot Malcolm flush in the chest. The impact of the shots at close range knocked Malcolm straight back. As Malcolm clutched his chest, his lean frame stiffened as he then toppled over backward into two of the empty guest speaker chairs. His head then struck the stage with a thud. Simultaneously two or three or maybe even four other gunmen rushed the stage and began emptying their guns into Malcolm's body. All told he was hit sixteen times in the arms, chest, legs.

Bedlam ensued as people scrambled to the floor for safety or ran out screaming. Tables and chairs were flying in every direction as the crowd ran for their lives out of the ballroom. A bodyguard named Gene Roberts, who was later positively identified as an undercover agent for New York's BOSSI (Bureau of Special Services) secret police division and an FBI informant, was seen giving Malcolm mouth-to-mouth resuscitation. Meanwhile, a pregnant Betty Shabazz, who witnessed the horrific tragedy with her four daughters, took a bloodied piece of paper from Malcolm's inside coat pocket that contained the names of the five hitmen from the Newark mosque, to whom Malcolm had been tipped off as being his eventual murderers. Malcolm had not known them.

When the smoke finally cleared, one man who had shot Malcolm and was unable to escape was taken into custody. Later two other men were also accused, arrested, and convicted, although the man who was caught initially, Talmadge Hayer (also known as Thomas Hayer), and some investigators testified that the two who were caught later were involved but not as actual assassins and that at least three other shooters got away. In any event, all the men who were arrested were convicted. To this day there is still widespread speculation by a number of reputable researchers that at least two, and perhaps three, of the actual murderers got away. Who hired them? Where are they? Elijah Muhammad, the NOI, the FBI, and the CIA all, of course, denied any culpability in Malcolm's death.

Coda

Malcolm X (1925–65) has gone on to become one of the most famous and revered figures in the world. Since his death there have been countless books, films, plays, book reports, and Ph.D. dissertations about his life, career, and contributions to twentieth-century history. He is taught about all over the globe and in a multitude of different languages. He is respected and celebrated as a political and religious leader, as a social activist and organizer, as an intellectual, and as a prophet. He is as well known in small villages and tiny island nations as he is in the major capitals of Africa, Asia, Latin America, the United States, and Europe. Denzel Washington, James Earl Jones, Al Freeman, Jr., and Morgan Freeman have all portrayed him in various films and plays. But more important than all the hype and media fascination generated by popular culture representations of him and his "image" have been the many anonymous men, women, and children throughout the world who have been inspired by his ideas, values, and exemplary example to dedicate their lives to the revolutionary pursuit of freedom, justice, self-determination, and human rights that marked everything Malcolm X did and tried to do in the course of one extraordinary lifetime. Thank you, Malcolm X, and long live El-Hajj Malik El-Shabazz!

Appendix

Bibliography

Breitman, George (ed). *By Any Means Necessary: Selected Speeches, Interviews, and a Letter by Malcolm X.* New York: Pathfinder Press, 1990.

———. *Malcolm X Speaks: Selected Speeches and Statements.* New York: Grove Weidenfeld, 1990.

Carson, Clayborne and Gallen, David (ed.). *Malcolm X: The FBI File.* New York: Carroll & Graf, 1991.

Clark, Steve (ed). *Malcolm X: The Final Speeches.* New York: Pathfinder Press, 1992.

Collins, Rodnell with A. Peter Bailey. *Seventh Child: A Family Memoir of Malcolm X.* New York: Birch Lane Press, 1998.

Davis, Thulani and Chapnick, Howard (ed.). *Malcolm X: The Great Photographs.* Stewart, Tabori & Chang, 1993.

Dyson, Michael Eric. *Making Malcolm: The Myth and Meaning of Malcolm X.* Oxford University Press, 1995.

Epps, Archie (ed.). *The Speeches of Malcolm X at Harvard.* New York: William Morrow & Company, 1969.

Evanzz, Karl. *The Messenger: The Rise & Fall of Elijah Muhammad.* New York: Pantheon Books, 1999.

———. *The Judas Factor: The Plot to Kill Malcolm X.* New York: Thunder's Mouth Press, 1992.

Gallen, David (ed.). *A Malcolm X Reader: Perspectives on the Man and the Myths.* New York: Carroll & Graf Publishers, Inc., 1994.

Goldman, Peter. *The Death and Life of Malcolm X.* New York: Harper & Row. Second edition, University of Illinois Press, 1979.

Greene, Cheryll Y. (ed.) and Strickland, William with Malcolm X documentary production team. *Malcolm X: Make It Plain.* New York: Penguin Books, 1994.

Haley, Alex with Malcolm X. *The Autobiography of Malcolm X.* New York: Grove Press, 1965.

Malcolm X. *Two Speeches.* New York: Pathfinder Press, 1965, 1990.

———. *Talks to Young People.* New York: Pathfinder Press, 1965, 1986.

Perry, Bruce. *Malcolm X: The Life of the Man Who Changed Black America.* New York: Station Hill Press, 1991.

———. *Malcolm X: The Last Speeches.* New York: Pathfinder Press, 1989.

Wiley, Ralph with Lee, Spike. *By Any Means Necessary: The Trials & Tribulations of the Making of Malcolm X.* New York: Hyperion, 1992.

Wood, Joe (ed.). *Malcolm X: In Our Own Image.* New York: St. Martin's Press, 1992.

Index

O

Kofi Natambu

Kofi Natambu is a writer, critic, and university teacher whose essays, reviews, criticism, journalism, and poetry have appeared in many magazines, journals, newspapers, and anthologies across the country. He has written extensively on American literature, history, politics, film, music, and cultural studies. He is the author of two books of poetry, *The Melody Never Stops* (Past Tents Press, 1991) and *Intervals* (Post Aesthetic Press, 1983), and was the editor of a literary anthology entitled *Nostalgia for the Present* (Post Aesthetic Press, 1985). He was also editor of a literary magazine of the arts, culture, and politics called *Solid Ground: A New World Journal*, which he edited and wrote for from 1980–87. A native of Detroit, Michigan, he lives and works in Oakland, California.